The Gender Order of Neoliberalism

With love and gratitude to our immigrant parents,
Rosetta and Giancarlo Solari,
BD and Sharada Radhakrishnan

The Gender Order of Neoliberalism

Smitha Radhakrishnan
Cinzia D. Solari

polity

Copyright © Smitha Radhakrishnan and Cinzia D. Solari 2023

The right of Smitha Radhakrishnan and Cinzia D. Solari to be identified as Author of this Work has been asserted in accordance with the UK Copyright, Designs and Patents Act 1988.

First published in 2023 by Polity Press

Polity Press
65 Bridge Street
Cambridge CB2 1UR, UK

Polity Press
111 River Street
Hoboken, NJ 07030, USA

All rights reserved. Except for the quotation of short passages for the purpose of criticism and review, no part of this publication may be reproduced, stored in a retrieval system or transmitted, in any form or by any means, electronic, mechanical, photocopying, recording or otherwise, without the prior permission of the publisher.

ISBN-13: 978-1-5095-4489-9
ISBN-13: 978-1-5095-4490-5(pb)

A catalogue record for this book is available from the British Library.

Library of Congress Control Number: 2022950232

Typeset in 10.5 on 12pt Plantin MT
by Fakenham Prepress Solutions, Fakenham, Norfolk NR21 8NL
Printed and bound in Great Britain by TJ Books Limited, Padstow, Cornwall

The publisher has used its best endeavours to ensure that the URLs for external websites referred to in this book are correct and active at the time of going to press. However, the publisher has no responsibility for the websites and can make no guarantee that a site will remain live or that the content is or will remain appropriate.

Every effort has been made to trace all copyright holders, but if any have been overlooked the publisher will be pleased to include any necessary credits in any subsequent reprint or edition.

For further information on Polity, visit our website:
politybooks.com

Contents

Acknowledgments   vi

1 Introduction: A Multicentric World Order   1
2 Neoliberalism's Pre-histories   20
3 Investing in "Empowered" Women   41
4 Neoliberalism's Gendered Architecture   65
5 Moving Toward Modernity   95
6 Manly Protectors   120
7 Conclusion: A Fairer Multipolar Future   149

Notes   161
References   179
Index   203

Acknowledgments

We owe an enormous debt of intellectual gratitude to Berkeley Sociology, a department and a tradition that brought both of us together and created the environment that made this book possible. We are grateful for the guidance and mentorship of Victoria Bonnell, Michael Burawoy, Gillian Hart, and Raka Ray, who inspired our passion to know one "area" of the world well, but never fail to put it in conversation with another geography.

This book has benefited from the feedback of multiple audiences, including the Gender and Power Theory Workshop, the American Sociological Association's Gender Inequality Session (2021), and American Sociological Association's Transnational Feminism's Session (2022). We appreciate the constructive critical feedback from Irene Brown, Helen Marrow, Joya Misra, and Natasha Warikoo in the final stages of the project as well as the helpful feedback from the three anonymous reviewers who did such a thorough reading of our manuscript. Jonathan Skerett from Polity has been an enthusiastic supporter of this project from its humble beginnings as a preliminary idea at the Eastern Sociological Society meetings in 2019. Karina Jákupsdóttir has been a wonderful collaborator in helping us realize the cover image for the book and many other production details along the way. Sijia "Scarlett" Qian spent a semester steadfastly helping us sort through vast literatures. Skylar Rathvon did a heroic job of intensive editing right before our final submission. Smitha thanks Cive Pillay for meaningful, radical, political perspective.

Our deepest thanks to our families for making us who we are, for giving us the rich heritages that have inspired us to think more deeply about our place in the world, and of course, for their tireless support and pride in our work. Cinzia thanks Davide Cis for a lifetime of love and companionship, for reminding her to slow down, for taking care of her when she felt slowing down was not an option, and, of course, for his *pasta alla ciociara*. Smitha thanks Ganesh Ramachandran who has been endlessly patient, kind, and creative in his support for this project and so much more. We have dedicated this book to our immigrant parents. At the same time, we look with pride and gratitude to our beautiful children, Selene, Giri, Eliano, and Abhigyaan, who remind us every day to work toward growing the fairer world we need.

1
Introduction: A Multicentric World Order

In the fall of 2000, two immigrant daughters met up in a Berkeley sociology theory class, our first as graduate students. We both felt out of place and wondered if there were others who shared similar life experiences. Over the years, we became friends and, increasingly, intellectual interlocutors. We took our qualifying exams in gender together and left for dissertation fieldwork around the same time. Cinzia researched domestic workers who left Ukraine to labor either in Italy or the United States and sent remittances back home, not unlike Cinzia's mother, who left Italy 40 years earlier to do domestic work in the United States.[1] Smitha researched information technology (IT) workers in India, who, like her father, had also left home to labor in the IT industry abroad.[2] After years of fieldwork, analysis, and writing, we found that our research participants had something critical in common: they were not just laboring for a living, they were laboring for their nations. This sense of pride in laboring for their nations, along with a sense of expanded choices for themselves and their families, made unfair conditions seem palatable and even justifiable. The women Smitha interviewed working in IT were at the helm of a new understanding of India. They understood their choices as consequential not just for themselves, but for the nation. The women Cinzia interviewed, laboring to care for the elderly in Italy and the United States, were Soviet grandmothers in their forties and fifties, pushed out of domestic labor markets and out of their familial homes. They also viewed their work and their choices as building the new, capitalist Ukrainian nation from the outside in.

At first, we regarded this similarity as a coincidence, noted it with interest, and moved on with our busy lives. We were researching social worlds with radically different histories, and we knew not to generalize. Smitha's context, India, a postcolonial nation, had become highly visible in the West as an "emerging economy" since the 1990s. New policy choices had produced a "new middle class" that was challenging naturalized assumptions about India as a "traditional" country. In the early 2000s, when Smitha's research started, India had become "modern" and "global," with a growing economy, global consumer goods, and a prosperous elite comfortable with western culture. Middle-class, caste-privileged women were especially drawn into new labor markets and new forms of consumerism, and thus were creating what felt like a new national understanding of India. Cinzia's context, Ukraine, on the other hand, a post-Soviet nation, was nearly invisible to western audiences in the early 2000s. Since the collapse of the Soviet Union in 1989, Ukraine was experiencing widespread poverty and was struggling to find its way under a radical policy regime that had abruptly turned from socialism to capitalism. Ukraine, too, was crafting a new understanding of modernity, but after a socialist experience in which women felt they were forced to work in the paid labor market. The nationalist call for women to return to the home felt like a modern "choice," at least for those who could afford to do so. India and Ukraine, we concluded, were distinctive places that could not be compared to one another.

As we moved from graduate school into careers as professors, we started to wonder whether there could be a systematic explanation for why folks in places with such divergent histories would end up justifying their circumstances through similar reasoning: expanded choices for women. Apart from our research, we were also experiencing life as mothers in US academia. We struggled with the taken-for-granted expectations for intensive mothering in the United States, alongside the pressures of our careers in academia. But when we looked around, our colleagues who were moms in academia also felt that we needed to figure it out for ourselves and somehow "do it all." We were grateful for the parental leave we received, leveraged the free labor of our own mothers for help with childcare, and did little to critique the system in which we struggled. Like those we had interviewed, we viewed our circumstances as fortunate, as part of the opportunity the United States was offering us. After all, we believed we had more choices than our mothers. With time, however, we began questioning these naturalized understandings. The convergence of these patterns of thinking from such different global locations at last prompted us to look closely at neoliberalism.

If anything, there is an excess of academic discourse on neoliberalism. In most US academic settings, neoliberalism is considered a bad economic system associated with reduced government social services, excessive corporate power, and hyper-individualism. Very often, an ill-defined understanding of neoliberalism infuses academic debates, serving as a catch-all kind of critique of contemporary economic and political conditions. If something terrible is happening, it is probably because of neoliberalism. There is also an abundance of scholarship that endeavors to theorize, critique, and describe neoliberalism. Even the most theoretical texts describe the system with the goal of exposing its inequities.[3]

Although we found ourselves sympathetic to these orientations, we found them inadequate to explain the gendered convergences we were finding in parts of the world with distinct national and regional histories. Most theories of neoliberalism center the West, especially the United States, and assume that the United States' version of capitalism spread to the rest of the world with the help of international institutions like the World Bank and the International Monetary Fund (IMF). But why, we wondered, did women and men experiencing unfair conditions around mothering, work, and identity in places as different as India, Ukraine, and the United States accept and even embrace these conditions? And furthermore, why did the nations they belong to not only accept but often actively participate in an unfair geopolitical system plagued by colonial inequalities, whether by sending workers abroad, by implementing policies that harm the majority of citizens, or by glorifying the arbitrary successes of a select few?

To address these questions, we knew that we needed to reconceptualize neoliberalism in a way that adequately accounted for the specificities of historical conditions, particularly those of colonialism as well as transformations. Colonialism refers to the conquest of a foreign people who are then ruled by members of the conquering polity.[4] Although colonialism no longer exists as a widespread political form, the long-standing patterns of power along axes of race, gender, and sexuality forged during colonialism continue to structure relationships within and between nation-states. We wanted to theorize neoliberalism in a way that viewed gender and nation as constitutive aspects of our current global political system because our research, as well as our understanding of colonial and imperial histories, suggested this to be true.

We began our work on this book by centering gender and nation as we examined our global political system. What came into focus was an international terrain of competition. On that terrain, colonial and Cold War histories are erased, and every nation-state, and even every individual, appears to have a fair shot at attaining high status. Historically powerless countries vie for power and status with historically powerful countries within fields of policy and expertise. Without the baggage of colonialism, there is no longer any external power to blame for those countries that do not manage to deliver goods and resources to their citizens. The very notion of "modernity," which implies linear progress, also suggests that peoples and nation-states can be ranked along a continuum. This is a key example of how colonial patterns continue to shape geopolitics and the experiences of individuals. This terrain of competition is crystallized in global institutions such as the United Nations (UN) and the IMF, but also in particular global fields such as economics, public health, climate, women and development, or education. To gain or maintain status on this terrain, nations must appear "modern" through the treatment of their women. The terrain of competition is also experienced at an individual level. Women, men, and gender-nonconforming individuals alike aim to advance their status within an unfair system that does not provide needed supports for childcare, education, or healthcare. Yet, instead of demanding better, there exists pervasive hope that hard work and luck will one day pay off. We found this pattern of reasoning in both our research and personal experience as mothers in US academia.

This book will illustrate neoliberal expectations and engagements on the part of individuals and nations – increased choice and a level playing field of competition over material resources and modernity status claims – have a hidden history involving three competing blocs that emerged from World War II (WWII): liberalism, socialism, and postcolonialism. The Cold War strengthened a struggle for geopolitical power that forced all other nations to pick a side: capitalist or communist. Both sides had imperial ambitions spurred on by the successes of the other side, whether in areas of education, women's rights, science and technology, or industrialization. The United States and the Soviet Union each led a regional bloc, the United States allied with Western Europe and the Soviet Union allied with Eastern Europe. The ever-growing list of newly independent postcolonial nations organized a third bloc, originally named the G-77, to create a third "team" that advocated for fairer trade terms in new global institutions and sought compensation for colonial legacies.[5] This hidden history also revealed to us transnational feminist organizing, linking postcolonial and Soviet Bloc countries that advocated for exactly the ideals that we found were lacking in the contexts we studied and lived in: support for mothers, universal education, economic and political equality for women.[6]

Introduction: A Multicentric World Order

With the collapse of the Soviet Union in 1989, capitalism came to be viewed as the victor of the Cold War. This ostensible victory rendered capitalism at once invisible and pervasive, making it difficult to examine the system of capitalism from any viewpoint outside of it. Without an ideological opponent, capitalism became the singular economic and political reality for all nations, despite their previous histories. Although critical histories of capitalism highlight its origins in the enclosure movements, the triangle trade, and the political economy of the British Empire, seldom do we remember that neoliberalism is still a form of capitalism, just the latest phase and one without a viable opponent. Once the opponent was obliterated, the terrain of competition was no longer contained by ideological blocs. This was the transformation that opened the competition so that each nation-state and every individual necessarily became a contender. Where previously nation-states new and old had to pick a team or bloc, now nation-states are free to articulate their own cultural identities in a global media landscape. Each country, then, is poised to conform to or challenge the very meaning of modernity. As a result, the cultural and symbolic space for imagining national and cultural belonging did not shrink as neoliberal capitalism became hegemonic – it grew.[7]

Not all aspects of neoliberalism are new. The naturalized order we experience today was cooked up in many global institutional, economic, and political deals over hundreds of years. Yet the very term "neoliberalism" is attentive only to liberalism as its precursor, erasing the other political blocs that helped create the policies and habits of mind that we now consider central to its functioning: intense individualism, a focus on an economically interdependent and unequal system of trade, and austerity policies that fundamentally block access to thriving for the majority. The erasure of how the Soviet Union and members of the G-77 interacted with one another at the close of WWII has left us with an academic understanding of neoliberalism that travels poorly to regions with histories of socialism and postcolonialism as a precursor to neoliberalism. An impoverished understanding of neoliberalism denies the constitutive character of gender and nation, making us ill equipped to organize transnationally to address the world's most pressing problems, as so many feminists endeavored to do and with some success in the mid-twentieth century.

Having uncovered these histories, which we narrate in detail in early chapters of the book, we return to the original question of convergence that prompted our study: Why, despite a situation of extreme hardship, do individuals, ourselves included, justify, internalize, and even defend a fundamentally unfair political and economic system? Our answer hinges on what we call the neoliberal feminist "cover story."

The neoliberal feminist "cover story"

A cover story, as defined by Arlie Hochschild, is a collectively constructed societal-level discourse that allows actors with disparate or even opposed interests to mobilize a similar "cultural toolkit" to address social problems on the ground.[8] A cover story conceals the gap between ideals and lived realities, obscuring the dynamics of inequality. In all three regions, we find that a limited, colorblind understanding of feminism that emphasizes individual "choices" for women regarding work and family legitimates the rigged competition. This unfair competition applies both to individuals competing for advancement and for nation-states jockeying for status in the global hierarchy of nations. This feminist cover story legitimates the neoliberal order by focusing on women's "choices" that allow individual and state actors to make claims about elevating women. Such claims, however, preserve the hetero-patriarchal values constitutive of neoliberal capitalism. The "feminist subject" produced in the context of neoliberalism, we suggest, is not solely or even primarily empowered through work, but rather through illusions of "choice" and "entrepreneurship," even as motherhood and reproductive labor continue to be compulsory.

The path to women's "uplift" and "empowerment" looks different across the regions we study due to historical trajectories that resulted in divergent positions within the global capitalist system. Nevertheless, individual actors, regardless of gender identity, must engage with racial and class-based constructions of "feminist," "empowered," and/or "liberated" women. Yet we will show that around the world, and most especially in the former Soviet Union (FSU) and Eastern Europe, neoliberal capitalism has become an engine for gender inequality.

In the aftermath of WWII, both collective and individualistic understandings of women's empowerment battled for dominance within the United States, the Soviet Union, and South and Southeast Asia (SSEA). Activists and politicians fought for their framing of empowerment in the nascent realm of international institutions. By the time of the Soviet Union's decline, however, we find that an abstracted understanding of women's empowerment focused narrowly on "choices" for women. By emphasizing choice, policy makers, scholars, and activists in diverse policy realms neglected to reveal the content and quality of those choices. Were the "choices" to be either a housewife or an entrepreneur or a domestic worker or a marriage migrant compatible with human thriving? Did such choices relate in a fair way to individual women's value systems in these three regions with different histories? The narrow focus on empowerment that took root precluded even the formulation of these questions, and an individualistic understanding of empowerment, derived from neoliberal feminism and, as we shall show, human capital theory, came to be constitutive of the global order. This outcome was surprising when viewed in context because collective understandings of empowerment were popular in most of the world. We show that although the narrow neoliberal version of "women's empowerment" is accepted in our three regions, it is an acceptance of women who do not challenge the politico-economic structure of neoliberalism. Women who threaten that order by organizing or seeking political power cannot survive easily and may even be targeted with misogynistic attacks.

Despite the preoccupation with individual choices within neoliberalism, a specific family form is fundamental to neoliberalism's gender order: the hetero-patriarchal family, consisting of a man and a woman who are married. Women are expected to carry out the reproductive labor required to raise children within a nuclear family for free, and this family form has been widely accepted and naturalized under neoliberalism because it is flexible in some ways. Part of neoliberalism's promise to provide "more choices" to vulnerable groups includes non-heteronormative choices; however, these "choices" are limited by the normative template of the hetero-patriarchal family. Same-sex marriage can exist as a part of neoliberalism and even be held up as a sign of morality, inclusion, and civilizational superiority (as we show in chapter 6), but the possibilities for non-heteronormative relationships are limited. Same-sex couples must still live in nuclear families where, if they have children, one parent must do the housework for free; thus the fundamental political-economic structure of neoliberalism remains intact. Following the literature on homonationalism, we argue that non-normative desire might be tolerated under neoliberalism, but not embraced. Communal living, multiple partners, or shared parenting, all of which could be part of a non-heteronormative political economy, cannot thrive under neoliberalism. Women and gender-nonconforming folks who refuse to perform free caring labor, like those who seek political power, can be targeted for misogynist attacks and experience physical harm.

The binary gender identities required for this kind of nuclear family form come out of colonialism.[9] In the neoliberal order, masculinities and femininities are privileged as organizing discourses, although binary gender is not inclusive of humanity's many embodied gendered identities. One gendered feature of the neoliberal order that is distinct from liberalism is that the cultural expectations for women have shifted. In a liberal order, women were asked either to be full-time homemakers or, for working-class women, to ensure that the necessity for paid work did not interfere with their mothering responsibilities. Under neoliberalism, women are still asked to do caring work at home for free, but they are also forced to craft entrepreneurial identities that result in additional labor that may or may not be paid. These entrepreneurial identities, which we explore throughout the book, could involve being a career woman, styled after Sheryl Sandberg or Ivanka Trump. But, depending on your social location and geography, expressing an entrepreneurial spirit also could include starting a home-based business with a micro-loan, mommy-blogging, or migrating abroad to care for children or the elderly. For men, instead, rigid notions of breadwinning persist, even as our neoliberal economy results in fewer men who have the economic means to claim the title of breadwinner. Thus, as the expectations for femininity have expanded, those for masculinity have remained the same or even contracted, leaving especially poor and working-class men anxious about their place in the world and in their families.

In the global race for an elusive, internationally recognized modernity, the performance of gender equality is key to achieving the high moral status necessary to be regarded as an "advanced" nation. Nation-states constantly negotiate what constitutes gender equality and how it is performed, but this too takes place on unequal terms. Global hegemons such as the United States can command status because of their imperial history as well as their insistence on having "liberated" women, while post-Soviet and postcolonial countries must perform gender equality through gender metrics, media discourses, or policy packages. All these countries must, in a neoliberal order, show that their women "choose" to live their lives the way they do, unconstrained by culture or history. The notion of free choices – and abundant choices – for women is the narrow, hollowed-out understanding of women's empowerment that has come to denote status in varied parts of the world while also legitimizing inequality.

We recognize that our discussion of gender and women in this book focuses almost exclusively on cisgender women and binary constructions of women and men. There has been little literature on trans communities in the times and places that we cover in the book. Although we do our best to retain a critical perspective toward the gender binary throughout our analysis, the assumption of its existence and its exclusion of the historical experiences of trans and non-binary persons pervades our analysis.

Theorizing a gendered, multicentric world order

Although we went into this project with area-specific expertise, as well as extensive knowledge of the United States due to our location and teaching responsibilities, putting these regions in conversation with one another was much harder than anticipated. Most of our area-specific knowledge assumed the nation-state was the most salient organizing category of knowledge for our ethnographic work, ignoring or minimizing the importance of transnational connections and influences. As a scholar of India, Smitha had expertise on the history of the Indian anti-colonial nationalist movement, the policies leading up to economic liberalization, as well as the cultural, economic, and political climate surrounding what has been characterized as "post-liberalization" India. As a scholar of Ukraine, Cinzia had knowledge of the history and nation-building efforts within Ukraine during and after the Soviet regime, but since Ukraine was so recently part of the Soviet Union, she also had deep knowledge of Russian and Soviet history and politics. Cinzia found that the value systems of her research interlocutors were deeply informed by understandings of Soviet versus capitalist selves. In some ways, then, Cinzia's training and research had prepared her for a regional approach to neoliberalism that theorized the actually existing character of capitalism from a point outside of it. Nonetheless, theorizing a global order that would systematically explore the extent to which such an order exists, and yet would remain attentive to and engaged with national and regional articulations of that order, required a new kind of thinking. Together, we had to acquire and organize new knowledge and to question the assumptions lurking behind the knowledge we thought we had.

We endeavored to meet this challenge by thinking both *horizontally* and *vertically*. We analyze horizontally by taking multiple places into account at the same time with attention to gender and nation. We analyze vertically by interrogating the interconnections between

(1) the global, including transnational institutions, global media spaces, and traveling policies; (2) the regional and/or national, including national and regional policies, discourses of belonging, and claims within particular fields of knowledge; and (3) individuals, motivated by a range of desires stemming from their diverse structured social locations and, in particular, their gendered, racial, class, and geographic identities.

Our effort to theorize *horizontally* pushes back against conceptualizations of neoliberalism that assume the United States constitutes the center of neoliberal policies, practices, and value systems from which concepts diffused to expand and sweep up less powerful countries. Instead, we propose a multicentric understanding of neoliberalism that reveals how the neoliberal order we see today was co-created by other countries and other visions of modernity. This understanding comes from detailed historical analysis that required us to rethink our areas of expertise in relation to other geopolitical formations. We needed to understand how neoliberalism was made, under what circumstances, and who was in the kitchen when the cooking was happening. There have been many "origin stories" of neoliberalism that we found convincing and useful.[10] But how were postcolonial and Soviet-bloc nations participating in the expert conversations and knowledge production in the lead-up to neoliberalism? How were they involved, if they were at all?

When we started asking those questions, arenas of transnational interaction, negotiation, and confrontation came into view. We found research on East–West networks of Soviet and American economists who designed the actual policy frameworks that would be adopted in the United States, Eastern Europe, and the FSU when socialism collapsed, and neoliberal capitalism was embraced. We gained an entirely new understanding of the political context that the various post-WWII UN institutions created, and we started to probe the divergent positions of these countries within that context. We engaged with an extensive literature about women's movements from the postcolonial and post-Soviet worlds that collaborated in the context of UN conferences to envision a radically different world order based on principles of democracy, healthcare, and education for all, and a substantive vision of gender equality. We discovered a critical policy and international relations literature that showed us how and why education and women's rights became key arenas in which geopolitical power was contested, with the United States and the Soviet Union battling one another for control over the rapidly decolonizing world.

Introduction: A Multicentric World Order

In all these interactions, US capitalism was affected by what the Soviets were doing, the Soviets were influenced by the policies of the United States, and postcolonial countries were fully cognizant of how their alliance with one side or another would affect their global standing. These, and many other historical examples, came out of our effort to think horizontally across countries and regions and to critically interrogate both the transnational production of a global order and the centrality of geopolitical competition in the production of our contemporary world. Geopolitical competition – first in the context of colonialism, later in the context of the Cold War, and most recently in the context of a multilateral interdependent neoliberal global order – requires us to be attentive to gender and nation as strategies through which nation-states and individuals naturalize domination and superiority relative to foreign others. Horizontal thinking required us to historicize and de-parochialize our preconceived understanding of neoliberal policies and value systems.

Horizontal thinking also required us to reconsider what we thought we knew about contemporary circumstances and conditions. As we thought about how we would articulate the characteristics of this neoliberal order and its consequences, we again had to explore vast literatures new to both of us, including both theoretical work on neoliberalism and examinations of materializations and manifestations of neoliberalism in particular places. Our work was to place these in relation to one another. As we are both ethnographers, we regarded critical qualitative studies as rich resources for expanding our understanding. A longtime scholar of domestic work and migration, Cinzia started researching more broadly why women migrate, apart from for work, and explored a rich literature on marriage migration that displaced women from postcolonial and post-socialist countries as they sought marriage to men in western contexts. More than other kinds of social scientific scholarship, scholarship on marriage migration considers the interplay between nations and conceptions of the hetero-patriarchal family in at least two locations to understand the decisions of individuals. Finally, we asked what consequences the neoliberal gender order might have on men, noticing the convergences between authoritarian men in leadership in the United States, Russia, and India. This set of questions also prompted us to navigate and critically analyze a relatively new body of work on the "crisis of masculinity" in all three locations. Keeping our eye on the horizontal relationships between each place, we exposed the geopolitical threads linking the frustrations of working-class men in these three locations, the rise of Trump, Modi, and Putin, and ultimately, the crystallization of what we call a conservative "manly protector" discourse that has resonance across multiple locations and broadens its base through media that does not require the legitimacy of established international institutions.

This project is not only a horizontal one, however. *Vertical* thinking required us to recognize how individuals, nation-states, regions, and the transnational arena all influence one another. Our interest in this project began with the conviction that the narratives of our interlocutors in divergent places in the global economy, as well as our own experiences, had a structural root that could be systematically investigated. Thus, in our later chapters, we consider how individuals navigate, respond, and rationalize both acceptance of and resistance to the neoliberal feminist cover story, the structural inequities that disadvantage them, and the uneven global terrain that sets up few pathways toward mobility and status for the majority. We lay out how these individual articulations are linked to the policies put forth within nation-states, and the larger competitive terrain of international politics in which all countries compete. Our vertical perspective recognizes that diverse social locations must be viewed in relation to one another and in their proper historical perspective on an uneven global stage. Vertical thinking requires us to ask: (1) What *are* the objective choices on the ground? (2) How does the set of choices that women have in less powerful parts of the world affect the options available for individual women in more privileged or dominant parts of the world? And (3) how does that interplay relate to nationalist discourses of modernity and cultural distinctiveness, which often hinge upon idealized understandings of gender and sexuality? To answer these questions, we synthesized literatures from diverse regions and put them in conversation with one another, using our existing regional expertise to contextualize relentlessly. However, we also recognized and highlighted across these studies the consistent patterns of discourse that other scholars have recorded and analyzed.

The past and present of neoliberalism's gender order

The chapters of the book are organized into two parts: (1) the history of neoliberalism's gender order; and (2) the architecture and consequences of neoliberalism's contemporary gender order. Our conclusion illuminates possible pathways out of our current system. We offer an overview of each section here and interpret the significance of each chapter.

Introduction: A Multicentric World Order

When we began historicizing neoliberalism, we initially thought it would be adequate to begin after WWII, but soon discovered that without understanding the zenith and immediate aftermath of especially British colonialism, we could not uncover the through-lines of colonial logics and legacies in the current system. Although there is no doubt that we could continue linking events in the twentieth century further and further back, we found that the New Deal in the United States (1933–1936), the Bolshevik Revolution in Russia (1917–1923), and the anti-colonial nationalist movement in India, which gained speed in the 1920s and culminated in the overthrow of British rule in 1947, were appropriate starting points for our horizontal comparison. As we narrate the national and regional contexts for these events in chapter 2, we reveal that the prevailing economic and political systems in each context hinged significantly on what we call a gendered "deal" in which women would make gains in some areas and compromises in other areas. The gains women made helped countries across the geopolitical system represent themselves as modern, but the compromises often came in the name of national or cultural preservation. In the United States, the gains of the New Deal and its aftermath presented contradictory options to women in the labor market. Women were included during wartime and then pushed back into the home or less desirable occupations when the war was over. The imperial United States wished to represent its women as liberated by capitalist modernity but nonetheless devoted to their families. The Soviet Union wished to emancipate women from the drudgery of housework by compulsorily drawing them into paid labor, especially factory work. The state took on the responsibilities of childcare, healthcare, and education, and extended its reach into families to displace men as "little tsars" at the head of their families. In India, the new anti-colonial nationalist government wanted to show the world that India's women, far from being oppressed by their culture, were modern, educated, and forward-looking. But in granting them equal civil rights, the new government strengthened patriarchal power within the family. These clashing gender orders comprised the backdrop to negotiations in the nascent international arena, a critical arena in which gender, nation, and economic systems were negotiated between the end of WWII and the fall of the Soviet Union in 1989.

The international policy arenas of women's rights and education take center-stage in chapter 3 as we consider the origins and contradictions associated with "empowerment" since "empowerment" is central to the neoliberal feminist cover story. Today, we understand this term to mean the upward economic and social mobility of individual women – not a broad social transformation that elevates all women. Yet, as we show, for decades in the postwar arena of international politics it appeared likely that the latter, more expansive definition of empowerment would "win" because it had the broadest support. In the three decades following WWII, the geopolitical order was divided up between liberal, socialist, and postcolonial blocs. These three blocs came to be known as the First, Second, and Third Worlds, respectively. We explore the lasting implications of these labels in depth in later chapters. In this context, "Third World" was taken up by activists as a radical departure from the hegemonic order. Led by Jawaharlal Nehru, India's first prime minister, the idea of the Third World aimed to forge a way separate from both the United States and the Soviet Union and was a significant force in global politics. Feminists from Soviet Bloc countries and Third World countries pushed against instrumental, capitalist interpretations of "empowerment," instead advocating for inclusive policies, ranging from paid maternity leave to universal childcare as foundational to empowerment. The United States and its allies, however, resisted, for if the United States were to yield to broad socialist visions of women's empowerment and education, the concession would cede geopolitical ground to the Soviets. Therefore, the United States needed to support different policies that provided protections for women and met the growing demand for education around the world. In this context, an increasingly influential policy paradigm, human capital theory, became politically useful.

Human capital theory suggested that human beings were economic resources that, when invested in, would yield economic growth. This narrow conception of human investment prompted US policies and discourses promoting women's rights and education within a framework oriented toward the production of economic value, rather than broad support for social progress. When the Soviet Union fell, US interpretations of empowerment, based on human capital theory, were the policy ideas available for deployment in the World Bank, as UNESCO (United Nations Educational, Scientific and Cultural Organization) programs stumbled and eroded without US support. As "gender" became "mainstream" in international development institutions in the 1990s and beyond, the version of "empowerment" that survived did little to address issues of "power" at all. It was reduced to narrow understandings of women entering labor markets under adverse conditions to take up entrepreneurial livelihoods. Thus, under neoliberalism's gender order, although we deploy the rhetoric

Introduction: A Multicentric World Order   15

of gender equality, we tolerate gender oppression. While "women's empowerment" sounds like "gender equality," the historical context we illuminate shows that the broader goals of gender equality are in fact better served outside of capitalism.

Having explained the geopolitical, discursive, and economic lead-up to neoliberalism's global dominance, we pivot to the second part of our book in chapter 4 with a characterization of the current architecture of neoliberalism's gender order. This characterization distills the core theoretical contribution of the book. We synthesize a vast literature to theorize neoliberalism to explain why these divergent regions can, in the twenty-first century, come to present seemingly similar aspirational possibilities for individuals. Before presenting this characterization, we acknowledge the transnational context in which the principles and economic policies of neoliberal capitalism were "cooked up." Economists, policy makers, and academics from Eastern Europe, the Soviet Union, and the United States were crafting neoliberal policies since the 1940s, and they met regularly to consider how Eastern European countries could be a "laboratory" in which such policies could be tried out.[11] After the Soviet Union collapsed, western scholars were surprised by the quick adoption of neoliberal policies across the region. However, this becomes less surprising when we recognize that the substance of neoliberal policies was created in collaboration with thinkers on both sides of the East–West divide. These interactions helped produce what we identify as the two *structuring conditions* particular to neoliberalism and the two *key actors* that come into view as the most important agents under neoliberalism's global gender order.

The two structuring conditions focus on the actions of states around the world and draw heavily from Slobodian's characterization of neoliberalism.[12] The first condition is that states become bodyguards for global corporations, capital, and elite groups. Through diverse policies, states around the world facilitate economic, social, and geographic mobility for those who can pay for it, privileging the ability of global corporations to participate in what Pietra Rivoli has termed, the "race to the bottom."[13] It is no longer nation-states that are roaming the world in search of territories to conquer. Instead, global corporations and the elites that benefit from those corporations can roam freely and stimulate economic growth in parts of the world with an immobile "local" majority. The second condition is that states strengthen their territorial borders by implementing laws that protect their territory from undesirable foreign laborers. While previously entry into the United States did not require documents, today an extensive system of border patrol, visas, and immigration laws prevents most from entering the world's most prosperous, dominant nation-state. We tend to think that distinctions between "legal" and "illegal" migrants have always existed, but in fact these distinctions are specific to the neoliberal order. By limiting the porousness of national borders, nation-states control labor flows, maintain a sense of national identity, and ensure that the nation participates in international trade as a cohesive, closed territory.

These conditions bring to the fore two key actors that have become particularly salient: individuals and nation-states. Individuals now hear the invitation to articulate their aspirations on a global stage. We are all invited to believe that the possibilities for local and global mobility are endless, and that hard work and luck can bring a comfortable life full of prosperity and personal thriving. An entrepreneurial approach to the self becomes paramount, yet this individualistic ideology hides the reality that the nuclear family, powered by the unpaid labor of women, becomes an even more crucial, but hidden, backbone of such individual aspiration.

Nation-states are the second key actor activated in a new way by the neoliberal order. Declared independent entities in the aftermath of WWII and the subsequent rapid decolonization of Africa, Asia, and Latin America, these nations are now invited to pursue economic prosperity within an interdependent neoliberal global order that appears to offer all nations, regardless of their history, a fair shot at success. Just as race, class, and gender hinder individuals within nation-states as they pursue their aspirations, structured inequities along geographic and historical lines prevent historically subordinate nation-states from pursuing economic policies that would make them economically self-sufficient. IMF policies require minimalist government expenditure from poor countries but not from the dominant countries that organize the system. Global financial systems thus encourage nation-states to find ways to participate in the global free market while at the same time preventing the world's majority from thriving. This contradiction is concealed by the illusion of "more choices" for individuals and nation-states alike, the core of the neoliberal feminist cover story. What new pathways emerge from this set of material realities? In the following two chapters, we address this question by exploring the consequences for women-led migration flows on one hand, as individuals aim to pursue modernity outside their home countries, and gendered resentment on the other, as men increasingly find themselves unable to fulfill their breadwinning roles within their families.

Under neoliberalism, women's ostensibly expanded vista of "choices" stems from their location in the global political economy. The distinctions between First, Second, and Third Worlds persist in the migration literature because the pathways available to women located in the Third World and the Second World are linked to those of women living in the First World and yet are divided along historical lines. Women living in the Philippines and former Soviet Bloc countries find two options available to them that both promise "modern" lifestyles: domestic work and (heteronormative) marriage. For Filipinas, pursuing domestic work abroad allows for economic and geographic mobility on a personal level while also uplifting the nation. The Philippines has organized its economy around the remittances of domestic workers, hailing them as heroes. Yet grandmothers from Ukraine face sanction from their nation when they migrate abroad, even as their social and material remittances provide a crucial foundation on which the "new" post-Soviet Ukraine is being constructed. Marriage migration presents other possibilities to move toward modernity. Women from former Soviet Bloc countries seek marriage to a man abroad to avoid working outside the home and acquire the protection of a "real" man who will take care of them. However, women seeking marriage migration from locations in Asia wish for an egalitarian marriage they believe is not possible at home. Both these quintessentially neoliberal "choices," experienced by individuals and nation-states simultaneously, pursue divergent conceptions of gendered modernity, even when the results can often be disappointing. The neoliberal feminist cover story legitimates these actions as honorable because both involve the perceived expansion of women's choices and an individualistic understanding of empowerment.

Neoliberalism's gender order does not provide a sense of expanded choices to everyone, however. Systematically, working-class men find that their opportunities for breadwinning have shrunk, but the expectation for "real men" to be breadwinners persists. In chapter 6, we examine how this set of conditions has given rise to what we call "manly protectors." Using the rise of the strongmen Trump, Modi, and Putin as an entry point, we trace a key consequence of neoliberalism's gender order on groups of men. Across many national contexts, strongmen inspire men to refocus their masculine identities on the protection of ethnic community and nation, giving rise to homophobic, misogynistic articulations of nation that aim to police and control historically subordinate groups. This chapter explores a range of topics and literatures that link geopolitics, ethnic nationalism, and masculinities together to argue that the "manly protector" ideal facilitates the rapid rise of an oppositional modernity that counters the dominant ideologies of the US-led neoliberal capitalist system.

As we look to the future in our conclusion, we identify possible pathways toward a fairer future. We aim to replace modernity and progress as organizing principles for an international order with the principles of justice and accountability. We center the twin crises of COVID-19 and Russia's war on Ukraine as we consider potential "portals" into a world in which justice is the aim of national and international policy making and individual aspiration. Touching upon the past successes of transnational feminist organizing around justice, current movements for grassroots transformation coming from abolition feminism, and contrarian voices within international institutions, we begin to imagine how global, decolonial sociology can help imagine a world that most of us cannot yet see.

We view this book project as a platform for other scholars. For example, we highlight a neoliberal "origin" story – with a lowercase "o" – that centers an East–West network of scholars "cooking up" neoliberalism. However, we acknowledge that there are other "origin" stories of neoliberalism that center on other world regions, particularly the global South. Horizontal thinking allows for this multicentric analysis in which agency is not only assigned to the United States in the production of neoliberal capitalism. This approach forces us to recognize that "neo"-liberalism does not grow out of western liberalism but is also rooted in the histories of socialism and postcolonialism. Using this multicentric, gendered approach attentive to both the existence of a global order and varied translations in specific contexts, we believe that other regions of the world can be brought into conversation with one another. Holding on to our framework of the multiple histories of neoliberalism, others might, for example, place Western Europe (liberalism), China (socialism), and West Africa (postcolonialism) into conversation with one another. This future study would deepen our understanding of the neoliberal order's history and everyday gendered workings. Similarly, an analysis that triangulates the United States, the Soviet Union, and Latin America would also produce complementary, essential knowledge about how individuals and nations from diverse geopolitical positions influence and navigate neoliberalism. We view the history and analysis we provide here, then, not as exhaustive but as suggestive of the importance of setting up the "First World," the "Second World," and the "Third World" in relation to one another and the importance of recovering socialist and postcolonial histories in the production of contemporary capitalist imaginaries and crises. In so doing, we hope that this book not only opens new possibilities for analysis but also for vital transnational political visions.

2
Neoliberalism's Pre-histories

Each of our three regions arrived at neoliberalism from divergent political and economic orders that comprised the global geopolitical landscape in the postwar period: liberal capitalism in the United States, socialism in the FSU, and postcolonialism in SSEA. This chapter focuses on the gendered "deals" that governments in the United States, the Soviet Union, and independent India made with women during the postwar period. These deals would support their respective states' approaches to political economy, cultural distinctiveness, and relative geopolitical position. National gender deals were thus embedded in the emergent global postwar order, which was organized through colonial understandings of modernity. These gendered deals affected the lives of women with different identities in divergent ways, producing both consent and protest over the decades between the end of WWII and the fall of the Soviet Union in 1991.

In the United States, the state called upon women to serve as a "reserve army" of labor that would enter or exit the paid labor market depending on national circumstances, and ultimately focus on supporting a consumer-oriented nuclear family with a male breadwinner as the head. In contrast, the Soviet Union needed full workforce participation to realize its goals. To make it possible for women to work full-time, the state undermined patriarchal authority in the family and provided meals, childcare and healthcare for families. Finally, in India, elite, anti-colonial nationalists sought to resolve the tensions produced by centuries of colonial rule as well as a citizenry stratified by caste and religion by providing women with legal equality but maintaining patriarchal control within families.[1] Each of these gendered nationalist projects contained contradictions and produced counterhegemonic responses. Ultimately, these

Neoliberalism's Pre-histories

projects ended up providing an affective justification for cultural distinctiveness that shored up the geopolitical projects of capitalism, socialism, and Third World non-aligned postcolonialism, respectively. We provide a shorthand for the key aspects of these three clashing gender orders in Table 2.1.

Table 2.1 Clashing Visions of Gendered Modernity: US/Soviet Union/SSEA (~1950–1991)

	Family	Waged work	Role of State	Freedom/Nation
United States	Hetero-patriarchal, nuclear family, racial endogamy to preserve White supremacy	Man breadwinner, woman homemaker, but women enter workforce as needed, a "reserve army"	"Liberal" capitalism: Provide access to economic mobility for especially White families through corporate-driven industrial modernity	Consumption, individual choice, economic opportunity, opposition to communism
Soviet Union	The state replaces men as the head of the family; state provides childcare, food preparation and education, private patriarchy undermined	All adults needed for the achievement of industrial modernity; women work full-time, men are servants to the nation-state to build socialism	Socialism: Provide childcare, education, and healthcare for all; centralized economy	Emancipation from the drudgery of housework for women, freedom from class oppression and exploitation for all, opposition to capitalism
SSEA (India in this chapter)	Patriarchal family structure, caste divisions and upper-caste dominance preserved, both nuclear and extended families included	Rural/urban distinction: male breadwinner model for urban families, manual labor of rural women required	Democratic socialism: state-driven industrial modernity, poverty alleviation	Formal equality between men and women, indigenous cultural expression on a global stage

The intertwined histories of these three regions uncover the importance of idealized visions of gendered relations in the ideological conflict between capitalism and communism that defined the Cold War.[2] The United States' "deal" with women promoted capitalism through a gendered modernity that emphasized the consumption of technological appliances to ease housework, a revered role as a mother, and middle-class prosperity, at least for White families. In contrast, the Soviet Union promoted communism through a vision of gendered modernity that emphasized liberation from the drudgery of housework and full incorporation into the industries that provide political and economic emancipation for all, emphasizing a "mother-worker" ideal. Postcolonial, gendered visions of nationalist modernity reworked those of capitalism, socialism, and colonialism to reflect indigenous national values, ensuring formal equality for women while also consolidating ideals of national culture.[3] In countries like India, the glorification of the figure of the modern Indian woman as the mother of the nation inspired cultural belonging.

All three contexts we analyze elevated their own visions of gendered modernity by denigrating the visions of competing "others." By emphasizing the separation between "us" and "them," nation-states offered an accessible, affective language through which to promote a desired political-economic order. This distinction was achieved to a large extent through the deployment of gendered ideals in policy and in culture. As we show in this chapter, however, these ideals were only partially realized in practice. Through imagery in art, cinema, advertisements, literature, and government propaganda, specific kinds of women and men were constructed as honorable and ideal national subjects, while other kinds of women and men were regarded as marginal or undesirably radical. Powerful women leaders, as well as characters in movies and literature, portrayed idealized women. Some ordinary women related to the struggles and triumphs of these idealized women and reworked those ideals to further their own life chances. However, other women rejected these ideals and organized social movements to enact large-scale social change. We illustrate this back-and-forth between policy, representation, and subjective experience throughout the chapter and the book. When successful, state-led projects of gendered modernity shored up countries' own statuses in the shifting geopolitical hierarchy of nations in the post-WWII global order. However, after the Soviet Union began crumbling in the late 1980s, a neoliberal understanding of women's empowerment emerged globally as a shared cover story, a development that we discuss in the next chapter.

The American "liberal" deal: modernity through economic opportunity for White families

Prior to the neoliberal order, the United States pursued three key phases of what may together be characterized as liberalism: the New Deal welfare state, the post-WWII period of economic expansion, and finally the Great Society of the 1960s. All these phases shared the vision that the United States needed to protect the liberty of their citizens by providing services that would ensure that individual citizens – implicitly White men – could live freely and realize their potential supported by the nuclear family. In contrast, women – implicitly White women – were to be available as a "reserve labor" pool when needed, as during WWII, but otherwise were mainly required to care for children and uphold the norms of hetero-patriarchal life. In this cultural conception of the American family, only White women were legitimately mothers due to their superior morality and their ability to produce "fit" American citizens. The "deal" that the United States government made with women engaged them primarily as mothers, but also as "modern" women willing to engage in paid work for the upliftment of the nation when called to action. From the 1970s onward, the feminist movement, birthed from the discontent of the restrictive prosperity that middle-class White women experienced in the 1950s, envisioned women's work as central to women's identities. This feminist vision, however, opposed the traditional nuclear family that was considered representative of capitalism at home and was deployed as a tool to fight communism abroad. Despite popular support for improving the positions of women in the labor market, the vision of women as both workers and mothers gained limited traction, and, instead, policies around childcare and labor doubled down on the ideal of White hetero-patriarchal society as iconic of America. Black women and other women of color were always prominent in shaping radical, alternative visions of American society that addressed the social conditions of their exclusion. Yet these women experienced the socioeconomic and political conditions of liberalism as second-class or non-citizens for whom the fruits of full economic and social belonging were always out of reach.

Following the Great Depression of the 1930s, Franklin D. Roosevelt's administration put forward the welfare-state policies of the New Deal program. The New Deal realized the values of liberalism by attempting to remove the obstacles of poverty, unemployment, and disease that stood in the way of individual and collective thriving.

New Deal legislation provided emergency unemployment assistance and temporary jobs, retirement and social security programs, and unemployment and disability insurance. New laws also provided restrictions for banking and finance industries and increased business regulation, with the intent of correcting the conditions that led to the 1929 Wall Street crash, one of the precipitating events of the Great Depression. These policies helped re-establish the United States' economic dominance in the world and put the country back on the road to prosperity. In contrast, African Americans and Latines were incorporated into the New Deal on a subordinate basis and did not benefit equally from this policy package.[4] The intertwined racial and class disparities of the early twentieth century thus extended through the New Deal recovery, compromising the seemingly expansive and neutral philosophy of state welfare liberalism.

The policies of the New Deal that set up the liberal welfare state were primarily oriented toward the production of "fit" "Americans" during a period of isolationism that characterized the interwar period in the United States. In this context, the US government regarded mothers mainly as conduits through which a strong American nation could be produced. New Deal welfare policies strongly re-established the ideal of the man as breadwinner and the woman as homemaker and thus rendered paid work morally and culturally incompatible with motherhood.[5] The logic of the family as the crucible for producing future Americans helped absorb new, European, immigrant groups into Whiteness, a category still being stabilized. Progressive reformers in the US Bureau of Children established intrusive policies toward poor women that established motherhood as a responsibility to democracy and to the American polity. The family would be the motor of cultural assimilation.[6] For example, mother's pensions, unconditional grants for widowed or abandoned women with children (divorced women and sex workers did not qualify) existed since the early twentieth century. These pensions were overtly aimed at alleviating the poverty of needy, single mothers for the sake of their children. Yet these policies were also deeply concerned with "Americanizing" the children of new immigrants through policies that directed mothers away from the culture of their homelands. This focus on the morality of the family further subordinated Black Americans who were growing in their cultural and political visibility following the Great Northward Migration beginning in the 1910s and continuing through the 1930s and beyond. Strong prejudices against African Americans meant that poor Black mothers were disproportionately excluded from the program based on their perceived immorality. Additionally, Mexican mothers were also refused pensions. Both these groups were viewed as unassimilable, unable to produce American citizens, and thus undeserving of pension support.[7] The impact of the seemingly progressive New Deal welfare policies, then, ironically concretized the White nuclear family as the epitome of culturally assimilated Americanness.

Furthermore, the labor laws that grew out of Roosevelt's landmark New Deal agenda cemented a "devil's bargain" that preserved the most oppressive working conditions for racialized workers.[8] While transforming the landscape of work for most, the lawmakers of the 1930s were intent on maintaining the racist order of the Jim Crow-era South. Thus labor legislation specifically excluded agricultural workers, predominantly Latine workers, and domestic workers, predominantly Black women. These two categories of workers were, under New Deal reforms, excluded from the protections of minimum wage, social security, and overtime laws that set a standard of low pay and a lack of benefits for decades to come.[9]

Buoyed by the United States' victory in WWII, the United States entered a period of unprecedented economic expansion that gave rise to another phase of liberalism that established a set of moral obligations between workers and employers. The postwar labor market operated according to liberal economic principles that suggested prices, wages, and profits should respond to market pressure and be negotiated between employers and workers.[10] Liberal principles also idealized a more just distribution of wealth and supported the expansion of individual freedoms. As a result, the postwar economy was characterized by a set of norms and obligations between workers and employers. For example, liberals continued to promote the greater power afforded to trade unions during the New Deal to maintain the balance of power between workers and employers. The idea of the "firm as family" and the notion that the firm and its workers had a long-term commitment to each other produced high levels of job security even within sectors of the labor market that operated with a nonunion model. Layoffs may happen during economic downturns, but a firm that was doing well could be expected to share the good fortune with employees. White-collar employees could expect a certain amount of employment security as well as upward mobility where workers begin in an entry-level position and work their way "up the ladder" within the same firm over their lifetime.[11]

However, these agreements between workers and employers solidified the understanding of women as secondary wage-earners at best, while also shoring up the nuclear family ideal further.[12] The prosperity for White families in the postwar era and the rise of white-collar jobs for men created an American culture that required a full-time wife and mother and a breadwinning man whose wages supported an evermore prosperous family that produced well-adjusted, confident children.[13] Women who were called into the factories during the war were told to go back to the home, even though many middle-class women did not wish to return to domestic life and many working-class women did not want to return to lower-status and lower-paying jobs such as domestic work.[14] Despite widening prospects for women in terms of education, sexual expression, and work, only women who were able to conform to the narrowing expectations of the hetero-patriarchal, White nuclear family were rewarded with the fruits of US modernity: single-family homes in newly expanding suburbs with technological appliances and the economic prosperity required to focus entirely on raising children. As Wini Breines has argued, the narrow expectations of femininity in the context of more expansive opportunities for women within view birthed widespread discontent that eventually gave rise to the feminist movement of the 1970s.[15]

The fruits of postwar liberal-democratic prosperity and morality were built upon racial separateness. Although all women experienced continuous discrimination in terms of the work that was available to them and the compensation they were offered, African-American and Latine women were restricted to the lowest rungs of the labor market, primarily domestic work and agricultural labor. Communities of color faced segregation in the workplace and continuous efforts on the part of employers to prevent cross-racial, cross-class coalitions in unions. Thus unions in key industries remained segregated, with employers using Black and Latine workers to break strikes and keep wages low. These workers were all but barred from white-collar jobs that could potentially offer more security and opportunity for upward mobility.

The Civil Rights Movement laid bare the inequities of the postwar economy and fueled the tumultuous social and political change of the 1960s. Yet the demands of the Civil Rights Movement were articulated in a way that aligned with liberalism's commitment to promoting individual self-determination. Racial discrimination came to be understood, like poverty, as an obstacle to individual thriving. Lyndon Johnson's Great Society legislation in the 1960s, a direct outcome of the Civil Rights Movement, reassembled aspects of the New Deal through a set of new policies. Great Society legislation declared a war on poverty, established the Medicare and Medicaid programs, and encouraged urban renewal. The United States passed landmark immigration reform, the 1965 Hart–Celler Act, which lifted the long-standing ban against migration from Asia.[16]

Amid the existential challenges around gender, race, and immigration at home, the United States entered into a heightened phase of the Cold War abroad, prompted by rapid decolonization in Africa and Asia and the rise of the UN.[17] The United States had long exercised imperialist policies, but the stakes of both "soft" ideological wars and military proxy operations had heightened by the 1960s. Indeed, the United States changed course on a key tenet of its stance against colonialism, established by Roosevelt in the 1940s in the context of India's freedom struggle. By the 1960s, US actions around the world promoted imperialist relationships of economic and political dependency, while opposing both Soviet and grassroots efforts to establish economic and political sovereignty, a topic we pursue in greater detail in the next chapter. All these factors led to a period of unrest and social transformation that laid the groundwork for the neoliberal policies that privileged corporations and eroded the moral and economic deal between workers and employers.

As economic growth stalled in the 1970s, economic and political discourses shifted from removing barriers faced by marginalized groups to addressing those government policies and programs that elites believed prevented the US national economy from realizing its full potential. The election of Richard Nixon brought new economic policy packages that began funneling rewards to the wealthy and a punitive approach toward the poor. This marked a sharp turn away from welfare-oriented policies that viewed poor families as centrally important for nation building. Pivoting away from an orientation of "sharing the wealth" toward a focus on growth rates, liberals increasingly used the government's power to tax and spend to grow the economy rather than to protect ordinary citizens against the busts of economic cycles. These shifts served to solidify and even exacerbate long-standing inequalities around racial wealth disparities, thus undermining the intended benefits of Great Society legislation and increasing the racial wealth gap.[18]

The creation of the suburbs emerged from a problem of political economy and geopolitics. After WWII, European markets were devastated, spurring US companies to create "new markets" at home. In parallel, the vision of US capitalism that was projected globally centered the nuclear family surrounded by its consumer goods. This nuclear family was supposed to be a bulwark against the spread of communism. Because the existence of a consumer-oriented nuclear family was so central to US economic and geopolitical interests, homosexuality was understood as treason. State-sanctioned discrimination against LGBTQ+ Americans, known as the Lavender Scare, was part of Joseph McCarthy's anti-communism campaign. The state justified this discrimination and homophobia by asserting that LGBTQ+ individuals could be blackmailed in a heightened moment of state-sponsored espionage during the Cold War. Thus, the US state carried out a purge of both actual and suspected LGBTQ+ Americans holding government positions.[19] LGBTQ+ citizens were also considered suspect because they did not contribute to the consumption patterns of nuclear families that were the basis for postwar American modernity. Gay identity seemed to threaten the nuclear family and did not require the new washing machines, vacuum cleaners, or cars that nuclear families, set up in the suburbs, were buying and displaying. In that context, the United States countered the Soviet Union's arguments about equality by emphasizing their problems of commodity distribution. The Soviet Union, to build "socialism in one country," had closed itself off from the rest of the global economy to create an economically self-sufficient supranational federation. Rather than have a debate about equality, the United States highlighted consumer choice and defined freedom as the ability to consume, all the while pointing fingers at the deprivation and lack of consumer goods behind the Iron Curtain.

White women's discontent with their domestic roles in the prosperous, Fordist family of the 1950s led to the women's movement of the 1970s. The daughters of "fifties mothers" sought to differentiate themselves from the oppression their mothers faced.[20] Betty Friedan's *The Feminine Mystique* made visible the gap between the ideal of the happy suburban housewife surrounded by her consumer goods and the malaise and unhappiness that White, middle-class women isolated in suburban homes reported experiencing, what Friedan called "the problem that had no name."[21] Friedan argued that women's oppression stemmed from their responsibility for unpaid labor in the home and their devaluation as "housewives." Thus the primarily White leaders of the women's movement envisioned women's freedom as tied to work outside the home. The key to liberation, according to Friedan and feminist activists, was access to paid work outside the home, which would make women economically self-sufficient and therefore free them from their dependence on men. For feminists of color, however, the workforce was a site of gendered and racial oppression, not liberation, due to the interconnected legacies of slavery, imperialism, and lack of legislation protecting women of color workers. As Black feminists have noted, while White, middle-class feminists were beholden to the reinvigorated postwar cult of domesticity, most women of color were already in the paid labor market, working in jobs that did not result in economic independence.

As greater numbers of women from all racial backgrounds entered the labor market, the need for state-supported childcare became evident, and, in 1972, a bill funding childcare for all children up until the age of five was passed by both the US House of Representatives and the Senate. However, due to the politics of the Cold War, which pitted US capitalism against Soviet communism, Republican President Richard Nixon vetoed the bill. Federally funded childcare, Nixon and his supporters argued, would have made the United States "communist." The veto of this bill, despite broad public support, ended any political possibility of state-subsidized childcare and legitimated the idea that, for the United States to be an exceptional capitalist nation, US women must care for their own children for free. This event has been largely erased from public memory, and support for state-subsidized childcare today has become a cause for politicians constructed as "far left."[22]

By the 1980s, citizens and policy makers under the presidency of Ronald Regan begin to understand the role of government in a new way. Scholars flag this as a key shift toward the neoliberal order: the role of government is no longer one of providing services to its citizens; instead it is to safeguard the well-being of its citizenry by maximizing their purchasing power and protecting their access to consumer goods. This shift in perspective had been in process since the start of the postwar period when white-collar jobs first started overtaking blue-collar jobs. Technologically driven products, as well as leisure, became sites at which to articulate prosperity and personal expression. But by the 1980s, the tenets of liberalism, contradictory as they had been, had given way to a new understanding of the state's role in allocating social good. Neoliberalism, as proposed by Reagan, suggested that the social good would be enhanced by maximizing the reach and frequency of market transactions, and thus neoliberal governance should ideally seek to bring all human action into the domain of the market.[23] In this framework, those who were poor were poor due to moral failings or a lack of hard work and were thus undeserving of state assistance. The domestic national ideology, as well as the international order upon which the New Deal welfare state was built, had transformed fundamentally. The United States needed to assert its global dominance and cultural distinctiveness through expressions of individual "choice" and "freedom" for both women and men, even as long-standing inequalities along lines of race and gender persisted and, in some cases, grew even starker. This ideological reconfiguration required, however, a socially conservative outlook that returned to the hetero-patriarchal family as the bedrock of national cultural identity.[24]

The Soviet Union's deal with women: "Build socialism alongside men"

As the nascent Soviet state[25] took shape after the October Revolution of 1917, 240,000 Bolshevik Party[26] members in a country of 145 million sought to transform a largely rural, peasant population used to being governed by a tsar into Soviet citizens with responsibilities for collective governance that required a new way of comprehending the world.[27] Marxist–Leninists prioritized class both in their immediate goal of creating a "dictatorship of the proletariat" that required a revolutionary class consciousness and as the interpretive frame for creating a Soviet moral order in which the collective was valued over the individual. However, gender was also important. Lenin and the Bolsheviks recognized that they needed women for both their political and economic projects to be successful. In laying out the project of radical democracy and inclusion required to staff a workers' state, Vladimir Lenin famously said in 1918, "Our task consists in making politics accessible for every laboring woman and in teaching every [female] cook [*kukharka*] to run the government."[28] To do this, Soviet ideology clearly and consistently stated that women should be liberated from their "patriarchal isolation" and the "stultifying world of housework."[29] Women must work with and support men in the collective project of building socialism. Official Soviet ideology suggested building socialism required women to cultivate a class consciousness that rejected bourgeois categories tied to gender identity in order to fully integrate women into all levels of the proletarian class struggle. However, political actors on the ground grappled with how to incorporate women into the Soviet project, and we can see this struggle in the political posters used to educate a largely illiterate population in the 1920s and 1930s.

The ideal Soviet man quickly and consistently emerged in Soviet iconography. The image of muscular, determined, proletarian men, whose labor provided the material riches of society – often depicted as blacksmiths – and whose political activism led the way to a bright socialist future, became ubiquitous.[30] Marxism–Leninism centered class status, privileged the urban proletariat, and remained wary of the revolutionary potential of peasants to embrace the working-class consciousness elites thought necessary to build socialism. Nevertheless, Lenin and the Bolsheviks recognized that they must build an alliance with the vast rural population. Rather quickly then, the heroic male image of the blacksmith worker with his hammer, leather apron, and boots was joined in the imagery by a bearded peasant with his scythe, peasant blouse, and woven bast shoes.[31] The category "worker" was gendered male, and the ideal Soviet man was consistently portrayed as the hero of the revolution, the protagonist of class struggle, and the champion of Soviet modernity.

It took several years for images of women as workers and peasants to join men in the political posters. When they were included, it was in subordinate positions that conveyed women's supporting role in building socialism alongside men.[32] Although on the surface, Soviet ideology was unambiguously committed to women's incorporation into the Soviet Union as full citizens with full gender equality, Lenin and other political elites worried that the "backwardness" of women would delay the state's project of propelling the region into Soviet modernity.[33] Thus, in the 1920s and 1930s, mock trials, performed by amateur actors and political activists, put fictional women on trial to condemn pre-revolutionary and "backward forms of behavior," and the "new" Soviet woman emerged as the heroine.[34] These courtroom dramas were to educate women on their new place in Soviet society.

Who was the ideal Soviet woman? Unlike the ideal Soviet man whose image changed little over time, the place of women was contested and the image of the ideal Soviet woman portrayed in Soviet iconography varied. The ideal Soviet woman was a "mother-worker." At times, the ideal emphasized motherhood, particularly when demographic anxieties due to loss of life during war surged, and at other times it emphasized her productive labor.[35] Nevertheless, the Soviet "mother-worker" was a proletarian who worked in the factory and was committed to the cause of socialism.[36] She was emancipated sexually and had the right to choose the size of her family – as long as she had one – for she was also a housewife who used modern, rationalized methods of work in the home.[37] She supported her husband and educated her children to adopt proletarian class and political identities. Thus the Soviet state sought to liberate women from private patriarchy and the drudgery of housework by making a gendered deal with women around these two issues, both because they wanted women engaged in the political work of building socialism but also because they needed women in the factories to support socialist economic programs of rapid industrialization.

As part of women's liberation, the Soviet state created an alliance with women as mothers to make them the direct beneficiaries of state services.[38] The state provided generous maternity leave, childcare, healthcare, and even socialized food preparation in collective dining halls.[39] Motherhood, therefore, was framed as a public service to the state.[40] Just one year after the Russian Revolution, the Family Code of 1918 attempted to equalize the rights of women and men in marriage.[41] It gave women the right to divorce their husbands without consent, access to abortion without the father's consent, undermined many aspects of men's authority in the home, and abolished the church's authority over family issues.[42]

Many scholars have investigated the question of whether women were actually "liberated," and most suggest that it is complicated. Answers vary by which women (for example, disabled mothers who could not attain the "mother-worker" ideal were disadvantaged in a workers' state),[43] by geography (policies and experiences varied by Soviet Bloc country, and nationality), and by historical period (gendered social policies shifted throughout the Soviet era). Additionally, some seemingly progressive reforms translated into the everyday lives of individuals in unexpected ways. For example, some aspects of private patriarchy were undermined, and Soviet women were not economically dependent on men for their and their children's livelihood. In addition, women reported that they felt "protected" by a state that guaranteed them stable work, free daycare, and free after-school activities.[44] However, the unequal gendered division of labor in the home was left intact since men were not expected to participate in housework and child-rearing.[45] The state replaced individual men as the head of the Soviet family and, in so doing, solidified women's sole responsibility for the family. Rather than economic self-sufficiency, women's dependency was transferred from individual men to the state.[46] Furthermore, discourses of women's "liberation" were mobilized to extend repressive state power into private family life.[47]

Women's access to paid labor had similarly mixed results. The region created a planned economy that spanned the republics to create an enclosed, self-sufficient economic region. According to the Soviet state, the progression to communism required policies of rapid industrialization and forced collectivization in agriculture.

Furthermore, the state needed full employment to meet production quotas in a labor-intensive, production-based, socialist economy. Thus, on the one hand, because the state was the primary employer, it could and did guarantee everyone full employment as a right of citizenship. On the other hand, the state also *required* everyone to work as a duty of citizenship. Although women were working in factories and state enterprises alongside men, because of their responsibilities at home, they were incorporated as second-class workers. Women were barred from top-level jobs, were channeled into sex-segregated occupations, and earned lower wages than men.[48] Women also did not feel "liberated" from housework because they could expect no help from men, and this left women alone to negotiate raising children along with the time-consuming tasks of managing the shortages of foodstuffs and other commodities that plagued the Soviet Union. Young mothers asked their own mothers for help.[49] Grandmothers stepped in to stand in breadlines and pick children up from daycare while young mothers worked. The Soviet state supported this extended family household by offering youthful retirement ages that allowed middle-aged women to help with the household labor and to provide childcare, often as the primary caregiver, to their grandchildren.[50]

Providing social protections was an important way the Soviet Union signaled its moral superiority to the West. Western "charity," offered by various private entities, was defined as an expression of bourgeois hypocrisy steeped in the exploitative domination of the ruling class. Instead, the Soviet Union offered *social* provision, protection, and care aimed at collectively guaranteeing emancipatory social justice.[51] Socialist welfare, linked to both collective social protections provided by the state and to the ideal of emancipation embodied by communism, was both the crux of socialist morality and the signifier of modern statehood.[52] Because mothers were constructed as a vulnerable population in need of social assistance and uplift, gender and women's emancipation became an important signifier of Soviet modernity.[53] Thus, in the gap between Soviet ideology and the varied lived experiences of socialism, many women did enjoy enviable social protections alongside severe hardship.

In recent ethnographic studies, women in the region often express nostalgia for the Soviet Union's social protections that guaranteed secure jobs, childcare, healthcare, and education, and they also deplore the lack of opportunities and choice.[54] The feminist neoliberal cover story in the FSU, which we explore in chapter 4, reframes emancipation as "choice." Many post-Soviet women find these "choices" – including the choice to be a mother without also being forced to be a worker and the choice to be a wife to a man who will "protect" the family – to be both modern and desirable.

India: forging indigenous nationalism between capitalism and socialism

Prior to the imposition of the neoliberal order, countries of SSEA experienced diverse colonial regimes imposed by the British, Spanish, Portuguese, Japanese, US, and Dutch – forces that all had distinctive characteristics and thus left behind divergent, intertwined legacies. Yet all forms of colonialism created economic and political structures of interdependency with the colonizer, as well as transformed cultural norms and ideologies shaped by colonial rule and nationalist resistance. When nationalist social movements overthrew colonial powers in this region, economic and ideological aspects of colonialism persisted. Newly independent governments were forced to confront the disorder, dispossession, and social unrest that colonial rulers left in their wake in their home countries.[55] Simultaneously, these new nation-states had to represent their national interests and symbolic projects in a global institutional sphere that had been consolidated after WWII. Representations of womanhood and family became key metaphors through which to represent postcolonial, nationalist projects both at home and abroad.

We focus on India's history in this chapter as a key representative of postcolonial nations' experience in the lead-up to the imposition of the neoliberal order. In doing so, we acknowledge that even within SSEA, countries did not necessarily experience a similar chronology of gendered and political struggles and that the timeline along which countries in the region wrestled with domestic crises and international power grabs in the context of the Cold War varied greatly. In the Philippines, for example, the legacy of US imperialism meant that the Philippines was a close ally of the United States in the two decades following WWII, and thus largely followed the model of the United States' liberal economic and political order. Gendered images of modernity and nation echoed those articulated by American gender ideologies of sexual freedom and consumerism.[56] When Marcos came to power in 1966, there was a marked shift both in international positioning and in gendered articulations of modernity because the Marcos administration forged closer ties with the Soviet Union and eventually became one of the founding members of the G-77 in

1971. This move distanced the Philippines from the United States in both political and symbolic terms, and notions of gendered Filipina modernity absorbed Soviet influences.[57] Acknowledging these variations, we contend that SSEA helps us uncover the global genealogy of the neoliberal order because of its confrontation with the legacy of colonialism at home and the compulsion to compete for status in global institutions abroad. In India, we gain the vantage point of a country at the forefront of anti-colonial nationalism worldwide and a leader in the formation of the non-aligned movement (NAM) and the G-77 even as India's articulation of gendered modernity was beholden to domestic articulations of indigenous authenticity and difference.

India's new government's state-centered social democratic vision defined the initial post-independence period. The challenges to this vision, which became apparent in the 1970s, revealed the failures of the new nation's political projects, especially in rural areas. By examining economic and political visions and gendered representations in parallel, we generate a fine-grained understanding of the connections between material and cultural struggles at home and the evolving hierarchy of nations, organized by perceptions of modernity that were always in the awareness of postcolonial leaders and policy makers.

India's leaders developed economic and political plans to drive the nation forward in response to pressures from within their borders and in response to pressures in the international realm. Gendered representations, such as Mother India on the one hand and heroines in films and literature on the other, legitimated political projects at home while also helping to envision a modern nation-state. Such representations were essential for shoring up India's soft power in the postwar international realm, especially because Orientalist imagery portrayed gender relations in India as perverse.[58] Gendered representations helped consolidate and articulate India's political resistance to British colonialism.

Anti-colonial nationalists struggled mightily over how an independent India would be organized in the aftermath of colonial rule. What would the nation stand for culturally and materially? How would independent India address layers of division within its diverse citizenry? How could rural India be modernized? How would India be fed and clothed? The elite men who controlled the anti-colonial nationalist movement debated these material and symbolic aspects of national identity amid the tactical challenges of political liberation. In the context of these debates, the "women's question" was central. Eventually, elite nationalists resolved this "question" in part through the discursive production of a gendered bifurcation between the public and private spheres that created an idealized Indian woman characterized by chastity, domesticity, modesty, and education.[59] In this nationalist formulation, the inner world of the home was considered to be the sacred space of Indian culture and identity, which needed to be preserved through a quintessentially Indian, Hindu, middle-class woman who embodied Indian culture and attended to the upbringing of children. In contrast, the outer world of men necessarily needed to modernize and incorporate the best of western science and technology.

During the anti-colonial movement in the early twentieth century, the respectable middle-class housewife became an ideal Indian woman, a keeper of culture and a marker of the moral superiority of the nation. She was an image that had to be constructed in opposition to sexier, explicitly "modern" formulations of Indian womanhood that were popular in the 1920s and 1930s.[60] This newer, more respectable ideal reflected the desire of the elite men who controlled the nationalist movement to show their support for gender equality in principle, but in practice to extend patriarchy and caste oppression.[61] Significantly, Indian women themselves, who were actively organizing around diverse anti-colonial causes, were not allowed to contribute to these ideologies. Instead, women's attempts to organize for full participation in every aspect of society were subordinated to the nationalist cause defined by elite men.[62]

As a result of these decisions, women of all backgrounds became both symbols of culture in nationalist ideology and active subjects managing the transformations wrought by anti-colonial nationalism. The conflicting imperatives of women's formal equality in the legal realm and strengthened patriarchal control in the realm of family life thus required a quintessentially gendered figure to consolidate the contradictions between tradition and modernity, authenticity and imitation, religion and science.[63] Nationalists depended on real women to act as signifiers of an "essential indigenous femininity" that stood in contrast to colonialism.[64] As in many other national contexts, in India the figure of the mother answered the call. Diverse and ever-changing representations of Mother India, or Bharat Mata, as a goddess attempted to consolidate and resolve the contradictions of the nationalist project through diverse images, media, fiction, and, later, cinematic representations.

By the 1950s, the early days after the overthrow of British rule, Jawaharlal Nehru, India's first prime minister, promoted a democratic socialist model of nation building that both nationalized the major industries and focused on poverty alleviation, particularly in rural areas.[65] Cinematic efforts, supported by state funding, bolstered this political vision through the production of emotional gendered imagery that created affective ties between Nehru's ideals and Indian citizens. Most significantly, the 1957 blockbuster film, *Mother India* (Khan 1957), reworked the image of Bharat Mata as a goddess, instead portraying this iconic figure as a sacrificing rural woman.[66] The film "celebrates [the] woman in the linked roles of daughter of the soil (soil = India) and mother of her sons." Drawing together influences from Pearl Buck's *Good Earth* (1931), Soviet nationalist films such as those of Aleksandr Dovzhenko, and Katherine Mayo's controversial book, *Mother India*, filmmaker Mehboob represented women as the soul of India in a way that was remarkably resonant with Soviet depictions of emancipated, rural womanhood and thus departed from representations of Mother India-as-goddess.[67] The film shows the protagonist, a peasant woman, struggling with the earth, often covered in mud and fighting the elements, all the while fulfilling her many familial roles without complaint. Ultimately, she sacrifices her own son to preserve the honor of the village and becomes a village matriarch.[68] By mapping the nation onto the body of a peasant woman, *Mother India* valorized collective national ideals for the nation's peasantry, all the while relating to the figure of Bharat Mata.[69]

Despite the explicit policy focus on poverty alleviation in rural areas, agricultural productivity stagnated by the 1960s, entrenching poverty further.[70] The 1960s brought a policy turn toward improving rural productivity with the rollout of Green Revolution technology. These improvements produced little in the way of redistributive change due to local elite control, lack of consistency over land reform in various regions of the country, and the reality that poor farmers did not have the support needed to take advantage of high-yielding seed varieties meant to fuel agricultural transformation. It was clear that the ambitious social goals set out by the country's postcolonial leaders had not been attained. In some areas of the country, such as West Bengal, these conditions fomented revolution. Women were heavily involved in leftist mobilizations, both as militant mothers and as cadre members, although their participation in these movements is understudied.[71] Their visions of struggle drew heavily upon the trope of the self-sacrificing mother and the heroic revolutionary son, even though they strongly critiqued elite nationalist economic and social policies. Like the film *Mother India*, these movements drew heavily from the ideology and imagery of communist peasant struggles in the Soviet Union. This was a period when the United States was anxious about the relationship between India and the Soviet Union, and especially about the rise of radical leftist movements. US policies heavily funded scholarship that would promote "village studies" during this time period, a structural-functionalist approach that viewed rural villages as a site of harmony, rather than strife.[72] These studies directly aimed to produce knowledge that would counter leftist framings of peasant struggles that had strong economic and affective appeal to a wide swath of Indian citizens.

Even though the Indian government made major investments in centralized industry, mirroring the economic strategies of the Soviet Union, this economic approach was never as successful as similar strategies deployed in other countries because the Indian state never completely controlled the business class.[73] Without control of the business class, successive efforts to reduce dependency on foreign markets failed. In the 1960s and 1970s, import substitution industrialization (ISI), a popular initiative across postcolonial countries that sought to eliminate domestic dependence on exports, was deemed a failure. Later, in the 1970s and 1980s, export-oriented industrialization, a strategy that achieved great success in Southeast Asia, also failed. Both poverty alleviation and industrialization efforts during the postcolonial period were dogged by the deep divisions along caste lines and the persistent rural/urban divides that were established under colonial rule and perpetuated by the new nationalist government. Legacies of colonial rule intersected with long-standing religious and social norms to reinforce the marginalization of the lowest-caste strata and tribal communities across the country that stymied national efforts toward "development."

Building upon the strategies of her father Nehru, Indira Gandhi's administration crafted policies to promote parallel economies to address these failures. One economy was oriented toward macroeconomic development and support for large industries, while a second economy aimed to promote social programs and rural economies. But, during Gandhi's time, it was clear that the latter was left behind due to underinvestment.[74] These discrepancies resulted in a series of political crises, and led to the imposition of emergency rule under Gandhi and, ultimately, her assassination in 1985. Between the 1970s and 1980s, diverse gendered representations in film and literature reflected the prevailing social crises. Gandhi's authoritative leadership itself challenged the idealized mother-wife-goddess trope of Indian womanhood. Representations of subaltern women's agency also contested this trope. In a popular short story by Mahasveta

Devi, for example (Srila Roy 2012; Spivak 1981), a Naxalite woman, Dopdi Mehjan, challenges her rapists through derisive laughter and mockery.[75] Iconic films in the 1970s and 1980s by master filmmaker Satyajit Ray represent women as amoral when circumstances demand it. His characters turn to cheating or prostitution to survive. In other circumstances, the women in his films are peripheral to the actions of men, who are the main agents. Both these representations depart from his earlier representations of the "new woman" as a moral agent of her own destiny.[76]

By the end of the 1980s, India's political and economic order had sustained multiple crises and only partially addressed the twin concerns of its nationalist founding: poverty and centralized industry. During this time period, India was at the forefront of organizing among the non-aligned countries and was working for a fairer economic order.[77] When Rajiv Gandhi took over from his mother in 1985, India started changing course, tilting toward a more capitalist orientation that set up the convergence toward a neoliberal order. New dominant representations of gender and nation that emerged in relation to the new global India, from the 1990s onward, will be explored further in chapter 4, where we characterize neoliberalism's gender order.

Conclusion

When the Soviet Union dissolved in 1991, it signaled the end of the Cold War and the triumph of a neoliberal world order designed by the United States and Europe. It also signified the start of a convergence between economic, political, and gender orders that were distinct, but, as we have shown in this chapter, constructed in relation to one another. The gender orders of the United States and the Soviet Union were, like communism and capitalism, constructed in opposition to one another because of the diametrically opposed "deals" they struck with women.

While the postwar prosperity that the United States experienced expanded opportunities for education, work, leisure, and sexual expression for women, the conditions of postwar prosperity and the opposition to socialism had the effect of constricting most middle-class White women to a domestic role as full-time mothers. Although this vision was undermined and questioned by the social movements of the 1960s and 1970s, its primacy in establishing a distinctive, American image of prosperity was supported by federal policies beholden to Cold War politics in the international realm. When Nixon vetoed the 1972 law for federally subsidized childcare because such a move would put the United States on a path toward communism, he highlighted the extent to which the United States' global engagements constructed its internal gender order.

In contrast, the Soviet Union built its socialist vision for the world on the emancipation of women from private patriarchy and the drudgery of housework. The Soviet state offered women full and equal participation in the labor market, and, through social provision, the state also assumed some of the burdens of childcare, housework, healthcare, and education. When formerly colonized countries gained independence, the Soviet Union vied for ideological and political power over the US-led capitalist efforts, and those battlegrounds centrally included gender. Claiming emancipation and freedom for its women in opposition to the oppression faced by American women, the Soviet Union articulated a vision of womanhood that elevated workers and peasants and rejected the bourgeois excesses of American prosperity.

India, like other newly postcolonial nations, consolidated a gendered vision of its independent nation as a part of its anti-colonial struggle. As the decades after independence proceeded, however, this indigenous vision for femininity was sandwiched between the appeals of Soviet-style poverty alleviation and rural uplift on the one hand and US-style prosperity for the urban nuclear family on the other. In this context, women became signifiers of the nation-state as well as everyday managers of the postcolonial condition to a more pronounced extent than in the United States or Soviet Union. Shuttling between ideals as goddesses, mothers, victims, and career women, Indian women were tasked with the production of a tenuous modernity that had to be communicated to a vast and diverse populace and publicized effectively abroad to counter Orientalist images that rendered all Indian women oppressed.

Building upon the context of these clashing gender orders, the next chapter examines how our three regions encountered one another in the realm of international institutions during the postwar period. We argue that the areas of gender equality and education became key terrains upon which the ideological battles of the Cold War were waged, with G-77 countries like India attempting to consolidate power in a changing global system that they had not built themselves. These policy battles in international institutions set up the discursive framework for "women's empowerment" that eventually became the ideological glue that would legitimize the neoliberal order.

3
Investing in "Empowered" Women

The distinct historical contexts that we have described in the previous chapter came into conversation with one another after WWII in the new realm of international institutions. The UN, established in 1945 by 51 member countries, constituted an unprecedented kind of transnational organization in which countries, regardless of their historical position, could dialogue with one another to maintain international peace and security while aiming to prevent a repetition of the atrocities of the war. In this chapter, we pivot from our focus on regional histories to the conversations that commenced between Soviet, postcolonial, and Euro-American countries at the UN and its many institutions. We find that this international realm comes to be a key area where we can witness the competition between nations and, in particular, the battle between two conceptions of empowerment, each with long political histories.

In our introduction, we argued that neoliberal feminism, and more specifically, a narrow, commonsense understanding of "empowerment" for women, constitutes an essential ideological building block of the neoliberal order. When we think about empowerment today, we take for granted that it refers to individual accomplishment, achieved through education, economic self-sufficiency, and expanded consumer choices, especially for women.[1] Its current dominance, however, obscures the long political histories of a much broader and more contested concept of empowerment that called for upliftment of the oppressed and a large-scale collective mobilization. After WWII, the United States, the Soviet Union, and postcolonial countries who had organized themselves into a powerful allied bloc called the G-77, fought ideological battles over which version of empowerment would be dominant in global and transnational organizations such as the UN and the World Bank. More specifically, the United States and the UN battled one another for decades over the issues of mass literacy, education for empowerment, and full inclusion of women in states and economies. The UN, with the support of most nations of the world, aimed to advance these issues, but the United States was firmly *against* these efforts. How, then, did we arrive at the set of associations with empowerment that we have today, and what are its consequences?

The tremendous upheaval and geopolitical turmoil of the Cold War, which unfolded in parallel with the rapid decolonization of countries around the world, presents us with a key context, too often forgotten, through which we may trace how empowerment came to mean what it does today in the global institutional sphere. Exposing these dynamics helps us uncover the gendered character of the neoliberal order that we regard as an inevitable outcome of global political history. In this chapter, we trace how empowerment became associated with individual economic choices for women, rather than collective mobilization and systemic transformation. The current associations we have with the term "empowerment" were never obvious outcomes. Instead, collective, radical understandings of empowerment had global support up until the end of the twentieth century. We identify the rise of human capital theory, an area of behavioral economics that emphasizes investment in individuals, as a key intellectual and discursive innovation that transformed empowerment into the individualistic concept we have today.

As we analyze how discourses of empowerment became real in the policy programs of global institutions, we find that the United States' policy priorities actively countered programs that promoted universal literacy and supported women's livelihoods and instead advocated for instrumental education policies ostensibly focused on economic productivity. Regarding education, the UN and the United States parted ways over the differences between "mass literacy" and "functional" education, a division that crippled the effectiveness of UN education programs in Asia, Africa, and Latin America for decades to come.[2] India and other newly independent nations were often ideologically aligned with the Soviet Union in their interpretations of empowerment. They aimed to implement radical policies that would eradicate poverty and illiteracy. Feminists from India and other newly independent nation-states established key political and social alliances with Eastern European and Soviet women to advocate for policies such as universal childcare at the beginning of the UN Decade for Women. In this arena, too, delegates from the

Investing in "Empowered" Women 43

United States withheld support for radical proposals as a way of pushing against Soviet influence.[3] Thus, diverse efforts to mobilize marginalized groups and strengthen the resilience of economies in newly decolonized nation-states were stymied by US policies about education and women. US interventions in global institutions thus fundamentally altered the diverse meanings of empowerment that were in circulation after WWII. As a result of these geopolitical interventions, an individualistic, gendered, and economistic understanding of empowerment became fundamental to the neoliberal world order.

But how did the United States legitimate and gain support for their proposals when most of the world opposed them? We identify human capital theory as the primary intellectual and political frame through which the United States and its allies forged its individualized vision of empowerment. Human capital theory focused on individuals by evaluating how investments in education could improve the individual productivity of workers, which in turn could fuel economic growth. Unlike the frameworks offered by collective conceptualizations of empowerment, human capital theory's foundation in economics presented nation-states around the world with a set of metrics through which they could gain status within a growing community of nations while at the same time transforming collective understandings of empowerment into individual ones. Human capital theory especially shaped meanings of empowerment in two specific policy arenas in the global institutional sphere: education, and gender and development policy. Between the 1960s and the early 2000s, in the policy areas of education and gender and development, we find that various applications of "empowerment" were tested and transformed by the framework of human capital. In the context of these debates, the United States, the FSU, and postcolonial countries such as India were all shaping and responding to the economic, political, and ideological shifts of a contested geopolitical order shaped by the end of colonialism and the Cold War. By the end of this timespan, the idea that empowerment could be advanced through the expansion of education and policies geared toward improving the lives of girls and women became common sense. High levels of literacy and education for women were able to confer status on previously colonized countries and allow them to appear "modern" in a hierarchical geopolitical order structured by competition and shared norms.

We present this chapter by first providing an overview of the ideological divisions that organized the global institutional sphere from the end of WWII until the beginnings of the neoliberal order. We found the postcolonial world to be a powerful force in international politics, one that threatened both capitalist visions of linear modernization theory and communist visions of emancipation for the masses through centralized planning. In the 1970s and 1980s, two varieties of empowerment discourse in relation to the management of marginalized groups began circulating in the global institutional sphere: individual empowerment discourse and collective empowerment discourse. We find that collective interpretations were diverse and had broad support from various countries, although individual interpretations were always sustained in tandem to these collective imaginings.

To explain exactly how the individual meanings of empowerment became dominant, we then focus on the policy debates of the 1970s, 1980s, and 1990s in the areas of education and of women and development to identify the ascent of human capital theory. In particular, global institutions such as the World Bank, the UN, and UNESCO were grappling with two parallel transformations that eventually converged: the shift away from investing in material infrastructure for modernization toward investment in education, and from "women" as a marginalized group to be managed or integrated to the "mainstreaming" of gender concerns throughout these sprawling institutions. Human capital facilitated these transformations in both these key policy areas, thus "taming" the unruliness of empowerment as a concept and disciplining it within a narrow individualist frame focused on access to formal education, paid work, and the potential for entrepreneurialism. By the turn of the century, human capital had become the master template for "soft" policies related to human development and democracy around the world.[4] These two policy areas, we argue, are the concrete sites at which global institutional actors affiliated with the United States mobilized human capital theory to eliminate competing understandings of empowerment by promoting spending priorities, donor requirements, and policy language that reproduced ideologies associated with capitalism and individualism.

The era of competing ideologies: postcoloniality, modernization, and communism during the Cold War

At the close of WWII, a global institutional sphere emerged from postwar institutions forged by the victors. In particular, the UN became an arena of global governance in which a new international system of nation-states, including many newly independent ones, could engage with one another to negotiate and converse on issues ranging from trade policy to land reform to human rights. This emergent sphere was shaped by three prominent geopolitical forces that comprised a postcolonial global order: the United States and its allies, who represented liberal capitalism; the Soviet Union and its allies, who represented socialism; and G-77 countries, a group of non-aligned countries, many of which were previously colonized. The G-77 bloc advocated for a fairer international economic system that would allow them to participate in the global economy on more equal footing while also meeting the primary needs of their own people.[5] But their decolonial aspirations took shape in the context of the Cold War when the United States and the Soviet Union were battling one another to preserve and extend their geopolitical influence.

These Cold War geopolitical dynamics, which presaged the neoliberal order, meant that contests over the meaning of empowerment were never just about finding the policy solutions that would best serve the interests of citizens or even nation-states. Instead, individualized interpretations of empowerment were understood to be aligned with the goals of liberal capitalism, while collective understandings of empowerment were understood to be aligned both with communism and postcolonial countries seeking redress for historical wrongs. In the context of these debates, further alignment emerged between collective understandings of empowerment and marginalized groups in nation-states throughout the world. We briefly summarize the range of positions in Table 3.1.

By the 1960s, most of Latin America, Asia, and Africa had won their political independence from their colonial rulers and were actively crafting policy packages that would strengthen local economies and dramatically curtail economic dependence on foreign trade. The anti-colonial movements that helped overthrow colonial powers around the world were based on nationalist notions of empowerment that stressed economic and political self-sufficiency for newly independent nation-states, a set of meanings that emerged from M. K. Gandhi's writings on self-rule during his time in South Africa.[6] Yet the policies of these new countries were constrained by the contests for power between the United States and the Soviet Union since both forces aimed to foster alliances with these new countries and prevent the spread of each other's ideologies. The Kennedy, Johnson, and Nixon administrations were

Table 3.1 Competing Visions of Empowerment in Geopolitical Perspective

	US-led	Soviet-led	G-77
Discursive language	Linear modernization led by private companies that would produce industrialization, science, and technology through economic growth	Emancipation for the masses through centralized planning that would lead to industrialization, science, and technology	Economic and political sovereignty/ self-sufficiency to support rapid industrialization and technological advancement
Desired system of trade	Interdependent system in which the United States could maintain its relative strength in managing resources and finance	Centralized system of interdependent states	A fair system of trade in which countries can choose to protect nascent industries through tariffs and other protectionist policies, NIEO
Education policy around the world, especially regarding newly independent nations	Not a priority until the 1980s; considered politically dangerous and not necessary for economic growth. Post-1980s, only "functional" education considered supportive of economic growth	Universal education viewed as a prerequisite for socialist society; Soviets supported and funded mass literacy projects	Universal education a priority for most postcolonial nations; required to support aspirations for a literate electorate and political sovereignty
Women and development	Focus on bringing women into productive industrial work to support economic growth and increase productivity	Focus on emancipation of women from patriarchal isolationism and the drudgery of housework by incorporating them as workers in service of building socialism	Collective vision of an economic and political system supportive of women as mothers and full citizens; forged by women's movements, not necessarily elites within respective nations

all centrally involved in crafting anti-communist policies around the world and through major multilateral institutions while funding proxy wars against the Soviets. Simultaneously, Soviet leaders were forging their own alliances in postcolonial contexts and promoting policies and programs that would expand the geopolitical power of communism.

Both dominant powers had compelling templates for modernity, progress, and development, and they were blatant in their efforts to expand their geopolitical reach. The ideological contests became more consequential because both the United States and the Soviet Union's visions of modernity and progress had many features in common: an emphasis on industrialization of agriculture and urbanization, a focus on science and technology, and a promise of education. Where they diverged, however, was on the purpose of these national projects. For the United States, industrialization, science, and technology were oriented toward trade and consumerism, while in the Soviet Union these goals were oriented toward the elimination of drudgery. Following Marx, the goal of technological advance was to reduce the number of hours citizens had to work to meet their basic needs so that they could enjoy more time in the "realm of freedom," living well-rounded lives.[7] While the United States' project of modernity was premised on a striving individual, Soviet modernity was premised on a collective culture in which everyone had their needs met. Because the Cold War was fought primarily on ideological terrain, the ideologically important "soft" policy areas of education and women were just as central to their geopolitical interests as control over territory or natural resources.

Resisting nationalist interpretations of economic self-sufficiency that were compelling for postcolonial nation-states, the Soviet Union championed understandings of emancipation that would support a union of centrally managed, interdependent states that collectively produced conditions that supported everyone. They provided free education and healthcare to millions who were only recently impoverished peasants, while also leading the world in technological innovations, a fact proven spectacularly by the successful launch of *Sputnik* in 1957 that won the global space race. These events only further intensified what was already an intense global competition between the United States and the Soviet Union as each government fought for influence in newly postcolonial parts of the world.

The United States, in contrast, sought to sustain an interdependent system of international trade in which the United States could maintain a position of relative power in managing the resources and finances of postcolonial nations. From the earliest postwar period, the United States leveraged its influence within global institutions like the World Bank to push modernization theories that posited a linear path to industrialization and development, a set of theories they believed would allow them to maintain some level of control over the postcolonial world.[8] In tandem with these policy packages, policies that we today would recognize as neoliberal – low tariffs, high levels of commodity specialization, few social benefits, a focus on exports – were crafted by a group of influential and well-connected economists who Quinn Slobodian identifies as the "ordoliberals." These thinkers long believed that national sovereignty was threatening to capitalism.[9] The ordoliberals wished to craft a world order in which new nation-states were compulsorily part of a global system of "free trade" that allowed the United States and its allies to retain their historical dominance and expand the global financial system. This vision was threatened both by the Soviet Union's political project of an interconnected, centrally managed union of allied states and by the demands of postcolonial countries to create a new international economic order (NIEO). For the neoliberal capitalist order to become widely accepted, the focus of "development" had to shift to individual economic opportunities. This shift required both anti-colonial visions of self-sufficiency and the interdependent internationalism of communist states to be erased in favor of a peaceful world of free markets.

By the 1990s, international institutions such as the World Bank had successfully redefined expectations for newly independent nation-states along lines favored by the United States and its allies, requiring austerity in social programs and a high level of specialization oriented toward export. This set of policy arrangements would insert all countries into interconnected trade circuits that would create webs of interdependence, ostensibly ensuring world peace. Thomas Friedman's bestselling 2004 and 2006 books, *The Lexus and the Olive Tree* and *The World is Flat*, represented the triumph of this neoliberal set of value systems most compatible with US interests. These books popularized what is now taken-for-granted knowledge in the most powerful circles of global policy making: that the interdependencies of a global system of free trade, far from being a continuation of oppressive colonial arrangements, are a prerequisite for individual striving, economic prosperity, and international peace. What role does the robust concept of "empowerment," long associated with the upliftment of oppressed groups, play in this triumphalist scenario?

Empowerment discourse: a brief genealogy

As the global institutional sphere became a key site at which contests for geopolitical power were underway, the concept of empowerment was starting to circulate in the hallways of the World Bank, the UN, and its affiliated institutions. Empowerment was conceived as a desired outcome for marginalized groups in the postcolonial world and in the United States. But the meaning of empowerment was contested in specific fields, most especially in policy making about women and education. An *individualized understanding of empowerment* focused on the improvement of opportunities for individual workers to access wage earning and commodities. In contrast, *collective understandings of empowerment* focused on guaranteeing a minimal standard of living for all, uplifting the most marginalized, and strengthening collective systems of production and care. These competing meanings of empowerment emerged in relation to education and women's movements in the global South and in the space of social work in the United States. In all these areas, collective interpretations of empowerment demanded structural changes that would fundamentally transform the position of historically marginalized groups. In contrast, parallel discourses in the Soviet Union of emancipation, not empowerment, were central to the communist project. Communist visions of emancipation were largely excluded from empowerment discourse in the emergent global institutional sphere, although, as we shall see, they influenced collective imaginings of empowerment coming from postcolonial contexts.

Women's empowerment

Women's movements in the global South had embraced the concept of empowerment at diverse sites around the world in a visible way for decades, eventually circulating in global institutional spaces by the 1980s. In a special issue of the journal *Development*, Andrea Cornwall and Nana Akua Anyidoho include narratives about grassroots women's empowerment movements from Brazil, the United States, Serbia, Sierra Leone, and the Palestinian Occupied Territories.[10] These transformative grassroots visions of women's empowerment, although distinct in each of the contexts they appeared, were oriented toward the disruption and eventual eradication of patriarchy and women's collective mobilization for structural change. As such, the "power" in "empowerment" was explicit.[11] Personal or individual empowerment, defined in terms of economic and social autonomy, was always a part of the concept, but never the focus.[12] For example, the grassroots activists in Recife, Brazil stated that empowerment was about women fighting together for safety, access to a livelihood, as well as personal autonomy to resist the domination of men.[13] Other feminist activists involved in grassroots understandings of empowerment describe a process of conscientization to realize and develop a collective identity that can be mobilized.[14]

At the global level, Gita Sen and Caren Grown articulated a vision of economic transformation based on collective understandings of women's empowerment from the global South that were drawn from a network of women's organizations from across the region called Development Alternatives with Women for a New Era (DAWN), a network we explore later in this chapter.[15] Sen and Grown link the persistent oppressive conditions faced by women in the global South with the macroeconomic structures of development policy and, in particular, the view that women need to be "included" in "mainstream" economic processes for empowerment and prosperity. They argue that the vision of empowerment needed to remedy this comes from organizations and women's movements on the ground centering the perspectives of poor women, a transformation that requires resources, skills, leadership formation, and dialogue, among other important efforts.[16] In this vision, individual empowerment is not equated with paid work for poor women but rather with mobilization within the context of broader political struggles.

The Soviet Union's ideology of women's emancipation was central to their political vision, and was informing, however implicitly, the specifics of empowerment discourse taking shape in the global institutional sphere. From as early as 1917, Leninist women pushed for women's education as a central feature of emancipation from classist oppression, a set of convictions and practices that influenced the entirety of the Soviet Union's experience of socialism. In Mikhail Gorbachev's *perestroika*, he specifies the high stakes for women's emancipation as both fundamental to the political order and to the relative status of one society when compared to another. "The extent of women's emancipation is often viewed as a yardstick to be used in judging the social and political level of a society," Gorbachev asserts. "The Soviet state put an end to discrimination against women so typical of tsarist Russia with determination and without compromise. ...Without the contribution and selfless work of women, we would not have built a new society nor won the war against fascism."[17] Because of this history, when FSU countries emerged onto a global stage after the fall of the Soviet Union, a highly educated population of women validated their relatively advanced symbolic position in relation to countries in the global South.

But as diverse conceptualizations of women's empowerment became incorporated into global development discourse at global institutions, feminists were deeply disappointed. Empowerment had been depoliticized. Cornwall and Anyidoho regard this "anemic" version of women's empowerment as "empowerment lite," or "em-ment" with the "power" taken out.[18] Cecilia Sardenberg specifies that this version of women's empowerment regards it as "an instrument for development priorities, be they eradicating poverty or building democracy."[19] Global organizations such as the United Nations Research Institute for Social Development (UNRISD), the World Bank, and the International Labor Organization (ILO) all incorporated concern for women's economic and social issues into their programming from the 1970s onward, but in the 1990s the notion of "empowerment" came to dominate discussions of women's issues. This version centered personal empowerment over collective transformation but was also appealing enough that it could be adapted to multiple cultural and ideological contexts. Once "mainstreamed" into various institutions, "empowerment" only became meaningful as a justification for investing in women's education when it became linked with the framework of human capital, a development we will explore below. "For many feminists," Cornwall and Anyidoho explain, "'women's empowerment' represents a sorry – but not unfamiliar – tale of how a once-radical concept was stolen by the high priests of neo-liberalism only to be foisted onto women in the global South as their putative salvation."[20]

Education for all

Empowerment discourse circulated in the global institutional settings of the post-WWII period in relation to education as well, setting up the most radical claim to the term and working in relation to women's movements around the world. Paolo Freire, the Brazilian philosopher, educator, and author of *Pedagogy of the Oppressed*, stressed a vision of education leading to political transformation that influenced DAWN's understanding of collective empowerment for women.[21] Freire believed that oppressed groups, through a participatory educational praxis, must become aware of the systems of subordination that constrain them. Freire believed that they had to start by analyzing the concrete details of the oppressive situations in which they found themselves and, through dialogue, develop solidarity among various groups facing oppression to work toward their own liberation. In this model, actors outside of the community were not to act as instigators of radical change – the change had to come from within. The radical education that Freire proposed required the full participation of the most marginalized groups in the design and practice of their own education and transformation. The oppressed had to, through their own effort, acquire consciousness of their situation of oppression to surmount it. This would require overcoming the hegemonic domination they are surrounded by and socialized into.

Freire's notion of participatory educational practice galvanized women's movements, non-governmental organizations (NGOs), and governments around the world. Aradhana Sharma has argued that, in India, Freire's perspective profoundly shaped a national program, called the Mahila Samiti (MS) movement, aimed at the empowerment of women in rural areas.[22] This movement emerged from a government policy program, despite it also being an NGO with the ethos of a social movement. Freirean principles informed the MS's understanding of women's education and placed the notion of participatory process and consciousness-raising at the center. But, as Sharma's research showed, the translation of these principles into practice sometimes undermined the stated aims because government programs required metrics and indicators for the success of empowerment programs. These requirements directly conflicted with a flexible pedagogical praxis. Sharma's work shows us that the Freirean understandings of empowerment, while influential, did not determine any specific understanding of empowerment in practice. Even the core principles of participation and conscientization merged with state and corporate imperatives on the ground that compromised or transformed those principles. On the ground in radical movements, empowerment was "unruly." Notions of collective and individual transformation collided in organizational settings, state policies and programs, and in the everyday lives of individuals and groups working with the most marginalized rural women in India.

When Freire's influential understandings of empowerment circulated at the World Bank, they became a key part of the reassessment and rethinking of modernization theories that were dominant from the 1950s onward. Developed by thinkers such as Walter Roscoe, Albert Hirschmann, and Talcott Parsons, US-led modernization theories were battling the equally ascendant communist views, since Stalin's role in the Allied victory had demonstrated the fruits of centralized planning that emphasized basic needs, literacy, and infrastructure. Freire's understanding of empowerment through participatory education sat uneasily alongside the World Bank's commitment to increasing worker productivity and expanding labor market participation in the postcolonial world. Yet to completely ignore these ideas risked the delegitimization of the Bank's role as a neutral expert fostering development.

American theories of social work

Although women's issues and education were contested policy areas in relation to empowerment at the World Bank and in the UN, the United States was internally grappling with how collective understandings of empowerment challenged domestic systems of power in the field of social work. "Empowerment" strongly influenced the field of social work, a field of praxis oriented entirely toward marginalized groups since its inception.[23] Early in the twentieth century, paternalistic approaches to these communities dominated the field, but after WWII there was a shift toward centering the needs of clients rather than the outcomes desired by the state. Practitioners and theorists of empowerment in American social work acknowledged the importance of social structures in shaping the lives of their clients even as they presumed that members of society yearn for freedom and fulfillment. Social workers seek to tell the "story" of "clients' own varied endeavors to gain resources that will enhance their 'mastery over their [own] affairs.'"[24] Over time, this empowerment-oriented approach to marginalization led to a strengthening of the social infrastructure, including strong unemployment benefits, welfare assistance programs, and education opportunities for marginalized communities throughout the country.

With the advent of neoliberal policies starting in the 1970s, however, social workers faced acute cutbacks to funding and resources as well as privatization measures that incentivized governments to purchase services from profit-oriented organizations. Thus the client-centric empowerment approaches central to social work in an earlier moment were transformed into more punitive systems of social control, especially for non-normative families and people of color.[25] These forms of social control extended into the expanding prison system, also a key feature of neoliberalism in the United States.

As the United States grappled with challenges to its geopolitical position in the international arena, the emergence of the concept of empowerment as a framework for including marginalized groups into national and international systems was familiar since the very same terminology, with the same ideological implications, had been implemented domestically. The imposition of neoliberalism internationally was inextricably linked to the rise and decline of empowerment discourse within the field most associated with marginalized groups in the United States, and especially women-headed households. Although we do not further analyze the field of US social work in this book, we regard the rise and fall of empowerment discourse in this field as a key indicator of how the United States' global bids for "soft" power were connected to the management of dispossessed populations within its own borders.

Human capital tames empowerment

In 1964, economist Gary Becker published his first treatise on human capital, an idea that had been in circulation for a few years prior. In *Human Capital: A Theoretical and Empirical Analysis, with Special Reference to Education*, Becker argued that investments in education, including formal education and on-the-job training, could improve "an individual's potential earning and psychic income." This work's publication spurred an outpouring of new research on human capital theory in behavioral economics and beyond, making it an influential paradigm for thinking about development in international contexts within a few years.[26] The term "human capital" pinpoints the notion that human individuals possess value, usually "untapped," that can be channeled into broader social and economic goals.[27] The conceptual orientation toward human capital knit together older visions of western liberalism that valued the notion of individual freedoms, conscribed by democratic values and institutions, with a vision of global neoliberalism that regarded capital as a proxy for value, both at the scale of the individual and at the scale of the nation-state. Human capital theory helped legitimize and redefine progress and modernity during the decades of the 1970s and 1980s, when the political and economic basis of the global neoliberal order was being established, helping pave the way toward policy environments that celebrate "free markets" and "small government." The framework motivated projects geared toward the education of women and girls around the world because it provided a way for powerful governments and the World Bank alike to transform the fundamentally political project of "empowerment" into an economic one that could focus narrowly on "investing" in the marginalized to improve their productivity. At the same time, human capital provided a convenient and supportive intellectual framework for corporations and nation-states to discourage investment in public works, welfare, and infrastructure, instead encouraging education that would produce a workforce for the new global economy.[28] Finally, the concept offered nation-states a new set of metrics through which they could now gain status within a growing community of nation-states. The rise of human capital theory was fundamentally shaped by the ideological divides of the Cold War. Thus the political compromises and commitments of that time continue to influence the narrow understanding of individualistic empowerment that today constitutes a key ideological building block of the global neoliberal order.

But how exactly was human capital theory used and by whom? By examining the policy arenas of education and gender and development in global institutions, we can understand how empowerment today has become associated with programs such as the expansion of schooling and gender equality as "smart economics." In particular, we show how and why the World Bank started investing in education, rather than only in the material infrastructure required for industrialization, and, during the same period, began "mainstreaming" gender into all aspects of their programming.

Freire's radical push for schooling for all, and why the United States eventually killed it

By the 1960s, in international organizations, debates and programming around mass literacy were producing huge geopolitical tensions because of Cold War divisions. In particular, UNESCO, the educational wing of the UN that had strong representation from the G-77 block of nations, experienced demands from its members for Freire-style literacy programs. Freire's radical ideas about education for the marginalized dovetailed nicely with postcolonial countries' left-leaning visions around the world. His new techniques for educating peasants and uplifting rural populations motivated mass schooling policies not only in his native Brazil but throughout Latin America, Africa, and Asia. These educational programs were political because they aimed to produce active, thinking adults among those who had been historically marginalized, a significant challenge to local power structures. As a result, programs motivated by Freire's understandings of local empowerment also often generated great resistance when implemented, sometimes leading to the jailing or execution of those who threatened existing power structures by carrying out such programs.[29] Left-wing governments in newly independent countries not only found a sympathetic audience and funding through UNESCO, they also received aid from the Soviet Union to enhance their education programs, all of which were geared toward "mass literacy." Since the Soviet Union had experience with mass literacy campaigns starting in the 1920s, this international goal aligned with their own policies and ideological priorities. The convergence between the Soviet push for mass literacy and the Freirean understandings of education for empowerment of the marginalized created a historically unique set of circumstances. There was great political will for a worldwide rollout of educational programs that had the potential to radically alter local, and perhaps global, structures of power, potentially threatening local and global elites.

But this rollout did not occur and was in fact stymied by US delegates to the UN. The fear from the United States was that large-scale political education, compatible with collective understandings of empowerment, would cede geopolitical ground to communism as an ideology, and to the Soviet Union as an ideological force in the Cold War world. Nonetheless, the United States was desperate to gain a toehold in the burgeoning political space of international education, which appeared to be an important pathway for putting the United States' own priorities into educational initiatives in parts of the world that were susceptible to communist ideas. After the successful Cuban Revolution in 1959, the Kennedy administration began funding Freirean programs in northeast Brazil, even though the logic of the program opposed US ideological interests. At UNESCO, however, US delegates from successive administrations leveraged human capital theory to insist that educational initiatives needed to be limited to "functional" purposes. This insistence eventually gutted the programming built around the existing demands of G-77 states.[30] As UNESCO's initiatives fumbled with inadequate funding and resources, Cuba and Iran successfully launched revolutionary educational programs of their own, based in part on Freire's writings and ideals, and without UNESCO support. This success brought into question the need for UN-funded literacy programs in the first place. Eventually, the lack of support from the United States for mass literacy, and the ineffectiveness of UNESCO's diffuse campaign, led to the eventual decline and extinction of UNESCO's literacy programs.

At the World Bank, the United States was similarly suspicious of investments in education, viewing them as beyond the purview of economic development. Nevertheless, due to the global ideological climate, the World Bank started to make small investments in education infrastructure as early as 1962. Although historically skeptical of the connection between education and economic growth, World Bank leaders found convincing evidence in Becker's work on human capital that education, when viewed as an investment in individuals, could be compatible with capitalist aims.[31] By 1968, the new president of the World Bank, Robert McNamara, led the bank away from a functional education approach toward "redistribution with growth," a strategy that promoted investments in education, so long as those investments could be shown to promote free markets.[32] Under McNamara's leadership, the Bank's funding for primary education became part of a larger package of poverty alleviation for nations and grew from US$883 million to US$12 billion when McNamara departed in 1981.[33] By the early 1980s, even though the United States had effectively undermined the UNESCO-led campaign to end illiteracy worldwide, the "human capital" framing was gaining significant traction, legitimizing investments in primary education beyond infrastructure. The tension persisted between US priorities, focused on productivity and economic growth, and the equity-oriented interpretations of education that motivated communist and postcolonial investments in education. The difference was that now the United States, as the prime funder of the World Bank, had more control over discourse and resource distribution than it had at UNESCO where G-77 countries had strong influence. In 1980, the World Bank published the "World Bank Education Sector Policy Paper", which outlined the economic, human capital-centered justification for large investments in education around the world. The paper advanced two parallel aims that reflected the political tensions surrounding the promotion of education policies at the time: education to contribute to the achievement of equity, and education to aid economic development by providing skilled labor power. In a commentary on the policy paper, economist Martin McLean argued that these aims were in fact incompatible with one another and paid insufficient attention to the political implications of implementing equity-focused educational programs, implying that an equity-oriented focus on education may conflict with the World Bank's mandated goals and the United States' national interests.[34]

Despite these contradictions, the World Bank continued to increase its funding. By the mid-1990s, education spending comprised 10 percent of the World Bank's overall lending budget. By the 1990s, the World Bank had emerged as the leading funder of education in developing countries with commitments in India, much of Latin America, and, notably for our project, the former socialist countries of Europe and Central Asia. In the sequel to the 1980 report, a 1995 report, 'Priorities and Strategies for Education,' adopted an approach that doubled down on education strictly as an input for economic growth, one that had to be evaluated in the same way as infrastructural investments. Furthermore, World Bank investments in education were understood to be assisting developing countries and transitional Soviet economies to "catch up" with OECD countries to meet the challenges of economic liberalization and transformed labor markets.[35] By the 1995 paper, the equity argument for education had disappeared from World Bank policy language, reflecting the dissolution of the Soviet Union and the triumph of a human capital-centric understanding of education. With the end of the Cold War, the World Bank could confidently steer the expansion of educational programs around the world that were geared strictly toward upgrading skills for the labor market, rather than toward the collective political empowerment that leftist campaigns for mass literacy had delivered with the support of the Soviet Union.

Gender equality and economic growth

Although international women's organizing got underway in the 1950s and 1960s, it only made its way into global institutions in the 1970s and 1980s. Once national-level women's movements started speaking to one another, they collectively started pushing the idea that women and gender as a system of power needed to be considered in every aspect of development policy making. The conception of empowerment in these spaces was contested, and diverse collective understandings of empowerment as transformation were discussed among powerful networks of women. As with education, Cold War politics shaped how issues related to women were articulated in the emergent global institutional sphere to a much greater extent than is usually recognized in feminist accounts of debates in this space. When the Soviet Union collapsed, radical proposals for a gendered reorganization of work and the economy, which were a part of Soviet global politics, were altogether erased. However, the United States' approach, oriented toward "gender equality" rather than a transformation of gender relations in the context of the economy, gained traction through the language of human capital and empowerment, especially in the World Bank. By the turn of the century and beyond, the idea of "gender equality as smart economics" has become common sense in World Bank programming.[36] This paradigm requires women to be "self-governing citizens who are empowered, entrepreneurial, and above all else, self-sufficient."[37] Despite the persistent advocacy of G-77 and Socialist bloc women for macrostructural change, the economic structures that persistently marginalize poor women within capitalist economies around the world have only gotten stronger since that crucial period of organizing.

Between the 1970s and the 1990s, the UN convened four major conferences on women: Mexico City in 1975, Copenhagen in 1980, Nairobi in 1985, and Beijing in 1995. These conferences began shaping the discursive terrain of women's rights and women's equality in the global organizational sphere. The debates that unfolded in these conferences influenced the agendas of all UN organizations in the decades that followed, including the World Bank, which from its inception was dominated by US interests. Because of a long history of organizing since the end of WWII, women were able to enter powerfully into the global institutional sphere, especially in the context of the UN, to advocate for specific policies, with key interests coalescing around motherhood.[38] One of the most significant women's organizations, often erased from women's history, was the Women's International Democratic Forum (WIDF), which had organized numerous conferences and workshops that brought together women activists in Eastern European countries as well as in the G-77 bloc. For example, for the WIDF's thirtieth anniversary in 1975, over 2,000 men and women from 141 countries gathered in East Berlin and discussed, among other important issues, how newly independent countries could pursue their chosen paths toward economic development without western interference, a topic viewed as directly related to women's issues.[39] In the context of WIDF, activists from diverse parts of the world formed solidarities around the need for feminism to address racism, imperialism, colonialism, and war. WIDF activists came to the shared conclusion, despite their many differences, that "equality" with men without concern for deeper political structures would be useless.[40] DAWN, mentioned earlier, was another example of a transnational network of feminists focused on envisioning and strategizing a new world order based on the perspectives of poor women. In the DAWN network, privileged women from global South countries were the primary organizers, but strong partnerships with NGOs and a radical outlook oriented toward the most marginalized meant that their visions were not monopolized by any single group.[41] Thus, by the time the

UN formally recognized and called upon women's movements to participate in a global conversation in Mexico City, women organizers had been having transnational conversations around issues of reproduction, sexuality, and work for decades, with some of the most critical and lively discussions occurring between women from newly postcolonial nations and women from communist countries.[42]

Cold War politics shaped the debates that took center stage in Mexico City and Copenhagen, and even more prominently in Nairobi, when Reagan's appointments displaced the more liberal women who had previously represented the United States at these conferences. US delegates came into conflict with the "Eastern bloc" of delegates and G-77 countries. They disagreed on issues relating to Palestinian women's rights, economic sanctions on South Africa's apartheid regime, and the concept of equal pay for equal work, and these disagreements prominently shaped the documents that came out of these UN conferences. Both sides suspected that the other was controlled by men on their side of the political spectrum. US delegates believed that socialist and G-77 women were controlled by central Politburos, while the allied socialist and G-77 women believed that the US delegates were beholden to the interests of the men in the US Congress.[43] Because the other side assumed that women representatives were not reflecting their own true interests, the many successes of Soviet and socialist countries in radically altering the gender division of labor and reducing vulnerability for women were overlooked and viewed entirely in ideological terms.[44] This climate thus rendered powerful interpretations of empowerment, fostered through transnational collaboration and organization over decades, as merely ideological battles that the United States and its allies were determined to oppose.

The United States and its allies were committed to an emerging policy consensus around "Women in Development" (WID), a perspective reflected in the Percy Amendment of 1970. This approach, often credited to the work of the Danish economist Esther Boserup, argued that women were an asset to the ongoing process of economic development, and simply needed to be included. Once women were included in the process of capitalist development, WID reasoning went, poverty could be alleviated, improving health and economic outcomes in countries around the world.[45] The WID perspective was particularly concerned with including women in industry and the mechanization of agriculture, challenging stereotyped assumptions of women's presumed association with the domestic.[46] Such an approach was entirely compatible with the capitalist vision for development advocated for by the United States and global institutions that directly represented US interests, such as the World Bank. Furthermore, the WID perspective was also compatible with increasingly influential understandings of human capital. WID helped make women visible because of their capacity to contribute to economic growth, a capacity that could be harnessed, in theory at least, with the right investments in education, training, and technology. At the World Bank, "gender entrepreneurs" committed to bringing more funding and programming to women's issues, molded gender issues into a form that would be palatable to the economists who dominated the World Bank. They conducted research that would highlight the "positive synergies between 'investing in women' and the Bank's main objectives – poverty reduction, increased productivity, more efficient use of resources, and social returns."[47] This had the effect of focusing entirely on the overlaps between gender equity and economic efficiency and displacing those visions of women's empowerment that required collective mobilization, access to political power, economic transformation, and a strong social safety net.

The WID perspective faced a great deal of opposition from especially grassroots women's groups who had been influenced by their associations and alliances with women's groups from communist countries. These groups from Asia and Latin America brought the framework of empowerment directly into conversation with policy makers at the World Bank. Indeed, Naila Kabeer has argued that it was the ongoing activism of grassroots women's movements in the international sphere that made it possible for WID to eventually gain traction in the realm of policy.[48] These thinkers challenged the "equality" argument of WID thinking and proposed a more radical understanding of women's empowerment, centering women's organizations, new economic policies supportive of women, and investment in a social safety net. This dynamic led to the World Bank expanding its engagement with women's issues beyond mere economic inclusion. Still, as with the issue of education, research and policy oriented toward economic efficiency had the strongest influence since such efforts were aligned with US policy preferences. The 1993 reorganization of the World Bank "mainstreamed" gender into all areas of World Bank functioning, establishing the primacy of efficiency-oriented, individualistic definitions of women's empowerment. The reorganization minimized, and perhaps even erased, the legacy of collective interpretations of what had historically been a deeply political term. The collapse of the Soviet Union facilitated this erasure and allowed human capital to become the organizing principle for neoliberal development policy. This framework also allowed women who are the targets of development policy – poor women in global South countries – to become the most visible agents of economic development.

As Sydney Calkin has argued in her extensive analysis of World Bank policies from the 1980s onward, human capital came to redefine women's empowerment to mean that women, within their socially defined roles in society, could be relied upon to deliver human development to themselves and their families without significant state investment in collective care.[49] This produces a new ideal hero of development in development discourse: the empowered woman, a racialized figure who would be resourceful, capable, and, above all else, would prioritize her family without radically transforming social or economic structures. This narrow interpretation of women's empowerment, focused on an entrepreneurial understanding of self and economy, comes into focus as a symbolic proxy for modernity and status around the world.

By the mid-1990s, the United Nations Development Project made gendered empowerment quantifiable through the Gender Empowerment Measure (GEM), a composite index that determines the level of gender inequality in a country by synthesizing measures for economic and political decision making and participation with a measure for power over economic resources.[50] The measure continues to play a critical role in a country's determination of the overall Human Development Index (HDI), a measure that ranks countries relative to one another, and is not alone in its effort to rank countries according to gender equality. The Gender Gap Index, the Gender Inequality Index, the Gender Status Index, and the Gender-related Development Index all aim to measure relative levels of gender inequality, considering both qualitative and quantitative measures. Through these global gender indicators, as well as women's empowerment-oriented policies and programming, media stories, and advertising that portray women in a positive light, countries have been competing for status. For countries with postcolonial histories, performing women's empowerment shores up claims to modernity and civilization in a global arena structured by legacies of colonialism.[51]

Conclusion

Our commonsense understanding of empowerment today not only acts as an ideological handmaiden to neoliberal capitalism but it also erases decades of organizing and discussion in grassroots movements all over the world and in post-WWII global institutions. Through a historical deep dive, we have shown in this chapter that the underlying principles of empowerment started out as collective and became individualized. The ideological context of the Cold War and the powerful organizing of postcolonial countries in the mid–late twentieth century provided us with visions of empowerment oriented toward the most marginalized while also regarding personal autonomy and security as central. Because of the tremendous influence of these visions of empowerment, the United States needed a compelling framework, palatable to economists, which would enshrine individualistic understandings of empowerment in US policy making at the World Bank and thus protect US policy interests and push back against the threat of communism. They found such a framework in Becker's human capital theory, a theory that promoted investments in "soft" issues like women and education. Human capital theory rendered the benefits of those investments in terms of individual flourishing and macroeconomic growth, rather than in terms of equity. Even though American rhetoric celebrates striving and economic success among marginalized groups, the US government opposed policies oriented toward uplifting the marginalized, educating the masses, or altering the power structures established by the neoliberal global economy in any way.

We show in this chapter that in the global institutional sphere, education and women become two key organizing terrains for Cold War efforts that greatly influenced how we understand empowerment today. The decisions that were made around educational policy and women and development powerfully shaped empowerment discourse and, by the 1990s, promoted policies based on individualistic and productivity-oriented presumptions about human worth and flourishing. This was consistent with the ideological priorities of the United States during the Cold War, and later, when the Soviet Union collapsed, the neoliberal world order, which was being constituted in a clandestine and systematic fashion not only at the World Bank, but also at the IMF and at the World Trade Organization (WTO).[52] Although feminist critiques of empowerment and its many meanings are commonplace, these critiques seldom recognize the global power dynamics that shaped its current form or the extent to which contemporary notions of empowerment displaced popular collective understandings. These collective understandings of empowerment emerged not only from communist imaginings of emancipation, but also from thoughtful, persistent, transnational, bottom-up organizing from 134 postcolonial countries coming in the G-77 together to challenge the prevailing neocolonial, capitalist system. Collective understandings of empowerment had roots in the United States as well. For decades, US-based movements had aimed to leverage government resources to center marginalized communities in the field of social work. Recognizing this history can help us challenge individualistic understandings of empowerment that dominate the discursive landscape in international institutions and everyday public discourse. Moreover, this history offers a powerful critique of how US power has operated in blatant opposition to the interests of the most marginalized, even as it continues to present itself as a moral authority protecting the vulnerable in a global arena. Our analysis here, then, invites a historically informed critique of human capital and a recuperation of the intellectual frameworks that the United States erased in its bid for sustained global dominance.

We now pivot from the first part of our book, the historical conditions and interactions that produced neoliberalism, to the second part of our book, the actual conditions and actors that comprise this order.

4
Neoliberalism's Gendered Architecture

How can we characterize the convergence of disparate areas of the global economy in the context of neoliberalism that were each experiencing distinct economic, political, and cultural conditions between the postwar period and the collapse of the Soviet Union in 1991? We have argued that the ideological glue holding this order together lies in a neoliberal feminist "cover story" that celebrates expanded choices for women and links them to narrow understandings of "empowerment." Leveraging and transforming the political language of empowerment employed by transnational women's movements, postcolonial countries, and reformist movements, the language of women's empowerment lays out a vista of individualized aspirations for men, women, and nation-states around the world. But what are the underlying discursive and material conditions that help consolidate the everyday assumptions and experiences within a neoliberal order? And, what are the transnational circuits, historical events, policies, and ideologies that represent the concrete, lived experiences of the neoliberal order in our three interconnected regions? In this chapter, we come to the central fulcrum of our book's argument by addressing these interrelated questions.

We begin by exploring the transnational circuits between the United States and the Soviet Union that generated many of the policies understood to be fundamental to neoliberalism. We explain how the interests of powerful groups in both places all could be served through this new set of policies, especially around trade. This context helps us counter the erasure of the Soviet experience and its transnational impact, an erasure that continues to exist within neoliberalism today. We then describe the discursive architecture[1] of existing neoliberalism, including two structuring conditions: (1) state protection of elite capital; and (2) strengthened national borders. This architecture has two key actors: (1) individuals; and (2) nation-states. Neither these conditions nor actors are "new" on their own. When we consider how they came together at the end of the Cold War, however, we recognize a "new" architecture that we identify as the neoliberal order, shaped by discourse and material conditions. Highlighting these conditions and actors helps center those who are most essential but most neglected, a focus that sharpens an intersectional critique and analysis of this order. Neoliberal ideologies embedded in media and policy appear to encourage and celebrate the empowerment of individuals from marginalized groups, yet these same groups are constrained by the extreme ways that the state protects global capital, elites, and borders. We explore the lived experience of those constraints and new "choices" in the following two chapters. In this chapter, we (1) identify the structuring conditions of the neoliberal order, (2) examine how they operate in our three regions, and (3) explore how they operate within individuals and nation-states to competitively advance their positions.

Once we lay out the structuring conditions and key actors, we turn to each of our three regions to explicate what these conditions and actors look like in their situated contexts and highlight how the architecture of neoliberalism helps produce a shared "cover story," which opens the possibility of "empowerment" for all, such that each individual comes into their own power. The clashing gender orders of the postwar period converged on a culturally adaptable understanding of women's empowerment as expanded choices; a break from what existed before. This understanding of a vast horizon of choices enables new aspirations and possibilities for both individuals and nation-states. For individuals, awareness of expanded choices – around employment, migration, marriage, romance, consumption, and travel – suggests that the gap between reality and a better life is temporary, and can be overcome through striving, creative thinking, and good luck. Similarly, for nation-states, the possibility of more choices promises an overdue coming-into-power, or an anxiety over losing power and influence. This is because, as we have shown in previous chapters and will become further evident in this chapter, the legacies of colonialism, imperialism and Soviet-style socialism persist as structuring legacies in international contexts after 1991. Circuits of development funding and ideology in the international arena encounter local gender politics and resistance to produce the facade of consensus around a cover story of expanded choices for all, a facade that belies the discontent, tension, and anxiety experienced by those who cannot access those promised choices.

Cooking up neoliberalism: East–West circuits of power and expertise

Our three regions, representing North American, Soviet, and postcolonial interests in the postwar period, all entered a neoliberal global order from the 1980s onward, with the solidification of this order from the 1990s especially. But how and where were the ideas developed that would define this order? And how did those ideas nearly erase our memory of Soviet-inspired social transformation so rapidly after the 1990s?

There were, no doubt, multiple key locations and historical periods that contributed to neoliberalism's theorizing, testing, and policy rollout. As Greg Grandin and Juan Gabriel Valdés have shown, Latin America, and especially Chile, was a strategic "workshop" in which the United States aimed to experiment with neoliberal policies.[2] In 1973, General Augusto Pinochet's coup led to the establishment of a range of authoritarian policies and dismantled Chile's democratically elected socialist regime. Some of those policies were compatible with US economic policy goals, and this made Chile one of the earliest sites for the application of neoliberal policies.[3]

While US–Latin American relationships were crucial to the establishment of neoliberal policies in that region, Chilean policies were based on the economic ideas that were also theorized, debated, and transformed within the historical context of the Cold War (1947–1991). This engagement with socialism is often overlooked, yet was fundamental to the development of neoliberal ideas and policies. Neoliberal ideas and policy recommendations did not simply spread from West to East but rather were produced and disseminated through exchanges that took place in a Cold War-era, transnational network composed of both US and Eastern European economists.

The transnational networks and discussions that laid the foundation of neoliberal ideology began as far back as the 1920s, following the Russian Revolution of 1917 that brought the Soviets to power.[4] Johanna Bockman and Gil Eyal argue that a network of US and Eastern European economists solidified in the 1940s and 1950s and saw socialism as a "laboratory of economic knowledge." The Great Depression created a debate in American economics about the need for states to intervene in markets to function efficiently. American economists were drawn to these East–West dialogues because socialism was a laboratory where the type and degree of state intervention could be tested, and the data then mathematically analyzed. Professionally, American economists were answering the Cold War call to study "comparative economic systems" for which there was government and foundation funding. The United States' political motivation underlying the funding of this network and its operation was the idea that academic exchange could undermine social regimes by infiltrating them with American ideas and values. Eastern European economists had a different set of motivations for engaging in this East–West network. They were anti-Stalinist reformers arguing for the introduction of limited market-based reform in the socialist command economy. Eastern European economists had their own professional pressures that included a struggle with bureaucrats and party officials over whose knowledge would form the basis of economic policy implementation. Eastern European scholars used the politically neutral language of mathematical economics to legitimate their claims of technical expertise. Despite different interests and motivations, both groups felt their needs were met by the co-creation of a shared metaphor in which socialism was given privileged status as a "laboratory of economic knowledge," where economists could test various theories of "reform economics" in a controlled economic setting that was not possible under capitalism.

Although neither side set out to create neoliberalism, both sides were shaped by the transnational dialogue. This East–West network produced neoliberal policies that, by the 1960s, came to be hegemonic among economists in both regions.[5] This explains why Eastern European reformers became strong, global advocates for neoliberal reforms and embraced neoliberalism so quickly after Soviet collapse. The origin story of neoliberalism most commonly told in the West, is one of western innovation and eastern passive acceptance.[6] It is true that institutional inequalities between East and West existed in the network. For example, the monies that funded their joint research flowed largely through western economists, many based at Harvard. Nevertheless, neoliberalism was not diffused to the region from the West but was already endemic in the region because of these sustained transnational exchanges. In fact, after the revolutions of 1989, the policies of "shock therapy" came from this network of US and Eastern European reformers and economists, and its adoption was, contrary to common belief, promoted by Eastern European reformers and not imposed by the West.[7] Shock therapy posits that a decisive change in national economic policy could initiate a rapid transition from a socialist economy based on central planning to a free-market economy, with the aim of curing the economic ills of socialism, such as hyperinflation and commodity shortages.[8]

Several Eastern European states readied themselves for a turn to open capital markets from as early as the 1970s, while others closed themselves off from those political and economic experiences, all derived from their varying experiences of the US-led postwar order.[9] Yet nearly all of them pursued policies consistent with globalization and neoliberalism through the 1990s. Western political elites had a different set of interests in promoting shock therapy: such policies would dissolve Soviet economic and political structures and attempt to remove Eastern Europe from Moscow's control. Western powers had learned an old truth from their previous imperial experience: "debt crisis provides a golden opportunity to supervise the reorganization of a country's socioeconomic structures in their own interests," a practice we will see repeated in SSEA.[10] Overnight, neoliberal stabilization and liberalization was implemented across the Soviet Union but without uniformity in form or effect. These actions resulted in an eventual total embrace of neoliberalism across the FSU.

After the collapse of the Soviet Union, neoliberal capitalism emerged as the victor in the battle of ideologies. Newly independent post-Soviet nation-states severed their ties to the larger Soviet federation, opened themselves to global markets, and adopted neoliberal policies. Neoliberal ideas took on an appearance of universal applicability because this network of economists aligned diverse political and economic motivations behind a shared set of policies. This helps explain later assumptions not only about the inevitability of neoliberalism, but also about the presence of Soviet sensibilities and knowledge experiments within the contemporary political system that comprises neoliberalism itself.

Structuring condition #1:
States protect elites and global capital

One of the primary structuring conditions of the neoliberal order results from a fundamental shift in the character of states and state institutions. While liberal states sought primarily to protect their citizens (see chapter 2), in the global neoliberal order, *states protect elites and global capital so that they may move freely and profit while neglecting most individuals, thus leaving them constrained.* As states orient their policies and institutions toward the protection of the capitalist global economy, they become particularly beholden to large global corporations. Dominant countries uphold support for global capital through international financial institutions. When historically dominant countries support global capital, historically subordinated nation-states are unable to pursue their long-term goals of economic self-sufficiency.

Many Polanyian conceptions of neoliberalism suggest that, when restrictions around the market relax, the market erodes protective aspects of society. Here, we instead follow Slobodian in arguing that *the state in fact protects the market* from social uprisings (including radical movements for racial and gender equity, migrant rights, and worker rights) and social policies that make claims on the market and "interfere" with its "natural," "free" functioning. Market-oriented policies, presented as race-and-gender-neutral, enrich elites who are often privileged in racial and caste hierarchies. Thus these elites can comfortably circulate throughout the world. The state and the market have historically been intertwined and jointly accountable for the provision of both social goods and economic opportunities to citizens. Under neoliberalism, specific policy packages cut off those interconnections to protect the supposedly "free" market from "distortions." New policies ensure that the market is not accountable for the provision of social goods or equitable economic opportunities for most citizens. This state-sponsored protection of the market, backed by coercion from international financial institutions such as the IMF, allows global firms to travel the world unfettered, seeking the lowest wages and the most advantageous tax conditions with minimum accountability.[11] The international financial system regulates and upholds this system through conditionalities that require austerity policies from postcolonial countries in a subordinate position within the interconnected global system of trade. Substantial scholarly literature has documented the harms caused by these policies on the world's majority.[12]

As states around the world have become bodyguards for global capital, the majority of the world's citizens have been rendered disposable, and chances of a viable livelihood at home have deteriorated for both women and men.[13] But the increasing availability of cheap, pliable labor pools around the world has de-incentivized corporations from extensive investment in any specific country, allowing conditions to deteriorate in a "race to the bottom."[14] Furthermore, state protection of capital and elites, and neglect of everyone else, has spurred gendered migration patterns within and among diverse countries. In formerly colonized countries, women migrate to do low-wage, stereotypically feminine work, such as domestic work or factory work, reinforcing global labor hierarchies. Thus this first structuring condition of neoliberalism has turned poor and working-class women into a low-wage, permanently subordinated labor pool typed feminine, and thus disposable.[15]

When postcolonial states depart from this model, they face punishment from global debt regimes such as the IMF. Driven by the aim of economic self-sufficiency, many postcolonial nation-states create policy regimes involving import substitution, tariffs, food subsidies, or restrictions on imports. Such policies protect domestic production from the vagaries of the global free market. Global financial institutions punish historically subordinate countries for such policies and demand austerity, but such requirements are not imposed on wealthy countries. In a recent report, for example, IMF, OECD, the World Bank, and WTO officials themselves acknowledge that subsidies are critical for supplying food to the world's majority. Such subsidies cushion citizens during emergencies, yet global financial institutions have prohibited such protective policies in postcolonial countries.[16] Massive protests against austerity policies around the world have done little to change the environment, but instead demonstrate the extent to which this structuring condition stifles democracy and exacerbates historical inequities.[17] The relative lack of control that subordinated countries exercise over their own economies becomes even more salient when we examine the second structuring condition, which strengthens borders but, like our first structuring condition, severely restricts economic self-sufficiency and even sovereignty.

Structuring condition #2: Strengthened national borders support global trade but restrict migration

In the neoliberal order, *strengthened national borders are required to promote trade and competition while also regulating labor flows.*[18] The collapse of the Soviet Union meant that new international borders, within what was previously a union of states, had to be constructed. Borders in historically wealthy nations become more restricted to regulate labor flows and ensure that poor countries demand lower wages, enforced by a favorable exchange rate. This makes immigration more difficult for those who are incentivized to migrate to cities or to other countries, due to the limited options in their local economies. In postcolonial nation-states, regional borders become both more rigid and more contested as long-standing struggles over territory and security accelerate and intensify.

International borders grew in importance under global colonial contests that sought to enhance the influence of empire-states, but these borders grew even more important in the twentieth century as colonialism came to an end and the nation-states became the organizing unit of the international political and economic system.[19] The British, among other empire-states, organized laws and regulatory systems around indentured labor to *facilitate* the movement of unfree labor across British colonial territories after slavery was outlawed. But today many nation-states have instead sought to impose *constraints* on citizens to shore up postcolonial and developmental nation-building projects of welfare and redistribution.[20] Through contestations between the logics of constraint and facilitation, an elaborate system of regulations around labor flows developed throughout the twentieth century and solidified in the technologies of the passport, the marriage license, the visa, and the institutions of country-level bureaucracies to generate various categories of deserving and undeserving migrants.

One important consequence of this new set of borders is the rise of the "competition state," a new kind of nation-state which, through various policy regimes, "liberalizes cross-border movements, recommodifies labor and privatizes public services."[21] These states compete for global capital, desirable migrants, and, ultimately, for a desirable national brand that commands status and attention in the global cultural economy.[22] But strengthened borders around territory do not necessarily enhance claims to sovereignty. As discussed earlier, the international political system blocks nation-states from fulfilling the long-standing ideal of economic self-sufficiency. Yet nation-states may build their own global cultural brands, which can compete with other national brands. Such conditions encourage ethnonationalist imaginings of identity instead.

Nation-states are constrained in their political and economic goals and must appear unthreatening in their aspirations for autonomy. This is ironic because it was a quest for economic, political, and cultural self-determination that drove the decolonization movements, which in turn generated the conditions that birthed neoliberalism. In the neoliberal order, postcolonial nations are corralled into a structuring system wherein they can only hope to compete with other nation-states for increased relative cultural power. Even as Brexit and "America First" policy regimes, backed by populist movements, make new claims to political and economic sovereignty, true self-sufficiency and self-determination are unattainable in the global neoliberal order.[23] This outcome erases the many significant political accomplishments of postcolonial nations organizing in international institutions in the decades following WWII.

Since the fall of the Soviet Union, there has been a proliferation of nation-states and an outward recognition of cultural autonomy, yet there is virtually no possibility of true economic self-sufficiency, especially for subordinate nation-states. Status for individual countries is instead derived from a race for modernity in which it appears that each nation-state has an equal chance. This race is outwardly an economic race based on trading and advancement up the value chain, as many economists theorize.[24] But in reality this is a race based on perceptions of status, influence, and cultural "coolness," extending long histories of cultural diplomacy into projects of national branding that involve states and private companies alike.[25] Postcolonial and post-Soviet countries enter the waiting room of modernity for a chance to appear high-status and modern within a global order that is ranked in terms of economic, political, and cultural power across different fields of policy, security, and economics.[26]

These structuring conditions, which protect global capital, elites, and historically powerful nation-states, have the effect of producing and justifying heightened inequalities. These conditions also call upon individuals and nation-states as key actors who must jockey for advancement and power within an inequitable system. Although the two structuring conditions appear to be gender-neutral and color-blind, our analysis of situated agents – individuals and nation-states – illuminates the striking inequities of neoliberalism's gender order, which preserves power and status for historically dominant nation-states while holding out the promise of advancement for all.

Key Actor #1: Individuals

Many scholars of neoliberalism have noted that the system emphasizes individual achievement and a corresponding individual responsibility for their own success and failure.[27] While most accounts of neoliberalism's emphasis on the individual make it appear that this individual is ahistorical and free-floating, here we note that the compulsion for individual achievement produces racialized, class-specific mandates for women and men. Neoliberalism has created a new set of imperatives for women's labor and identities while continuing to emphasize breadwinning for men. To be recognized as "modern" and "empowered," women must labor in their families for free and create entrepreneurial identities that engage the marketized public sphere. Men, on the other hand, must navigate the pervasive anxiety that comes with the expectation to be a breadwinner and the reality that makes that expectation unattainable for most.

Emphasizing individual achievement is not only an ethos that pervades neoliberal economic and social life, but it also results in a particular form of governance. Neoliberal governance requires the state to protect individual rights and freedoms rather than looking after societal well-being as a whole.[28] This shift in governance has intensified and extended precarity. The middle-class, whose formal education and professional status had previously provided a buffer from uncertainty, now join the poor in job insecurity.[29] While governments scale back the use of debt to spur economies and maintain social welfare supports, neoliberal citizens are encouraged and compelled to take on student loans, mortgages, and consumer debt – and the incumbent risk.[30] Neoliberalism has thus ushered in a new "enterprise culture" that celebrates self-reliance, risk-taking, and competition around the world.[31] Policies supporting neoliberal governance as well as the discourse of self-reliance have together democratized the figure of the entrepreneur. "Entrepreneur" now applies not only to those starting a small business but to anyone who embraces risk or innovation, so that "we are all entrepreneurs."[32]

This idealized entrepreneurial self is a path to "empowerment" for mothers in particular, providing an aspirational figure for women who can "have it all." Mothers face discrimination in the labor market due to their disproportionate unpaid labor in their families, a situation exacerbated by reductions in state services and the need to work in low-end factory or service jobs to make ends meet for their families. Nonetheless, entrepreneurial ideology suggests that women can "do it all" with grit and creativity. An "entrepreneurial mindset" can allow women to combine unpaid reproductive labor with work outside the home.[33] This theme rears its head at diverse, interconnected sites: Ivanka Trump's memoir, the Nike Foundation's programming for girls, and the World Bank's funding priorities, to name just a few examples.[34]

"Mompreneurship," heralded by many as the "new feminism,"[35] appears to connect well-to-do entrepreneurial women in North America with marginalized women in the global South. Mompreneurs might be paid or unpaid; they may be working as party planners, life coaches, mommy bloggers, homeschoolers, leaders in parent–teacher associations, or founders of community charities in North America or Europe. Mompreneurs may own a tailoring business, a chicken coop, or offer beauty services to neighbors in global South contexts, thus combining income generation with childcare. Politicians, policy makers in international institutions, and microfinance executives tout a racialized construction of an ahistorical Third World Woman, capable of pulling not only her own family but her country out of poverty so that the whole world can benefit from this capitalist expansion.[36] Supported by the increasingly feminized world of financial products, neoliberal feminist ideology invites women around the world to combine their roles as mothers, entrepreneurs, and financial managers of the family to regulate their time, plan for the future, and end global poverty in the process.

While a feminist, entrepreneurial self provides a path for women to navigate neoliberal precarity and aspire to or even attain the status of "empowered woman," men lack access to a countervailing individual aspirational discourse, even though men too are subject to gendered understandings of individual achievement. Men's worth continues to be measured by the breadwinner ideal, which means that they must be successful in the paid labor market so that they may be breadwinners for their families.[37] This ideology is not new to neoliberalism; what is new is the growing gap between this ideal and men's ability to achieve or sustain it. Economic precarity means most working-class and poor men are unable to attain breadwinner status, whether in the United States, the FSU, or SSEA. Ironically, when they *do* attain breadwinner status in the United States, men are riddled with anxiety since professional degrees and jobs no longer offer the promise of economic security.[38] Economist Joanna Syrda found, in her longitudinal study of 6,000 heterosexual households in the United States, that men still aspire to the breadwinner ideal. Men experienced anxiety and psychological distress that was detrimental to their health both when they were not the breadwinner (the tipping point for men was wives contributing over 40 percent of the family income) but also when they were the sole breadwinner burdened with the financial well-being of their family.[39] Thus, the difficulty of attaining breadwinning status significantly structures the experiences of men under neoliberalism.

These gendered discourses around "individual achievement" appear to be "colorblind," but are lived out through race, caste, sexuality, class, and geography. The aspirational entrepreneurial woman in the United States is constructed as White, middle-class, cisgender, heterosexual, and married, with a man's salary to lean on. The economic realities of racism mean that people of color, depending on their intersectional identities, find it even more difficult than those with dominant identities to achieve lasting economic success in neoliberal labor markets.[40] Moreover, these groups have less intergenerational wealth to rely on, due to histories of exclusion from housing markets and ongoing patterns of predatory lending.[41] The trope of the entrepreneurial (implicitly White and upper-class) woman requires the cleaning and caring services of "nonaspirational" women of color for her empowerment dreams to come true.[42] But poor and working-class men of color in the United States are disproportionately subject to incarceration, deportation, and other practices to control surplus population.[43] In India, the notion of women's entrepreneurship, among especially rural and poor women, appears to provide a pathway out of poverty, but these ideas oversimplify the constraints of a highly stratified labor market in which women have few options for crafting a livelihood apart from a breadwinning spouse.[44] In the Soviet Union, women's labor market participation rates far surpassed those in Western Europe, and it is worth noting that under socialism, private enterprise was largely illegal.[45] However, in the FSU today, states call on entrepreneurial women to maintain their families' survival through post-Soviet institutional collapse by selling what they can.[46] At the same time, women are deemed "redundant" in the labor market and come to see their exclusion as a "choice" to spend more time with the children.[47]

As this discussion implies, neoliberalism requires a particular family structure to support "individual achievement": the hetero-patriarchal family. Because women are most often responsible for the functioning and reproduction of that hetero-patriarchal family, the fundamental building block of neoliberalism, they find themselves in a structurally disadvantaged position in the labor market. The ideal of entrepreneurial, reproductive motherhood reinforces the heterosexual nuclear family unit. Because of this ideal, women with entrepreneurial identities pursue "choices" in their public and private lives, whether as small business owners, mommy bloggers, corporate executives, or migrant domestic workers. Poor and marginalized women rarely have the material resources to be stay-at-home mothers and are likely constructed as "lazy" if they do not also have paid work. In a previous historical moment, elite women were celebrated for "choosing" full-time motherhood as both a difficult and noble job.[48] In a neoliberal order, however, it is no longer enough even for elite women who dedicate themselves to full-time childcare to simply embrace the identity of stay-at-home-mother as their "choice." They must also be entrepreneurial to be a "feminist" or "empowered" subject.

Key actor #2: Nation-states

The second key agent of the neoliberal order is the nation-state, which must compete with other nation-states in an international arena governed by free trade. While the ideology of free trade and the growth of multilateral global institutions makes it appear as if these countries are competing fairly, nation-states are instead competing in an unequal arena structured by the lasting legacies of colonialism and imperialism.[49] We suggest that nation-states are engaged in an "every country for itself" competition in a global hierarchy of nations, a view supported by critical international relations scholars.[50] Status in the international arena is cultivated through various cultural and political fields in which gender dynamics are prominent or central. Nation-states deploy gendered discourses about "their women" to construct themselves as "modern," a key criterion in negotiating the boundaries between "First" and "Third" World, "developed" and "developing," or "modern" and "traditional" nation-states.[51] In the neoliberal order, nation-states are invested in being considered modern countries with desirable cultures on a world stage. To pursue this modernity, they borrow and transform colonial associations between civilization and an enlightened gender order. While in an earlier moment, nation-states in different regions struck different gender "deals" with women, in neoliberalism's gender order, nation-states from across the global system aim to prove that "their women" are "empowered" by showing to the world that they are free to make their own "choices."

Gender politics have long constituted an important basis for determining the status of a society, nation, or culture relative to others. The status of women has been arguably the most important symbolic terrain upon which relations of power between countries and cultures has been contested.[52] Colonial rule legitimated itself through the propagation of a supposedly "modern" gender order, resting upon a hetero-patriarchal marriage in which women were respected but dependent upon both men and colonial state power.[53] In the words of Gayatri Spivak, colonialism was about "white men saving brown women from brown men."[54] Colonialism promised an elevated form of culture and civilization premised on the idea that western, upper-class gender norms were "natural" and produced a superior social order in contrast to the cultures of racialized others which sought to oppress women. Although anti-colonial nationalist struggles around the world endeavored to reject these claims, these associations nonetheless informed gendered constructions of nationhood around the world in the mid-twentieth century as new nations aimed to elevate and legitimize their own gendered values as distinct from, but still related to, their colonizers.

Constructions of modernity are gendered because gender is an effective signifier of power; it allows for macro-level power relations between nations to be distilled down to the scale of the personal and intimate, intelligible by individuals within their own lives and translatable to specific bodies and experiences.[55] This remains true even though modernity is not a unified concept. Indeed, the aspiration to modernity on the part of especially postcolonial nation-states is explicitly *not* an aspiration to be "western." Different countries with divergent economic and political systems have envisioned many alternatives for modernity: Marxist, fascist, or capitalist. As we will argue in chapter 6, Vladimir Putin is engaged in formulating a historically distinct, oppositional modernity through Russia's war on Ukraine. Despite the divergent content and claims to modernity, particularly since the twentieth century, this notion has been the terrain upon which nation-states compete for status. The principle of modernity organizes hierarchies between countries in which some are deemed "ahead" and others are "catching up."[56]

Under neoliberalism, countries actively promote policies and circulate discourses that appear to elevate the status of women in their countries and thus help their nation-state rise above other nation-states competing for cultural power, influence, and attention. Previously colonized countries in particular aim to project an image of themselves in which "empowered" women are the norm within their specific cultural context, often as a counter to colonial norms.[57] While there is cultural specificity to performances of gender that vary from country to country, there is a common assertion of "women's empowerment" that seeks to project modernity and civilization around the world.[58] Such performances, shored up in developing countries through quantitative measures such as the Gender Empowerment Measure (GEM), legitimize the "soft" power and status of some countries relative to others.

In the most powerful countries, such as the United States, the presumption that women are "liberated," a complex discourse circulated throughout the world through media and consumer products, legitimates the United States' dominant status in the world.[59] In the FSU, where women had previously experienced near full employment, neoliberal capitalism has resulted in the expulsion of women from their previous positions in the labor market. Post-Soviet women "choose" to prioritize motherhood. In many nationalist discourses throughout the region, women are described as being "liberated" from the Soviet "triple burden" of housework, wage work, and civic duties to reign as empowered "matriarchs" in their families.[60] And in postcolonial countries, notions of empowerment are embedded in both microfinance development projects targeting poor women in rural areas as well as "knowledge for development" projects that promote high-tech.[61] While the United States and other Western European countries constitute the gold standard for what it means to be "modern" through their take on gender equality, the FSU and postcolonial countries continuously modify and retool gender performances of "their women" as they compete for status in the global waiting room of modernity.

Imperialism, hegemony, and aspiration in US neoliberalism

The US iteration of our first condition of neoliberalism – *states protect elites and global capital so that they may move freely and profit while leaving everyone else constrained* – emerged in the 1970s within a new understanding of the role of government that was consolidated during the Reagan administration and the resolution of the Cold War in the 1980s. Domestic economic restructuring in the United States led the processes of global economic restructuring. Key domestic policies included deregulation, privatization, and a withdrawal of the state from social provision.[62] US companies moved manufacturing abroad in search of cheaper labor and established Export Processing Zones (EPZs) in developing countries. The state embraced a new mandate: to safeguard the US citizenry's access to cheap consumer goods.[63] At the same time, the US government, along with other western states, enacted policies that limited the mobility of people across borders. These policies had myriad destabilizing effects in poorer nation-states. EPZs, along with the movement of capital, spurred mass emigrations as well as mass internal migrations from rural to urban areas.

The post-WWII economic order's version of liberalism was premised on a "deal" between companies and workers wherein the interests of companies were intertwined with the interests of labor, supported by generous social policies. From the 1980s onward, this "deal" was shattered in the United States. Access to cheap labor abroad and the rise of new financial instruments that allowed companies to distribute unprecedented levels of profit to shareholders through financial speculation resulted in a shift in management culture and in the level of commitment employers were willing to make to their labor force.[64] The balance of power shifted in favor of management due to weakened unions, increased economic insecurity, and reduction in the role of government in policing the labor market.[65] Kathryn Dudley further suggests that meritocratic individualism became a new form of the Protestant work ethic: it is no longer God, but the economy "that rewards those of good character while punishing the shiftless and improvident."[66] Deindustrialization involved a "transformation of our cultural character" and created a new neoliberal value system.[67]

This transformation created a skewed economy with a radically different opportunity structure than existed in the post-WWII landscape. The loss of unionized factory jobs all but eliminated jobs for working-class men and women that had provided stable wages and supported middle-class livelihoods. For these workers, most without university degrees, deindustrialization was what Dudley called a "status degradation ritual" in which laborers were told their class standing and self-worth were lower than they previously believed.[68] As the US industrial economy transitioned to the service economy, job growth was concentrated at both the top and the bottom of the labor market, with growth in high-end service jobs in finance and technology and in low-end service work. Former industrial workers, squeezed out of a shrinking middle class, found themselves downwardly mobile in the new "hourglass economy."[69] This not only meant lower wages and less job security, but also less mobility from the bottom of the earnings distribution to the top over the course of workers' careers.

This transformation affected working-class communities of all racial backgrounds but hit Black and Brown communities the hardest. By the 1990s, policy transformations at the national and local levels had gutted decades of welfare policy, blocked access to homeownership for communities of color, and decimated a range of community-based institutions in urban inner-city areas, leaving their residents "hyper-segregated" with almost no paths open for social or economic mobility.[70] Furthermore, Black and Brown workers, previously a "reserve army" for industrial labor, were rendered disposable and became targets for new policies of social control, including incarceration.[71] New policies at the federal and state levels expanded the carceral system to carry out the "war on drugs," a set of policies that targeted impoverished neighborhoods suffering from job losses, encouraged the flight of affluent residents to better-off interracial suburbs, and resulted in the collapse of urban economic and social institutions. This constellation of circumstances led to the mass incarceration of Black and Brown men living in marginalized communities and the expansion of carceral logics to the streets and schools of these neighborhoods.[72]

Deindustrialization in the United States worked together with our second condition of neoliberalism: *strengthened national borders that serve to promote trade and competition between countries, even as nation-states give up on the dream of self-sufficiency.* The creation of EPZs led to increased emigrations from developing countries to receiving countries like the United States but, simultaneously, a strengthening of national borders. In the United States, the term "illegal alien" did not exist before the 1960s. In the late 1970s, with political elites pushing narratives of "border protection" and "strengthening national borders," the term became commonplace and pejorative.[73] At the same time, neoliberal economic policies increased the geographic mobility of capital, a process that begins in the 1970s but consolidates in the 1990s. By the early 1980s, Keynesian economics, which maintained there should be a just degree of state intervention within systems of open markets, was purged from the IMF and the World Bank. Instead, US economists advised in favor of neoliberal policies that emphasized control of inflation, sound public finance, and reduced taxes and regulations for corporations. The emphasis on full employment and social protections that was emphasized in the liberal post-WWII period receded. This shift helped set up a competitive global free-trade environment in which countries were forced to specialize in producing specific goods and to compete in a global market.

The growing consensus around free trade in the most powerful countries was imposed upon the rest of the world through international institutions. The Washington Consensus of the 1990s consolidated support for free trade through the WTO and NAFTA and the reduction of tariff barriers. With the United States at the helm, the World Trade Agreements of 1995 forced all states to consider how "business friendly" their markets were to remain competitive and, in 1996, the General Agreement on Tariffs and Trade (GATT) was transformed into the permanent WTO.

A key tactic by which international institutions imposed free-trade policies on the rest of the world was through the conditionalities associated with debt.[74] IMF bailouts required free-market reforms as a condition of receiving monies. The IMF and the World Bank used the "degree of neoliberalization" as a measure of good business climate, thus increasing pressure on all states to adopt neoliberal economic reforms. Although decolonialization had already occurred, powerful international institutions, led by the United States and its allies, imposed their belief in free trade to force countries to specialize in goods and services where they have a comparative advantage. This meant that developing economies, previously controlled by colonial powers focused on the extraction of raw materials, would now have to continue producing raw materials or other products at the bottom of global value chains. Alternately, they could use the export of their population as laborers (domestic workers, for example) as a commodity in the global market. This new global economic architecture, led by US interests, thus undermined many of the goals of decolonization as well as the institutional norms established in the postwar period.[75]

Turning now to how the key actors of the individual and the nation-state come to the forefront of public life, the US context provides perhaps the most important national context for understanding *the ideology of individual achievement*, closely associated with capitalism and baked into US policy packages throughout the postwar period. The United States was already leading the way in holding individuals, communities, and nation-states to the meritocratic ideal during the post-WWII period we have previously identified as liberalism. The American Dream is built on the idea that talent and effort are enough to ensure upward mobility. But the definition of individuality and meritocracy intensified under neoliberalism, supported by social policies that disinvest from the protection of society.

Particularly since the 1980s, meritocracy has become "neoliberalism's handmaiden," facilitating the atomization of individuals while extending competition and entrepreneurial behavior into all areas, even the most intimate, of everyday life.[76] This has led to an intensification of social stratification and hierarchy in US society. Neoliberal meritocracy has erased traditional political divisions between left and right, so that both the political parties of Barack Obama and Donald Trump converge around a strikingly similar belief in competitive individualism and entrepreneurship. These discursive practices of "meritocracy" and a "level playing field" obscure deep inequalities and discrimination along the axes of race, class, gender, and citizenship status. Yet it is these very categories of disadvantage that disrupt the US narrative about claims to modernity and linear progress. In fact, neoliberal meritocracy's entrepreneurial success stories, such as Facebook's COO Sheryl Sandberg and her advice that women emulate her success by "leaning in," are offered as solutions to the very racialized and gendered disadvantages perpetuated by neoliberal meritocracy.[77]

In this context, the notion of women's empowerment through paid work has become the ascendant narrative in the United States and around the world, a transformation that we traced in chapters 2 and 3 that began as early as the 1960s. What is new about these discourses under neoliberalism is that public discourse around women has shifted from conversations about national-level policy transformation and resource redistribution to raise the floor for all women to conversations about work–life balance, "leaning in" and the "end of men."[78] As women are increasingly left to figure out how to tackle childcare, work, and family demands on their own, the Nixon-era policy battle around universal childcare has been erased from public narratives. This erasure hides from view the fundamentally political, capitalist, and American character of the requirement that women care for children for free within the structure of the nuclear family, and makes it appear instead that American women, especially elite women, have virtually unlimited choices. They can be mothers or workers or both if they can just figure out the right "balance." The structural issue gets experienced as a personal set of choices that rests on the shoulders of women.[79]

The so-called "empowerment" of elite women through paid work in the United States did not liberate them from the expectation of free caring labor in a nuclear family due to the global policy environment in the early 1970s. However, the legitimization of women as default caretakers for the family perpetuated the growth of poorly paid, dead-end service jobs at the bottom of the US "hourglass" economy once the transition to the service economy was complete.[80] These jobs, which tend to be associated with caring labor, have become typed as "feminine" jobs and thus are associated with flexibility, dexterity, and a secondary-earner status. This set of conditions created a servant class, disproportionately comprised of migrants, whose existence is critical for sustaining the possibilities of self-realization and empowerment for elite White women and men.[81] Despite these structural conditions, the US state and corporate media have been able to represent the United States as a space of liberation for women, where even working-class immigrant women have ample choices leading to upward mobility. This representation makes the United States a magnet for gendered migration, the consequences of which we explore more closely in the next chapter.

The mandates of neoliberal meritocracy extend from individuals to nation-states. A similar logic of competition, entrepreneurship, and merit applies to justify nation-states' access to wealth, cheap labor, and status location in the hierarchy of nations. It also justifies the reinforcement of neocolonial relationships between nation-states. The United States and the West continue to exact "tribute" from developing countries – considered by neoliberal political and economic elites as less deserving, less modern, less entrepreneurial – in the form of massive debts, labor exploitation, and financial policing from external entities. As the WTO and other institutions set neoliberal standards and rules for interaction in the global economy with the explicit aim of opening as much of the world as possible to unhindered capital flow, neocolonial relationships of power allowed the United States, along with European nations and Japan, to "exact tribute from the rest of the world."[82] As a global hegemon, the United States could externally appear self-sufficient, but internally the economic reliance of the United States on China, evident in a long-standing trade deficit, and the reliance of consumers on ever cheaper and higher quality goods from around the world has exposed just how dependent the United States is on other countries in the new global economic order.

It is in this neoliberal context that Trump's assertion that the United States will "build a wall" and have "Mexico pay for it" is intelligible. This reality, considering the continued effects of deindustrialization and growing inequality, planted the seeds for Trump's "America First" agenda, which foregrounded economic and political self-sufficiency and American isolationism and exceptionalism.[83] Such a conception, still powerful under neoliberalism, was diametrically opposed to the prevailing norms of neoliberal economic policies in favor of specialization and comparative advantage. We return to a discussion of this backlash against free trade and the concomitant assertion of national sovereignty through populist authoritarianism in chapter 6. We regard it as part and parcel of the consequences of neoliberalism's gender order.

A complete break from the socialist past in the FSU

Although the specific policies of "shock therapy" and the transition to neoliberal capitalism were created in East–West circuits of expert knowledge, much of the discursive architecture of neoliberalism was set up by US leadership on a national stage and within global institutions after the Soviet Union collapsed. In the FSU, this architecture took shape in distinctive ways. Even though economists and other elites in the FSU had long been in consultation with US economists to set up the policies that would usher Soviet countries into the global capitalist order, these policies were largely without precedent and, from the perspective of everyday people, were imposed through a "shock doctrine." This "shock doctrine" caused an immense and sudden rupture in the entire social order, with a range of implications for gendered articulations among individuals and nation-states, both at home and abroad.

The first structuring condition of neoliberalism, *state protection of elites and global capital so that they may move freely and profit while leaving everyone else constrained*, was particularly pronounced in Ukraine. In fact, while Ukrainian elites formed a "super-class" of so-called "oligarchs," the creation of a society of mass consumption occurred in the near absence of a middle class and an acute impoverishment of most of the population.[84] Ukraine saw catastrophic declines in economic output, and, as in many other post-Soviet countries, privatization, deregulation, and liberalization drastically increased social inequality. The decline in Ukraine's GDP over the 1990s was 54%, worse than Russia's at 40%, and twice as severe as the general estimate for economic decline in the United States during the Great Depression of the 1930s.[85] Over ten years after Soviet collapse, Ukraine did experience some improvement in the country's devastating poverty rate, and in 2003 Ukraine's poverty rate was 37.7%, comparable to Mexico's 40%.[86] However, Ukraine's poverty rate began to rise again with the global economic crisis of 2008 and is expected to increase dramatically after Russia's 2022 invasion.[87]

Although foreign direct investment (FDI) soared in some post-Soviet countries, in order to attract investors, many states reduced labor protections, maintained low taxation of capital, and supported laws around the protection of private property and the right to expatriate profits bolstering the mobility of capital.[88] Ukraine, however, did not have the inflow of FDI that some other countries in the region experienced. Economic elites, often with political clout, pushed measures that would help preserve their status and obstructed policies that would endanger their interests. They favored the privatization of strategic assets but blocked the liberalization of banking activity that would have allowed an influx of transnational capital, a development that elites found threatening.[89] This "insider" privatization of former state property and enterprises produced a local ruling class of "oligarchs" whose wealth was generated by "special exemptions on economic regulations" and the "expansion of ownership," rather than through productive activity or new investment in development projects. As a result, well into the post-Soviet period, the economic elite was still identified with the state apparatus.[90] While the "Soviet descent into capitalism" has been a success from the standpoint of global capital, the deterioration of the Ukrainian economy has fueled mass emigration and frustrated aspirations for a "postcolonial renewal."[91]

The Soviet Union was a closed and largely self-sufficient federation. The collapse of the Soviet Union left the countries of the region newly independent and in many cases severed economic and political ties between them. Thus the second structuring condition of neoliberalism, *strengthened borders for purposes of competitive trade*, came with regulations that were experienced as entirely new in Ukraine. A passport and visa regime was implemented so that newly formed states could strengthen their borders and regulate the movement of people. However, strong borders were further required to support the nation-state building projects of post-Soviet countries. States strengthened borders to be able to face the new economic reality of trade and competition, which replaced the Soviet economic system based on regional self-sufficiency.[92] Although some post-Soviet countries looked toward Russia for a Eurasian Economic Union (EAEU), others looked to the European Union (EU). Ukraine continues to knock on the door of EU membership but has not been admitted for many reasons, including poor economic performance and autocratic political tendencies.[93]

Neoliberalism's hailing of *the individual as a key social actor in national and global history* was salient in the dramatic new morality introduced by free-market capitalism after the collapse of the Soviet order. Neoliberal capitalism offers radically different status and value systems according to which individuals judge themselves. The end of state paternalism and the collapse of Soviet social protections ended the social contract between working women and the state, forcing them to search for new life strategies and identities.[94] After the collapse of the FSU, it was not just states that took the neoliberal turn; individuals did as well. In her study of single mothers in Russia, Jennifer Utrata shows that Russian single mothers are surprisingly supportive of the neoliberal capitalist ideologies of independence and self-reliance.[95] Despite the significant structural constraints they face, these women work hard to transform themselves into post-Soviet people who control their destiny and can "make it" in the New Russia. In this version of the feminist cover story, women believe they "make" their own destinies and perceive expanded "choices," but in practice, live far more precarious lives.

In Ukraine, market ideologies at first seemed to provide many "choices" for women, but in the end they offered women only two possible identities: housewife or businesswoman. They mobilize myths of Ukraine's traditional past associated with the revival of independent statehood after years of Russian colonization.[96] In the West, a relegation of women to housewives may be understood as "backward," but, in a post-Soviet context, this identity is framed in popular discourse as a progressive move forward from socialism to capitalism. The identity of "housewife" confirms a "matriarchal" society where women rule the private sphere as one that is separate but equal to that of men in the market. The second identity, the successful "female entrepreneur," legitimates the new market order by assuring the public that women – just a handful are needed – will introduce the ethics and morality lacking in the capitalist system. This marginalization of women is attached to the "transition to market" project in which the institutions of market society are presented as universal, natural, and fair, rather than based on a socially constructed and unequal gendered division of labor. Instead of Soviet mother-workers, in the neoliberal capitalist system women must choose to be either a housewife or an entrepreneur – motherhood or career – but they may not have both. These visions of empowerment make up a cover story of expanded choice that obscures the hardened inequalities along lines of class and region that make it appear as if life outcomes are deserved, a fair result of individual striving.

Meritocracy, free markets, and an emerging economy: India's neoliberal turn

Unlike the FSU, India's turn to neoliberalism did not occur quickly in the context of institutional collapse. In India, abiding internal divisions and political crises converged with the ruptures of the global political economic system to produce a new identity for India in the international realm. No longer a rabble-rouser organizing Third

World nation-states for a new international economic order in international institutions, by the 1990s India had acquired the status of an "emerging economy." The country started to open its markets to free trade and was forced to relinquish its long-standing friendship with the Soviet Union.[97] This new status came with a transformed vision of gendered modernity and a new commitment to meritocracy, a set of developments that once again marginalized decades of anti-caste struggle that had shaped the postcolonial period. The new vision for neoliberal India also pushed aside overt efforts to reduce poverty that had been central to government policy since independence.

As early as the 1960s, as the central government attempted to manage multiplying political and economic crises, India's policies shifted away from the centralization of state industries and the sustenance of two parallel economies, one for poverty upliftment and another for growth. As state policies increasingly became oriented toward promoting economic growth, the first structuring condition of neoliberalism, *state protection of elites and global capital*, started taking shape through policy regimes that enriched elites through foreign capital-driven industrial growth. By the 1980s, Rajiv Gandhi started crafting policies that would allow foreign direct investment in India to fuel a global tech sector, arguably the first set of policies implemented in India consistent with neoliberal principles.[98] In parallel, Gandhi rolled back banking regulations, lowered tariffs, and opened India's consumer markets to foreign goods. As the government started investing in new software tech parks and EPZs that would encourage foreign companies to set up operations in the country, new policies allowed Indian tech talent to travel to the United States for specific technical projects, allowing a highly skilled segment of the Indian workforce to seek wages outside India and then return.[99] This arrangement also greatly benefited US tech firms, who needed the relatively cheap tech skills to grow their businesses. The advantageous exchange rate, a feature of the neocolonial system of free trade that was consolidated in the 1990s, allowed US companies to tap Indian talent at a much lower cost than would be possible if they only had access to domestic talent, a phenomenon known as "labor arbitrage."[100]

Over time, these policies fueled massive rural–urban migration, widening inequalities, and acute crises of malnourishment and hunger.[101] Currently, India has one of the highest levels of inequality in the world.[102] The 200 million-strong, "new" Indian middle class that has emerged post-liberalization enjoys levels of wealth and status that were unheard of a generation ago, but the floor has not risen for the vast majority, as the state has made minuscule investments in education, healthcare, and rural economies. In the context of the COVID-19 crisis, the mass migration of workers from urban areas to their rural homes was the cause of a protracted humanitarian crisis, laying bare the conditions of extreme precarity and vulnerability that most workers find themselves in during an era of nationwide prosperity.[103] Women workers from vulnerable communities were hit especially hard, experiencing sudden loss of employment, rupture in social and familial bonds, and a rapid return to their native villages.[104] India's efforts to protect elites have left its most vulnerable neglected and thus constrained, arguably undermining many of its initial aims as a postcolonial nation-state.

India has also gone to great lengths to adopt our second structuring condition of *strengthened borders and a focus on ethnonationalist identity, while compromising on key aspects of political and economic sovereignty*. These moves have generated significant contestation and reflect the heightened importance of regional geopolitics in postcolonial settings. In India, the apparent desire to expand trade comes into conflict with security concerns over territorial sovereignty and exclusionary constructions of ethnonationalist identity in the region. The Look East policy, an important feature of liberalized India's foreign policy, sought to expand infrastructure projects as well as cooperation in regional organizations. Since 2014 this policy has been refocused and intensified under Narendra Modi's nationalist regime.[105]

But these seemingly "open" policies that appear to effectively break down borders may only be paying lip service to a system of border policing that enforces territorial sovereignty while also drawing strict lines between "insiders" and "outsiders." These contradictions increasingly form the basis of Indian belonging, which has become increasingly nationalistic. The South Asian regional context is one that has been rife with struggles over borders throughout the twentieth century, whether in relation to Kashmir, the contested regions between India and Pakistan, Bangladesh, and China, the latter a border that has been particularly contentious in 2020.[106] Furthermore, the lived experience of racism in India's borderlands and among migrants from neighboring countries in India's cities suggests that the borders around who gets to claim Indian identity are tightening rather than expanding.[107] Ethnonationalist framings have increasingly become crystallized in laws and practices that privilege dominant-caste Hindu groups who appear racially "Indian," and exclude "Northeastern" migrants.[108] In parallel, new unconstitutional legislative acts curb the citizenship rights of Muslim migrants.[109] Yet neoliberal India has strengthened its ties to wealthy Indian diasporas abroad, creating new categories of Indian citizenship to encourage investment and absentee property ownership.[110] This has helped fuel Hindu nationalism while favoring the enrichment of industries supported by the state.[111]

In this social and political context, a merit-based understanding of the striving individual has ascended to organize politics and morality in India. The antecedents of this idea go back to colonialism. Under colonialism, logics of individual merit dominated public institutions, legitimating the education and promotion of elite class and caste groups into the upper echelons of India's bureaucracy. Those same institutions were reproduced in postcolonial times through the continuation of the Indian civil service and the establishment of the Indian Institutes of Technology, meant to build up a pool of technical talent that would serve the new nation's industries. But during the transition to neoliberalism, the objects of merit-oriented public institutions changed. Government jobs came to be associated with caste-based reservations, a postcolonial policy aimed at redressing historical inequities that has faced heightened scrutiny under neoliberalism. In parallel, the global technological services industry boomed, and India's market became flush with consumer goods and media from around the world. New ideals of worth and belonging emerged, valorizing the striving individual with cosmopolitan tastes, a strong sense of family, and capitalist sensibilities oriented toward personal and family enrichment.[112] These values have been shown to be emblematic of India's so-called "new middle class." This ideology finds expression among middle-class women through gendered modes of comportment, work–life "balance," and putting family first.[113] Among working-class and poor women, rather than a focus on rights-based political mobilization, the state, in collaboration with financial institutions, promotes values oriented toward entrepreneurship and financial management.[114] When women achieve these ideals, they appear "empowered" to the nation and to the world, advancing India's symbolic position within a hierarchy of nations.

India's position as a nation-state in global hierarchies has shifted considerably in the lead-up to the neoliberal period. During the postwar period, India was a prestigious founding member of the NAM but became a less credible member of the NAM club when it established closer ties with the Soviet Union.[115] In 1991, in order to qualify for a loan from the IMF, India implemented prescribed liberalization policies from above.[116] But the implementation and acceleration of these policies was considerably more cautious than in Latin American countries and was stalled by the East Asian crisis in the late 1990s. Despite these caveats, India's liberalization drew significant global attention, as analysts, policy makers, and the public began viewing India as a global superpower competing with China. This was due to new economic forecasts in the 1990s that developing countries, some of which were now reframed as "emerging markets," were now prime destinations for FDI and would soon outcompete the western powers in terms of overall economic growth.[117] India was predicted to replace Germany as the fourth largest economy in the world by 2020.[118] Powerful global South countries, led by an elite G-15 (of the original G-77) that included India, had accepted that global capitalism was the prevailing system within the global economy and that postcolonial countries would have to adapt to that reality.[119] There was a contradiction in this newfound status: the "emerging economies" of Brazil, India, and China were now politically powerful and economically formidable, yet a large proportion of their populations suffered from entrenched poverty.

India's rising political and economic status in global hierarchies was accompanied by new gendered representations of women's empowerment and status in a liberalized economy. Starting in the 1990s, for the first time women from India became prominent participants in Miss World and Miss Universe beauty pageants, capturing both titles in 1994, a historic event that was celebrated throughout India.[120] This event not only signified the cultural arrival of Indian women to the cosmopolitan modernity that was fast becoming a hallmark of neoliberalism, but also a break from India's "traditional" cultural identity, which publics at home and abroad often regard as inherently oppressive toward women. The trope of respectable femininity, which commanded status in the postcolonial cultural landscape, continued to exercise considerable cultural power in this new moment, but she had been transformed. The neoliberal icon of an "empowered" woman became a new ideal among India's new upwardly mobile middle classes. This idealized upwardly mobile, implicitly Hindu, upper-caste woman, internalized some aspects of western comportment and "global" value systems, often marked by a "modern" job outside the home, but she retained her essential cultural identity.[121] Everyday women working in upwardly mobile occupations view these transformations as an expansion of choices, such that they can now have more of a say in their own future.[122] During the same period, India began experimenting with new strategies of poverty alleviation that required women to take out loans in groups, following the successful example of Bangladesh. By the early 2000s, microfinance programs targeting vulnerable women in rural areas of India had saturated the countryside, enmeshing private and public financial institutions in predatory debt.[123] Despite many of the deleterious effects of these poverty policies, the icon of the empowered Indian micro-entrepreneurial woman provided a compelling justification for neoliberal policies that had largely left India's agricultural sector behind. Women from many class and caste backgrounds, then, have been able to both be represented to the world as "empowered" and have been able to experience a sense of expanded choices, even though they may personally experience a more contradictory and limited set of livelihood options than those representations suggest.

India's symbolic rise as a nation-state has been accompanied by a steady strengthening of its ethnonationalist identity as a Hindu majoritarian nation, a trend that has strengthened in parallel with the political, economic, and cultural transformations signifying neoliberalism in India. Indeed, transformations such as the spread of cable television across the rural countryside and the widespread proliferation of culturally specific consumer goods have strongly supported the goals of Hindu nationalist politicians.[124] The rise of Narendra Modi, which we discuss further in chapter 6, represents the culmination of neoliberalism's discursive architecture in India because of his simultaneous support of global free-market capitalism and an authoritarian strongman identity, built upon a populist base of discontent with India's secular past, a past that much of the constituency now deems elitist and out of touch.

Conclusion

In this chapter, we have provided a theoretical basis for understanding and interpreting the discursive and material architecture of neoliberalism. Indeed, this complex yet well-defined convergence constitutes the "gender order of neoliberalism" that is the title of this book. Focusing on two key structuring conditions and two key actors, we have created a matrix of concepts from which to understand how divergent historical circumstances in the United States, various FSU countries, and India nonetheless share discursive and material conditions that, while not identical, are related to one another. Together with other competing nation-states, these dynamic conditions and actors comprise the gender order of neoliberalism, which requires the neoliberal feminist cover story to paper over the significant global inequalities that persist across the world.

We have argued that in the United States, the FSU, and India, neoliberalism has called into focus *individuals* and *nation-states* as primary actors seeking status and upward mobility in a competitively structured field. The dominance of these two social actors has had the effect of diminishing, though not completely erasing, the importance of other kinds of subnational, sociocultural, or political formations. Collective understandings of empowerment, for example, or Soviet-style emancipation discourses that require a large-scale societal transformation in order to open up new possibilities for the marginalized have been at best sidelined. At worst, such understandings of empowerment and mobilization are unthinkable in the neoliberal order. They receive relatively little support from the state, the market, or global policies, and they do not constitute a field of aspirations on which social actors imagine their futures. Instead, aspirations and hopes can be imagined only within the context of an individual story or the story of a nation-state. What those aspirations look like differs considerably across the many contexts we have examined, yet the structure of these aspirations is similar. When individuals and nation-states are primary actors, their perceived gender in a local and global power matrix significantly impacts future trajectories, which we explore in the next two chapters.

We have also identified two structuring conditions that come together to set up the gender order of neoliberalism: (1) the state's protection of capital and elites; and (2) the strengthening of national borders primarily for the purposes of global trade. These conditions go together with an imagination that views individuals and nation-states as primary actors, and a global system in which the dominance of the market is supported by a system of trade that requires closed borders that only capital and the privileged can traverse with ease. These dynamics create a captive labor pool that is consistently seeking modernity, affluence, and status elsewhere, and a permanent underclass of nation-states that lack true political autonomy in a globally interconnected neoliberal landscape. Here again, there is tremendous variation among countries, and there is a dynamism to what individuals and nation-states do under these conditions. In the following two chapters, we provide an initial exploration of what this gender order of neoliberalism produces for gendered individuals and gendered nation-states which are ostensibly "empowered" to craft their own destinies, even where the real conditions inhibit autonomy and thriving for the vast majority. We first examine, in chapter 5, how individual migrant women and nation-states aspire to status and modernity abroad through domestic work and marriage. In the following chapter, chapter 6, we examine a more recent culmination of neoliberalism's gendered architecture: the emergence of a "manly protector" cover story that aims to create a new vision of modernity built around community and nation which rejects the dominance of the market altogether.

5
Moving Toward Modernity

For those located in postcolonial countries, migration is a project of transformation, driven by both nation-states and individual migrants. Colonial regimes utilized the discourse of "civilization" to justify forced migration, slavery, and labor extraction. Postcolonial governments, in contrast, pivoted to celebrate inward-looking domestic and regional modernities shaped by the politics of the Cold War.[2] Since the 1970s, however, these modernity projects started to engage outward-facing discourses and practices of transnational migration. The economic imperatives of neoliberalism increasingly required postcolonial and post-Soviet countries to incorporate mobility into their understandings of modernity. These new conceptions of modernity, we find, are often in conversation with both real and imagined opportunities in wealthier receiving countries. Nation-states and migrants alike view migration as a project of pursuing modernity, whether through exposure to new places and ideas or changes to income level or lifestyle.

Images of women, family, and home are central to most national and ethnic cultures.[3] In nationalist discourse, women are often constructed as the symbolic bearers of the nation, responsible for both its biological and cultural reproduction.[4] Women's centrality to nationalist projects around the world, and especially postcolonial and post-Soviet projects, makes emigration policies an explicit target of concern.[5] The feminist cover story suggests that there are lots of choices available to women, provided that nation-states embrace neoliberal policies and the underlying value system of the global neoliberal order. The logic of merit and fair competition within neoliberalism obscures inequality at both the micro and macro levels to create the illusion that all players are on an equal footing. The reality of inequality at multiple scales is that both individual migrants and nation-states move within an uneven global geography shaped by histories of imperialism and colonialism. The neoliberal feminist cover story, steeped in the logic of merit, suggests that striving individuals who have invested in their own human capital may – with an enterprising spirit, hard work, and a little luck – convert their human capital into greater productivity, and thus wealth, in the global labor market. The feminist cover story further suggests that there is an even playing field for socioeconomic mobility that allows for advancement toward empowerment and modernity. Working in tandem with these discourses, migrant-sending states use discourses of gendered nationalism to portray their citizens, whether at home or abroad, as modern, entrepreneurial, and upwardly mobile in the global arena. Having internalized these ideas in the face of few other opportunities for economic advancement, individual migrants seek to convert their human capital in the global labor market. When they do, migrants find that ideologies about gender and race at once facilitate and curtail that conversion. Thus we carry forward the theme that the neoliberal order requires both nation-states in the global arena and individuals in their locales to compete for wealth and moral status, often articulated through idioms of gender and sexuality.

In this chapter, we ask: (1) what choices become available to nation-states and individuals coming from postcolonial and post-socialist contexts once these actors embrace neoliberalism? (2) how are these choices experienced by actors situated in the so-called "Second" and "Third" Worlds? And (3) how are these choices linked to the choices available to nation-states and individuals located in the so-called "First" World?

Many women located in migrant-sending countries think of migration as moving them closer to or farther away from modern lifestyles. Ethnographic studies reveal that what modernity means to these women is varied. For example, for some women migrating from the Philippines or Vietnam, "modern" means egalitarian relationships between men and women and especially husbands and wives. For many post-Soviet women, "modern" means women, previously subject to the exhausting Soviet mandates of mothering and paid labor, are now free to choose to focus on being wives and mothers and dream of a "real" man who will "protect" and "care" for her and their children. Despite these seemingly opposing expectations of life in a modern country, we find that the aspiration that women should have "choices," what we call the neoliberal feminist cover story, is ubiquitous. These aspirations are grounded in a particular political economy and a set of material conditions, each of which limits the possible pathways toward modernity for women in migrant-sending regions. The intensification of the world's visa regimes, the constraints of the global economy, and the interconnections of gender and racial systems transnationally have narrowed the options for the majority who seek to migrate. Thus two interlocking choices are most accessible to them: migrate to do cleaning and caring labor as a domestic worker or migrate to become a wife.

In what follows, we first lay out the politico-economic conditions that produce the categories of domestic worker and marriage migrant as vehicles of mobility. Although migrant-sending states have, with variations, adopted policies of investing in women, we begin by explaining why the lived conditions of global economic restructuring curtail the promise of human capital as a path to upward mobility. The neoliberal feminist cover story of "choices" makes these mobility paths appear aspirational for individuals. Nation-states hoping to propel their country to a higher status in the international arena then aim to capture migrant remittances, thus incorporating migration into national economic development plans.

Next, we examine two mobility pathways to modernity: domestic work and marriage migration. Of the two options, domestic work is a "choice" being mobilized by some nation-states that systemically export women as domestic workers to improve their economic standing but also their national status. However, in both postcolonial and post-Soviet contexts, the mass emigration of women to perform cleaning and caring labor abroad simultaneously represents a "modernity threat" to be negotiated. Individual migrants find themselves caught between patriarchal gendered nationalisms that require women to remain committed to both mothering and aspirational understandings of modernity (including self-transformation, egalitarian or "protective" marriages, new patterns of consumption, and uplift for their families and nation-states) that draw them into the landscape of "choice." Migrant women must then negotiate the unexpected realities of "modern life" in their receiving countries. Rather than a modernity threat, marriage migration is seen as a "modernity promise" by both individuals and sending states. Although receiving states might worry about racialized migrant mothers, sending countries pay this mobility pathway less attention than the domestic-worker migrations because marriage confers respectability and is recognized as an honorable option in a global order that values the hetero-patriarchal nuclear-family form. Individual women experience both options as a "choice" that moves individuals and nation-states toward modernity.

Our usage of the terms "First World/Third World," "developing/developed," or "global North/global South" throughout this chapter especially varies to reflect the terms used in the migration and development literatures. As we use these terms, we remain aware of their geopolitical history, the terrain of competition that all these terms imply, and their racist, classist connotations for varied audiences. At times, our usage highlights the problematic transformation of "Third World" as representing a radical alternative to capitalism or communism to a representation of poverty, brownness, and low status.

Global economic restructuring and the limits of human capital theory

By the time the Soviet Union collapsed in 1991, global economic restructuring had been underway in the United States, Europe, much of Asia, and in large swaths of Africa. This process accelerated the commoditization of women's labor in new ways, drawing women at the bottom of national and global hierarchies into paid work outside of agriculture – in factories, in low-wage service work, and in homes as migrant domestic workers.[6] Capitalist theories of human capital and empowerment, which won out over socialist theories of collective uplift (see chapter 3), promised upward mobility through paid work for marginalized groups if they invested in education and hard work. But the emerging reality of neoliberal capitalism undermined that promise for all but a few. Migrant women filtered in at the bottom of the US labor market and encountered systemic and interpersonal racism, a surprise for many migrants who expected the United States to be a "modern," First World country in which "investing in women" might translate into moving up the economic ladder. Yet migrants found that they were largely unable to convert their education at home into high-paying jobs abroad, even in wealthy receiving countries, due in part to the limited opportunities for mobility between the lower and top tiers of the "hourglass" economy.[7]

Because of structural constraints and the constraints imposed by visa regimes, a second pathway for upward mobility opened up: marriage to men living in wealthier countries. The experiences and choices of individual women migrants within the unequal global economy that emerged after neoliberalism exposed the fantasy of human capital theory. Nation-states and individuals, both key actors in the neoliberal landscape, have thus endeavored to leverage any advantages they can from the limited pathways to modernity and progress that the new system offers.

Global economic restructuring that began in the 1970s created an "hourglass" economy with expanding job opportunities at the top and bottom of the labor market and a constriction of middle-class jobs.[8] At the bottom of the labor market, there was a dramatic expansion of jobs coded as "feminine" without a corresponding expansion of work coded as "masculine." This economic reality has unmasked the limitations of human capital theory. Women in the Philippines and the FSU, for example, with high levels of education were not able to convert their human capital into high-paying professional jobs. Instead, they work as domestic workers abroad, a move that only makes economic sense because of exchange rates that privilege historically wealthy countries. In fact, some studies found a small minority of migrants resisting the notion that educating women would lead to empowerment and uplift. These informants reported they decided to save the time and expense of attending university since they ascertained that all women, regardless of education level, would end up in the same place – as domestic workers abroad.[9]

During the colonial era, migration paths moved largely from colonized to colonizing countries. Economic development is often dependent on the recruitment of cheap labor from other places. However, Saskia Sassen registered a shift since the mid-1960s and noted that capital mobility created new conditions for the mobility of labor.[10] Increases in direct foreign investment in the development of export manufacturing transformed migration streams from colonial routes to migration pathways that followed capital investments like invisible bridges back to diverse locations in the global North. Colonial routes turned into migration pathways that satisfied the labor needs of global North countries. US economic policies have played a disproportionate role in refashioning the global political economy, and particularly labor flows, since the 1970s.[11] US companies have increasingly moved manufacturing abroad – reducing domestic middle-class job opportunities – to create Export Processing Zones (EPZs) in developing countries.[12] This spurred processes of proletarianization that included large internal rural-to-urban migrations in many areas of the developing world.[13] These manufacturing sectors operated according to a gendered logic tied to feminized patterns of racial and regional inequality and sought to employ "cheap," "docile," "nimble-fingered," brown women.[14] Women from rural areas in the Third World have been migrating to EPZs, where they have become "disposable workers," discarded after sustaining injuries in factories.[15]

This transformation expanded economic opportunities at the bottom of the labor market for women, but not for men and, further, left rural men to struggle since they lost women who were their partners in agriculture to factory work.[16] These displaced women then became a reserve army of labor that followed capital flows as migrants from the Third World to developed or rapidly developing countries. Between 1960 and 2000, the number of women migrants worldwide more than doubled from 35 million to 85 million and, in 2022, the number of women migrants increased further to 134.9 million.[17] According to the World Bank, women comprise about half of the world's migrants, with expectations that both the number and percentage of women migrants will continue to increase.[18] This pool of women migrants is differentiated by educational attainment, but also by nation-state. Nation-states that have high levels of acceptance of paid work for women outside the home and the farm are more likely to send women abroad to labor or marry. In her cross-national, comparative study of migration within Asia, Nana Oishi found that, compared to Asian countries that do not send women migrants abroad, Asian migrant-sending countries have higher levels of women's education, higher numbers of women in the domestic labor market, and higher levels of social legitimacy for women's inclusion in the domestic paid labor market.[19] Thus nation-states that send women abroad to labor have transformed the promise of human capital. The promise for education and work is no longer that "investing" in women can make women more productive. Education and a cosmopolitan embrace of paid work for women, however, can allow individuals and nation-states to leverage foreign-exchange rates in wealthier countries through labor migration. Gendered labor migration allows educated women to access pathways for upward mobility that are cut off at home because of the stratified global system.

What are the jobs to which women and men, constructed as "enterprising subjects," migrate in these new economic and social conditions? They are predominantly low-end service jobs, including domestic work, childcare, elder care, fast-food service, and landscaping. These low-status precarious jobs lack paths for advancement. They are "made" for undocumented immigrants who construct their status in relation to their sending, rather than receiving, contexts.[20] Since the 1970s, middle-class women in the First World – here we focus on the United States – have been incorporated into the labor market with limited or no childcare or eldercare services provided by the state. First World women, unable to convince their men peers to share domestic labor, have outsourced much of this labor to Third World migrant women, exacerbating inequalities along the vectors of race, gender, and citizenship status.[21] In this context of privatized mothering, individualized caregiving, and the links of gendered inequality between nation-states, enterprising migrant-sending states have recognized a labor niche and moved to fill it.

Like women located in migrant-sending countries, many women in migrant-receiving countries also find themselves caught between patriarchal gendered nationalisms that require women to remain committed to mothering and aspirational understandings of empowerment. Among middle- and upper-middle-class families in the United States, a "stalled gender revolution" since the 1980s has transformed expectations for mothers to include paid work and an expanded set of responsibilities for "good" mothering, while the expectations of men and fathers, largely centered on breadwinning, have remained the same.[22] Middle- and upper-middle-class women asked: Who would cook, clean, and raise the children? Facing a resounding silence from the men in their lives, the United States, along with other developed and developing nation-states, tugged on the macro-level chains that linked together unequally placed women according to race and citizenship in a global gender order. As a result, the labor of migrant women subsidizes the empowerment of middle- and upper-class women, often White US citizens, whose household incomes can pay for the livelihood of a nanny, thanks to increased inequality that concentrates wealth at the top of the income ladder. These households can also afford to pay for services that middle- and upper-class women simply do not have time to provide, such as house cleaning, laundry services, pre-made meals, grocery shoppers, help driving children to after-school activities, and so forth.

The promise of human capital thus collapses in the face of a transnational "hourglass" economy structured by inequality both between and within nation-states. Migrant women's education and English-language skills contribute to the "empowerment" of White, middle- and upper-class women, while these migrant women remain trapped at the bottom of the labor market within a wealthy receiving country like the United States. Even then, migrant women pursue migration not only for economic and physical mobility but to participate in a process of self-transformation that promises personal empowerment and access to the goods and cosmopolitan attitudes that comprise modernity. The empowered First World woman and the empowered Third World woman, both alluring ideals, set up a dichotomy that obscures Eastern Europe and the FSU entirely.[23] The dichotomous contrast *requires* inequality between and within nation-states, naturalized through race and gender hierarchies, for it to be achieved. How, then, do migrant-sending countries, many of them postcolonial and/or post-Soviet, and thus invested in ideas of cultural distinctiveness and self-sufficiency, justify the mass export of women for domestic work abroad?[24] Migrant-sending countries, recognizing that gender is a signifier of modernity, deploy discourses of gendered nationalism to make claims to modernity and status, even as the emigration of their women exposes the precarity of those claims.

Modernity threat: migrant domestic workers

Although the decision to migrate is often presented as an individual choice, this choice is in fact being mobilized (and at times blocked) by nation-states to improve their status in the global hierarchy of nations. On the one hand, nation-states see that they can fill a gap in the international division of labor by meeting the demand for domestic workers. On the other hand, nothing screams "Third World" quite like the mass emigration of women to perform cleaning and caring labor.[25] Although no country has moved from the Third to the First World on the backs of domestic workers, the belief that nation-states are competing on an even playing field makes this remittances-as-development strategy appear plausible. Nation-states also realize that the terrain of competition is not solely about economics. For example, many Middle Eastern countries are wealthy but are still not judged by the international community as "modern." How nation-states "treat their women" – judged by western institutions and ideals – matters significantly in making modernity claims.

Postcolonial and post-Soviet nation-states manage the contradictions and challenges of this historical moment in divergent ways. Their strategies are shaped by both their unique histories and their potential location within global status hierarchies. Their commonality is that, relative to previous eras, migrants today come from countries at more advanced stages of economic development and nation-state building.[26] As a result, migrants leave countries to which they have strong attachments, and states expect even migrants that settle permanently abroad to continue to be actively involved in their origin country. In this way, nationalist discourses have more power to shape the behavior of emigrants abroad than in previous eras, and in some cases state bureaucracies have evolved to enforce the obligations and privileges of national membership.[27] In all the cases we examine below, gendered nationalism and the allure of the perceived links between migration and modernity shape the meaning-making terrain in which we locate nation-states and individual migrants as actors.

Philippines: the labor brokerage state and "export quality" women

Beginning in the 1970s, the Philippine state transformed itself into what Robyn Rodriguez calls a "labor brokerage state."[28] The Philippine state negotiates temporary labor contracts in the global market with states looking to import what the Philippines has to offer: "export quality" women.[29] The Philippine state promotes leaving the country to earn wages abroad as a nationalist contribution and even designates a week-long holiday in June, Migrant Heroes Week, where it organizes formal activities to celebrate the nation's emigrants. This is supported by a state discourse of "global Philippine citizenship" that justifies a robust web of overseas offices and consulates. This transnational bureaucracy offers Philippine migrant workers a measure of protection abroad while simultaneously enforcing the obligations of citizenship, including the transfer of monetary remittances that are taxed by the state.[30] In fact, the state officially calls migrant laborers "overseas Filipino investors" in recognition of their individual contributions to the economic development of their home country.[31] The Philippine state asks its migrant women to pay its IMF debt and behave as "ambassadors" to bolster its economic development strategy. Migrant women, through their example of sexual modesty, hard work, and ethics, will convince foreigners to join them in investing money in the Philippine economy.[32]

Filipina migrants are also expected to be mothers who reproduce the Philippine nation. The imperatives of gendered nationalism are not only enforced through laws but also link migrant women's feelings of maternal duty to their children and families left behind with feelings of obligation to the Philippines as a nation-state. Both the Philippine state and migrant-receiving states prefer long-term labor contracts that encourage transnational families. This adds another incentive for Filipina migrants to send home monetary remittances and return to the Philippines when labor contracts expire, while wealthy countries, which do not bear the cost of reproducing this workforce, benefit from a captive, low-wage immigrant labor force without the rights of citizens.

This institutionalized, state-run labor export system has a CEO. In May 2003, the Philippines' President Gloria Macapagal-Arroyo stated, "Not only am I the head of state responsible for a nation of 80 million people. I'm also the CEO of a global Philippine enterprise of 8 million Filipinos who live and work abroad and generate billions of dollars a year in revenue for our country."[33] Arroyo represented herself not just as a head of state but as an entrepreneur. The state actively invests in its women to produce citizens that are "export quality" – well-versed in cooking the national cuisines of the destination country, trained to use modern equipment such as vacuum cleaners, and skilled English-language speakers.[34]

Filipina migrants fulfill the trope of a global, neoliberal ideal hero of development: the racialized empowered woman pulled into the capitalist labor market who has the potential, through self-sacrifice and entrepreneurship, to lift both their family and their country out of poverty. Although there is not yet an empirical example of a country propelled to global North status through migrant remittances, many other sending states have emulated this development strategy, including Guatemala, El Salvador, India, and Indonesia.[35]

The Philippine state "invests in women" to prepare them for export. Nonetheless, the strategy is not free from angst around gendered nationalism. The kind of policy a state enacts to regulate the emigration of "its women" reflects national values and identity and is also an indicator of where the nation-state lies with respect to the global markers of modernity: democracy, human rights, and gender equity. Mistreatment of migrant women abroad poses a modernity threat.[36] This is not equally true in the case of men who migrate. For example, in 1995, Flor Contemplacion, a Filipina domestic worker in Singapore, was accused of murdering a fellow Filipina domestic worker and the child in her care and was executed by the Singaporean state. Filipinos in the Philippines and around the world rallied to protest as many of them believed Contemplacion was framed by her Singaporean employer. The case exposed the vulnerabilities that Filipina migrants faced abroad. A Philippine state investigation found that "irreparable damage" had been "inflicted to the reputation of Filipina women in the international scene.... Our nation has gained the embarrassing reputation that we are a country of DHs [domestic helpers], entertainers, and even prostitutes."[37] The Philippine state temporarily blocked Filipina migration to Singapore – concerns about national status superseded economic need.

In contrast, the labor exploitation of Filipino migrants, such as men working on fishing rigs who were left on islands to die by employers who sought to avoid paying their wages, did not incite national indignation.[38] This suggests that although "we are all entrepreneurs" under neoliberalism, it is gendered understandings of women that prop up the system. Women are perceived as the symbolic property of the nation, thus their sexual or labor exploitation abroad is experienced as a humiliation for the nation-state[39] and a modernity threat. To address this bind, nation-states develop institutions and practices to protect the material and symbolic status of their citizens abroad and use nationalist discourses about "their women" to both manage their populations abroad and bolster their nation's status in the global arena.[40] These discourses are powerful because they effectively sustain economic, political, symbolic, and emotional ties between individual migrants and their home countries.

The other key actor within the neoliberal order, the individual, in this case the migrant woman, also advances a discourse parallel to the nation-state about the terms of her migration: moving toward modernity. For individual migrants, spatial mobility, strongly associated with social mobility, helps constitute narratives through which individuals aspire and dream of something called "modernity" and "progress."[41] Prospects for mobility itself constitute what modernity stands for in many parts of the world.[42] For those located outside of the First World, the "readiness to be mobile" is a key requirement of the "modern" individual.[43] The economic motivations of individuals and nation-states are important, and migrants actively link their labor to national goals. For example, Rhacel Parreñas noted that the migrant Filipina domestic workers she interviewed understood themselves as "the Mercedes Benz" of international caregivers and thus a competitive commodity in the global market.[44] Nicole Constable found that Filipina domestic workers in Hong Kong also linked their labor to nationalism and used nationalist discourses to discipline each other's behavior in order to combat unflattering Chinese stereotypes of Filipino poverty: backwardness, loose sexual morals, and inclination for gossiping and loitering.[45] One domestic worker wrote in a publication written for and by Filipina domestic workers:

> If we still have . . . the feelings of a true Filipino, let us join hands to prove to the whole world that Filipino maids still have moral values though how lowly we are in this foreign land . . . let us realize that whatever misbehavior we show in our sojourn is a disgrace and a shame to the whole Filipino race.[46]

Although migrants recognize the constraints of gendered nationalism and global economic inequality, migrants also tell researchers that they are hoping to "progress" in general.

One Gujarati man was persuaded to move by his uncle who said, "If people stay in one place there is no progress."[47] Many migrants from the region migrated to Britain because they expected to find a modern, clean, "civilized" country with high morals and plenty of opportunities.[48] These sentiments suggest that for individual migrants, as well as for nation-states, migration itself is a project of transformation in which new identities are being forged and existing orders are being challenged. Pei-chia Lan found that when Filipina women migrate to Taiwan for domestic work, a locale that is wealthier than the Philippines and also considered by migrants as more modern, they do so not only to "escape poverty" but also to "expand life horizons and to explore modernity."[49] One Filipina migrant woman with a college degree in pharmacy described "other compensation" beyond money that made her want to stay in Taiwan. She said in a group discussion,

> I think there is also other . . . how to say . . . compensations people receive when they are in Taiwan. If you are in the Philippines, you are a mother, a plain housewife only. This will not happen – going to the disco every Sunday and having your cellular phone! [Everybody laughs]. Yes! That's true! Joking, eating in McDonald every Sunday – can you do that in the Philippines? [Others shake their heads]. Yes, this is the difference. We are wearing jewelry, short skirts – you cannot wear that in the Philippines! In my hometown, people are very conservative. If I wear [clothes] like that, people will stare at me! That's why we want to stay abroad because of these compensations![50]

Lan argues that migrant domestic workers sought material affluence but also sexual liberation in societies considered modern. Thus individual migrants both conform to and resist gendered nationalism.

By portraying migration as motherly sacrifice, the Philippine state encourages even educated Filipina women to embrace the neoliberal feminist cover story as enterprising subjects and to use laboring as migrant domestic workers to uplift their family and country. At the same time, the state trades women as commodities in the global labor market. For former Soviet Bloc countries, the modernity threat posed by the mass migration of women to perform domestic work abroad is even more difficult to manage because these countries seek admission to the EU, which requires states to treat women, and other minority groups, according to international standards of gender equity, standards that would be undermined by sending women abroad to work in low-wage jobs.

Former Soviet Bloc countries: becoming European

"Second World" countries, precariously placed between the First and Third World, use gender to prove First World status. Whereas the Philippines, and many other nation-states in SSEA, create labor brokerage states as an economic development strategy, many post-Soviet states stigmatize migrant domestic workers while benefiting from their remittances. Post-Soviet states are engaged in capitalist transformation. Chapter 2 outlines the gendered "deal" the Soviet state made with women and shows that the ideal Soviet woman was a "mother-worker," building socialism alongside men. Women's emancipation was tied not only to economic projects of rapid industrialization, where young mothers were needed to labor in factories, but also to Soviet morality and modernity projects. The collapse of the Soviet Union has meant not just an economic retooling from a planned economy to the free market, but a new moral order. In the Soviet system, "businessman" was an insult that referred to a dishonest person who profited from exploiting others. However, in the new moral order of capitalism, "we are all entrepreneurs."[51]

Gendered expectations have also changed. Women's emancipation from "patriarchal isolation" and the "stultifying world of housework" was integral to the Soviet project and resulted in extended family households where grandmothers performed much of the childcare and household labor while young mothers performed paid labor. But, in post-Soviet discourse, women's emancipation now symbolizes much of what went wrong with the Soviet experiment. In this juxtaposition, women's emancipation is labeled "Soviet" and blamed for many social ills: the creation of "weak" men and "masculine" women, the demise of the ethnonation threatened with extinction due to low-birth rates, and the rise in men's unemployment and alcoholism.[52] Additionally, the heteronormative nuclear family has been identified by political elites and everyday denizens of the region as necessary to effectively compete in neoliberal capitalism where states call reproductive labor "housework" and ask women – not the state as under socialism – to do it for free.

Therefore, the ideal of the private, patriarchal family with women dependent on husbands and primarily responsible for raising children is being rehabilitated across the region, even if the economic realities mean most women still work for a wage in the formal or informal labor market.[53] Mikhail Gorbachev, the eighth and final leader of the Soviet Union, famously argued that many of the Soviet Union's problems could be attributed to women's employment, which resulted in "weak families." He called for women to recommit themselves to their duties as wives and mothers and "return to their purely womanly mission." Gorbachev wrote, "Many of our problems . . . are partially caused by the weakening of family ties and a slack attitude to family responsibilities. This is a paradoxical result of our sincere and politically justified desire to make women equal with men in everything."[54] This rhetoric of "traditional family values," and the reification of the nuclear family form, is portrayed as foundational to pre-Soviet cultural heritages and has found resonance across the region. Policy makers have called for women to "return to the home" to fulfill their "biological imperative."[55] Newly independent states, engaged in processes of nation-state building, also find this gendered framing useful in constructing ethnic and gender identities. They use them both to signal a break with their Soviet past and to create political and cultural boundaries that emphasize their separateness from Russia, often cast as a colonizing state.[56]

Growing ethnonationalist movements across the region, including in Romania, Poland, Hungary, Slovakia, and Ukraine, have enacted pro-natalist policies that glorify mothers as the cultural bearers of the nation and the source of ethnic purity.[57] For many post-Soviet nation-states, joining the EU is a path to modernity as well as an act of disassociation from Russia. Ironically, post-Soviet countries must fulfill the requirement of nearing gender equality in the labor market, something socialism had largely if imperfectly attained, to be considered for EU membership.[58] The neoliberal project of divesting state services and benefits has resulted in the privatization of motherhood and the transfer of responsibility for reproductive labor, once shared with the Soviet state, onto the shoulders of individual women to create barriers to women's labor market participation.[59] Many women have left to labor as domestic workers abroad, despite states stigmatizing women migrants as contributing to the "degradation of the family," the abandonment of children as "Euro-orphans," and even men's moral debasement by driving them into the arms of mistresses.[60] Which women migrate varies by country. For example, in Ukraine, it is predominantly middle-aged grandmothers, whereas in Moldova it is young mothers.[61] For a region seeking a neoliberal transformation, the links between gendered understandings of mobility, Europe, and modernity are thrown into stark relief not only for nation-states but also for individual migrants.

Cinzia Solari, in her study of Ukrainian migrants in Italy and the United States, found that migrant women borrowed Gorbachev's language of *perestroika* to describe migration as a process of "restructuring."[62] As in the case of the Philippines, individuals not only understood migration as an individual process of self-transformation but also saw themselves as agents of Ukrainian nation-state building. Inna, a former language teacher from Ukraine, explained that she left Ukraine to do domestic labor in Italy to earn money, but also to help her adult children and Ukraine learn the new norms of neoliberal capitalism. Inna explained:

> Imagine, Cinzia, that all the rules change, that all the things that you learned growing up about what you were supposed to do are gone. I am supposed to tell my children what to do to be successful, to live a normal life, and to be respected. How will I learn these new rules so that I can teach them? Some of this I learn here in Italy. My children will stay in Ukraine and help build the new Ukraine. I do not want them to have to go abroad. I must help my sons and also our Ukraine from here. This is why I study and take classes: to learn the rules, understand?[63]

Inna felt her migration moved not just herself but her children and country toward modernity. For Inna and many other Ukrainian migrants, moving toward modernity meant joining "Europe."

Lydmyla managed to bring her husband and young children with her to Italy, but she wanted to make clear that she still feels an "obligation to Ukraine as a nation," not just to her family there. She bitterly recounted that once Ukrainians were freed from Russian rule, she thought "we would *join* Europe, not *migrate* there to do [domestic work]." Lydmyla explained that many Ukrainians still had a "Soviet mentality" and had to learn to be European, so she personally worked hard to learn to be European for her sons and for Ukraine. She noted, "I am a patriot . . . Ukraine is becoming European, and we must help Ukraine in this. My boys, they may not ever be Italian, but they will be European."[64] The Ukrainian nuclear family was often used to signal cultural synergy with Europe and distance from Russia. A Ukrainian talent show, which aimed to show Italians that Ukrainians were European, opened with the portrayal of a hetero-patriarchal nuclear family in embroidered Ukrainian peasant garb where the traditional expected roles of father, mother, brother, and sister were explained. Oksana, a Ukrainian migrant observing the performance, explained:

This is what makes us different from Russians. Russian women are cold and selfish. Do you think a Russian woman would come to Italy and make the sacrifices that our Ukrainian mothers make for their families? Do you think they would lower themselves to do the work we do here [domestic work] even if there is great need? No! Ukrainian women are different. They do everything for their family, everything! Ukrainian women are nurturers, it is in our blood. That family on stage: that is Ukraine.[65]

Thus migrants replaced the Soviet "mother-worker" with a new ideal Ukrainian woman, embodied in the national goddess, Berehynia, whose statue soars over Kyiv's Independence Square. Berehynia, infused with Catholic links to the Virgin Mary, repudiates the "unnatural" Soviet gender order and connects Ukraine to European colonial gender discourses where high levels of gender differentiation and specialization were thought to be a marker of modern civilization. In this gendered nationalist narrative, men and women are celebrated not for being the same but for performing different tasks in equally valued "separate spheres." The "empowered" women of Ukraine are juxtaposed against the "oppressed" women of "patriarchal" Russia and are foundational in Ukraine's claim to Europeanness.

Like Ukraine's Berehenyia, Poland is also represented by the Catholic iconography of the "Our Lady of Częstochowa," a national symbol known colloquially as "Queen of Poland." She is both symbol and protector of Polish identity and an ideal mother, the standard to which Polish women are held.[66] She is considered the protector of the ethnonation. In one Polish nationalist narrative, when the Soviet Red Army attacked Warsaw in 1920, the nation prayed to Our Lady of Częstochowa, and the Virgin Mary appeared in the clouds above Warsaw, resulting in the swift defeat of the Russians. This gendered nationalism is central to the traditional idea of the Polish family and the position of women as mothers in the household, and it is used in post-Soviet discourse to restrict reproductive and employment rights for Polish women.[67] Poland and Ukraine use gendered nationalism to signal a break with their Soviet past and draw boundaries against Russia by juxtaposing the traditional family and intensive mothering with Soviet "mother-workers." Indeed, Poland draws on discourses of "separate but equal" and "choice" to construct modern women who "choose" to put mothering first. This current-day gendered nationalism clashes with Soviet sensibilities. Poles who remember the Soviet Union tell the younger generation, now free of Soviet mobility restrictions, to use their new passports to be "free" and "modern."[68]

Yet, migration set off a moral panic in Poland about abandoned children, dubbed "Euro-orphans," due to the migration of young mothers.[69] Nevertheless, the Polish state emphasized "the family as a bastion for the market in a changing neoliberal society" and was allowed to join the EU in 2004.[70]

As the cases of Ukraine and Poland suggest, the migration of women signals deep gendered anxieties. The Moldovan state also blames its women who have left to labor as domestic workers abroad for social disorder inside Moldova, deploying the trope of "mothers as the key to social order" and stigmatizing migrants as "prostitutes" or "trafficked women."[71] In the post-Soviet context where racial and religious hierarchies, Soviet modernization projects, and aspirations to join Europe intersect to precariously place the region between the First and Third Worlds, migration can be read as both moving toward and away from "modernity" within a taken-for-granted global order. Leyla Keough finds that inside Moldova, those migrating to Russia or Western Europe are viewed as moving toward "civilization," while those migrating to Turkey, despite its relative wealth compared to Moldova, are seen as moving "backward," away from civilization and modernity.[72] We can see the complicated interactions of mobility and modernity in an exchange between a Turkish employer, Keough's grandmother, and her Moldovan domestic worker, Lidya:

> For instance, my grandmother would say to Lidya, "We were so afraid of you ["Russians" or "communists"] and now look – you are working for us!" And Lidya would reply smartly: "And us, too – we were afraid of Turks – but now you are under our care!" This pithy exchange indexes the continued problematics of power and gender in the Turkish household, but also new frames of meaning – issues of communist versus capitalist, Turk versus Russian, and Muslim versus Christian.[73]

Concerns about migrant women, and whether they are moving toward or away from modernity, are heightened by Moldova's aspirations to Europe where gendered performance is part of the criteria for entry. Moldova, although not yet an EU member, was granted EU candidate status in 2022.

Modernity promise: marriage migrants

Neoliberal economic restructuring produced domestic work as one way of linking migration and mobility, but a second mobility pathway to modernity privileges transnational marriage markets over transnational labor markets, although the two are often intertwined. The juxtaposition between domestic workers, marriage migrants, and the continuum between the two – the "maids" who might become "madams" – reminds us that acquiring stable residency rights or citizenship through labor migration is nearly impossible.[74] From the perspective of sending states, marriage migrants do not pose the same modernity threat caused by the mass migration of women to perform low-status cleaning and caring labor. Instead, marriage markets offer a "modernity promise" to individual women located outside the First World. Marriage agencies and commercial brokers have long linked women from less powerful countries to men in wealthier countries, and marriage migration has increased under neoliberalism.[75] Beginning in the 1970s, the (re)entry of middle- and upper-class women into paid labor threatened the gendered underpinnings of the patriarchal nuclear family. Therefore, an increasing number of men in the United States and other wealthy countries longed for a return to a "traditional" gender order. This pattern of upwardly mobile First World women created two parallel demands that drew women from postcolonial and post-Soviet contexts to wealthy countries as domestic workers but also as brides. Global inequalities between nations, not just developing countries but also within world regions, are thus reproduced in a burgeoning transnational marriage market in which men from developed countries are dominant and able to share their wealth with less privileged nations and individuals, so long as migrant brides agree to adopt the ideas of democracy, capitalism, and civil society while maintaining more conventional gender relations.[76]

Although western feminists often depict marriage migrants as "mail-order brides," a uniformly oppressed and vulnerable group seeking to escape Third World poverty only to be duped, abused, and "trafficked" and thus in need of saving and protection, ethnographic studies of marriage migrants reveal more complexity.[77] Many marriage migrants, like their domestic worker counterparts, seek "adventure" within a "postcolonial, global imagination of modernity."[78] The neoliberal feminist cover story of "empowered women" with expansive choices allows for contradictory understandings of what constitutes modern marriage. Many marriage migrants from SSEA, particularly the Philippines, include love, choice, and gender egalitarianism in their definition of modern marriage, although there is variation by class.[79] For Filipinas coming from rural or working-class backgrounds, whose day-to-day lives involve a combination of hard work in shops, factories, or rice fields combined with domestic chores and responsibilities for an extended household, work in the paid labor market does not feel liberating.[80] Instead, the idea of working only at home, with the help of time-saving devices, and of being responsible for their own husbands and children may constitute for them an attractive and "modern" alternative.[81] Post-Soviet women rarely define modern marriage as a search for gender equality. Instead, they seek economic stability, reliable visa status, and sometimes romance.[82] The understandings of "traditional" versus "modern" marriage also vary among the men engaged in transnational marriage markets. Just as migrant women understand the geography of migration as moving toward or away from modernity, the geographic location of the men searching for brides also shapes whether they believe they are getting a "subservient" or a "modern" bride.

For example, earlier we noted that inside Moldova, women migrating to Turkey, despite Turkey's higher economic status, are seen as moving "backward," a fall from modernity. Intimacy, mobility, and modernity intertwine with discourses of "love" and "choice" to make post-Soviet migrant women something more than domestic workers in Turkey because Turkish men also see post-Soviet countries as closer to modernity, in part due to shared "socialist ideals, cultural imaginaries of secularism, and Islam."[83] Post-Soviet women from Moldova, Russia, Belarus, and Ukraine are seen by Turkish men as desirable because they signify "modernity" by being well-educated, "cultured," and beautiful without "complexes around sex."[84]

Men located in the United States and Europe may have an opposite vantage point. Some men located in the West consider western women "too liberated" and complain that they place their careers ahead of marriage and family.[85] This is an interesting parallel to post-Soviet discourse that also views Soviet women incorporated into socialist economies and politics as "too liberated." Thus these men seek more "traditional" wives who they believe are untainted by western feminism, faithful in the face of rising divorce rates, and find caring for their own family "easy" compared to caring for other people's children as domestic workers. Acquiring dependents through marriage and children has often, in the US context, been thought to help men "grow up," be more responsible, and become better workers.[86] Thus migration, as a project of self-transformation, also touches these men as they seek women who will dedicate themselves to making them "better men."[87]

How do migrant women frame their participation in these transnational marriage markets? We turn first to examine the experiences of women from SSEA. In a study of the transnational Vietnamese marriage market, Hung Thai found that two groups of "unmarriageables" emerged. Vietnamese women living middle-class lifestyles in Vietnam, supported by monetary remittances and pursuing higher education, became "unmarriageable" due to both the limited pool of men with equally high education levels and to what was perceived as their "advanced age" because they put off marriage for schooling. In the United States, Vietnamese men, despite high education levels, experienced downward social and economic mobility and found that low-status service work was the only work available to them. Their low wages, the small numbers of Vietnamese women in the United States, and US racial regimes excluded them from local marriage markets. These two groups of unmarriageables found each other in a cross-national marriage market. Thus, although the dominant storyline in the West is that women who choose to become marriage migrants are looking to escape poverty, researchers found that many women are living middle-class lives prior to migration.[88] These women may be excluded from local marriage markets because they are considered too old, divorced, or already have a child. Filipina, Chinese, and Thai women expect western men, and even immigrant men living in the West, to have absorbed modern notions of gender equality and to overlook these characteristics that disadvantage them in domestic marriage markets.[89] However, Hung Thai found that it was more likely that there was dissonance between the gender ideologies of Vietnamese women who sought egalitarian marriages and the Vietnamese men located in the United States. Thanh, an educated woman living in Vietnam with a soft spot for Ann Taylor clothing, explained her idea of a modern, egalitarian marriage: "I don't want everything split fifty-fifty. For example, I like to cook. But it's important for me as an educated woman not to be controlled by my husband . . . [the men in Vietnam] feel like their wives are like their domestic workers."[90]

While Thanh wanted a respectful marriage based on principles of gender equality where both she and her husband worked in the paid labor market, Minh, the man sponsoring her migration to the United States as a wife, had a different idea. Whereas Thanh engaged in First World consumption patterns in Vietnam, Minh struggled to make ends meet despite working long hours. He longed for a wife who would bolster his manliness. Minh explained: "I mean that husband and wife should not be equal, the wife should listen to the husband most of the time. That is how they will have a happy life together. If the woman tries to be equal they will have problems."[91] It is unlikely that Thanh's life in the United States will feel "modern." She likely will not find an egalitarian marriage with Minh, nor will she find a life where she can engage in consumption patterns associated with modernity. While Thanh sought "America" in the United States, other marriage migrants sought "America" through marriage markets within Asia.

The United States represents to many a place with modern amenities, modern government free from corruption, modern values and attitudes toward marriage and gender relations, and more sexual freedom in contrast to the imagined shortcomings of the homeland. And this is particularly true for Filipina migrants steeped in a colonial past with the United States.[92] Nobue Suzuki found that "America is a source of empowerment in the popular Filipino imagination."[93] Indeed, the United States loomed so large in the imaginaries of modernity that Filipina women in Japan – "export quality" women, many laboring as entertainers – saw marriage to a Japanese man as providing them with an opportunity to enjoy an "American life" in the "First World," both in terms of consumption patterns and in everyday interactions where men care for and protect their wives. Leah, a Filipina migrant in Japan explained, "I like people who follow American ways. [Americans] are romantic, aren't they? In foreign countries, a man cares for you. Caring and protecting make men manly!" Leah, like many other Filipina wives in Japan, was surprised by her husband's long work hours that made her feel neglected, laws that limited her legal citizenship status in Japan, and both state-based and interpersonal social exclusion as the Japanese state and everyday individuals sought to police ethnic boundaries and guard against "unfit" foreign mothers.[94] The modernity promise was a broken one for these Filipina wives in Japan.

Like Japan, South Korea also imports Filipinas but specifically as wives rather than laborers. Minjeong Kim finds that the internal rural-to-urban migrations of women have left men in rural villages without wives.[95] In addition to rural men's low economic status, mismatched gender ideologies also exclude them from the larger domestic marriage market where Korean women are often unwilling to marry rural men due to the hardships involved in farming and conservative familial expectations regarding cohabitation with in-laws. Thus the South Korean state promotes the marriage migration of Filipina and other SSEA women assumed to be more subservient than native-born Korean women to address both the "bride deficit" and the resulting low Korean birthrate. This state strategy is also not free of gendered anxieties as the "incorporation of the immigrant wife aggravates *prior* anxieties about the rural economy under Korea's neoliberal globalization and industrialization."[96] The Korean state's anxiety about racially mixed children and immigrant mothers unable to transmit Korean culture to their children negatively shaped the sense of belonging for these immigrant Filipina wives and mothers. These marriage migrants often do experience some level of upward economic mobility but not the fantasy of "love" marriages and economic plenty they imagined of life in a "modern" country.

Instead of love, the extreme precarity resulting from Soviet collapse has left many post-Soviet migrants seeking "stability" through migration. Post-Soviet women often note the ironic relationship of mobility to first socialism and then neoliberalism. In the Soviet Union, mobility was restricted. Soviet citizens were denied the freedom of movement between cities, much less the right to travel abroad. Now people in post-Soviet countries no longer have mobility restrictions imposed by their state but are facing an increasingly robust external visa regime that severely limits their mobility under neoliberalism. Marriage migration is one of the few options for legal stability abroad.[97] The large migration of Ukrainian women in their 40s, 50s, and 60s to Italy, along with a visa regime that keeps these migrant women undocumented or precariously documented, has led to an increase in marriages between Ukrainian migrants and the elderly men, often 75+-years old, that they care for.[98] Due to Italy's low birth rate, most migrants in Italy care for elderly Italians. Ukrainian women may seek marriages, in part, for the right to remain in Italy, especially when they are no longer able to work themselves. Additionally, these women felt that permanent legal status helped equalize power imbalances within the couple.[99] Although Ukrainian women entered relationships with immigrant men of their own or other nationalities in Italy, only Italian men could make them a *Signora* (Madam), which links ideals of social respectability to economic security.[100] Olena Fedyuk recounts an interaction from her fieldwork in which a study participant, Irina, 50, was to marry a 75-year-old widower, Gianni.[101] In a conversation with Irina's friend, Fedyuk wondered if Irina loved Gianni. The friend replied:

> I mean, listen, we are almost 50 . . . what are we doing here, in Italy? We work, but how much longer can we do it? With all this rushing, cleaning all day, hands bleeding from the detergents we use daily . . . Don't we deserve something better, something that we need [for ourselves]? Irina will get her papers, she'll get the support. Otherwise, should she just go

home now after all these years in Italy and do what? Start all new? She already cannot work as hard [as she used to]. She has had surgery . . . what kind of prince should she be waiting for? Who else would like to spend his life with her?[102]

Irina and others like her felt they had worked hard to earn the right to think pragmatically about marriage options. They thought carefully about what each partner brought to the marriage so that they felt it was a moral and equitable exchange.

In her study of post-Soviet women in Turkey, Alexia Bloch also found that these women navigated the constraints of money and borders and thought pragmatically about liaisons with Turkish men.[103] Marriage was not always the most sought-after arrangement since many women reported losing leverage to negotiate men's contribution to their material well-being once they were subjected to the rules of marriage that dictate women should provide domestic labor without remuneration. Depending on the women's visa status, being a "kept" woman or a mistress, both understood as modern forms of intimacy, could be considered preferable to marriage.[104] In fact, many post-Soviet women who were deported from Turkey entered into marriages of convenience in their home community and then re-entered Turkey on a passport issued under a different family name so that marrying foreign men was not seen as the only way to secure documents.[105] The Turkish state continues to increase its "raid and deportation" missions that target the workplaces where post-Soviet women labor and, with few other means of regularizing their status, the state indirectly continues to push women to seek the protection of "marriage" in whatever form it may take.

Conclusion

Both nation-states and individuals must manage gendered anxieties about presenting "empowered women" to the world to move the nation-state out of the waiting room of modernity and into the First World. Gendered nationalism has contradictory work to do in the neoliberal order. It needs to shore up a cultural and ethnic identity tied to a national version of ideal womanhood that aims to elevate women as a source of pride and identity for its people. Gendered nationalism discourses must also respond to the neoliberal economic order that dangles the possibility of improving the status of countries through exporting enterprising women who send back monetary remittances to uplift their family and their country. Thus, as states compete for status in the global arena, post-socialist and postcolonial countries find themselves positioned differently vis-à-vis dominant tropes. The Philippine state, along with other enterprising nation-states in SSEA, undertakes development/modernization projects that produce enterprising subjects on a bureaucratic assembly line for export as domestic workers, yet that same process creates the very modernity threat they seek to avoid. The neoliberal feminist cover story produces the aspirational, upwardly mobile, White, middle-class woman in the First World whose success is made possible by outsourcing cleaning and caring labor for children and the elderly to racialized, poorer, Third World women with precarious legal status. (The FSU does not exist in this narrative.) The cover story suggests that these Third World women are empowered, enterprising subjects benefiting from a potpourri of neoliberal choices that allows them and their countries to move toward modernity.

Post-Soviet countries are in a different bind. Post-Soviet women already think of themselves as modern working women. Global racial and religious hierarchies intersect with notions of "East" and "West" and First and Third World so that the racial groups and the religious designation of "Muslim" assigns those groups to modernity's waiting room while the designated Whiteness and Christianity of many, but certainly not all, post-Soviet people bolsters their modernity claims. For many former Soviet Bloc countries, this is expressed as trading in the supranational identity of "Soviet" for the supranational identity of "Europe," a powerful signal of moving from Second World to First World status. Post-Soviet migrant women and Filipina migrants alike, who have internalized neoliberal ideals of economic self-reliance and entrepreneurship, find that, even in locales they consider "modern," they are unable to convert their human capital into upward mobility. Post-Soviet women in Italy and Turkey, for example, despite the advanced degrees made possible by the free Soviet education system, still find migration as domestic workers or wives as the two possible paths to modernity in their search for economic and legal stability. Migrant women must compete for wealth and moral status, usually articulated through idioms of gender and sexuality, and often find they are on the losing end of both. Migrant domestic workers – whether celebrated as "heroes" of the modern economy in the Philippines or vilified as "prostitutes" and "bad mothers" by the Polish and Ukrainian states – find "wealth" is elusive and their status as respectable women under siege. Marriage migrants might find a modicum of respectability as a *Signora* or Madam, but they also experience social exclusion by both interpersonal and state practices (policies that limit marriage migrants' access to citizenship or permanent legal status, state-sponsored courses in cultural practices of mothering, and so forth) that see them as a racial threat to the nation, unfit mothers, or "gold diggers." For both migrant domestic workers and marriage migrants, the neoliberal feminist cover story conceals multiple systems of inequality between nations, between men and women, and between differently positioned women.

6
Manly Protectors

We have argued that neoliberal feminism has radically transformed expectations and aspirations for women. The empowered woman ideal, a neoliberal cover story, has motivated economic competition between nations and argued for the inclusion of women in capitalist labor markets. Aspirational White women can be both CEOs and mompreneurs, immigrant women of color can be included as enterprising subjects, and racialized Third World women can become the economic saviors of their families and countries, potentially pulling their entire nation out of poverty and into the First World. This neoliberal cover story, however, contains within it the seeds of its own destruction. Women now appear to be competent, feminist, neoliberal subjects no longer in need of rescue because they can save themselves. If women are "doing it all" and no longer need to be saved by men, where does this leave men?

In this chapter, we turn our attention to men who perceive a loss of power in diverse parts of the world. Although we might assume that transformed expectations for women also alter expectations for men, we find that neoliberalism has instead produced expectations that double down on breadwinning as men's primary obligation. Global economic restructuring, however, has made breadwinning more difficult and even impossible for most men to achieve. The discrepancy between gendered expectations and economic realities has created gendered anxieties. Some women are harried and overburdened with both caregiving and financial responsibilities for their children and thus long for a benevolent patriarch.[1] Men, especially those from historically privileged groups, also manifest gendered anxieties as some of them experience downward mobility and a loss of status. Because men perceive lost authority in the labor market as well as in the family, we show that diverse groups of men have begun to turn away from breadwinning. Instead, they locate their status in the protection and maintenance of national and community borders, often articulated in racial-nationalist terms.

Although scholars of gender and nation have traditionally explored the relationship between gendered ideologies of womanhood and nation-state building, we argue that neoliberalism has shifted the terrain of gender and nation so that men and manliness are now at the center of neoliberal nation-state building projects. In the post-WWII era, liberal, Soviet, and postcolonial states, despite their many ideological differences, all implemented policies that aimed to alleviate inequality around issues of race and gender. The postwar international community viewed leveling the playing field for women and other historically marginalized groups as a central feature of liberal modernity. Four decades of global neoliberalism, however, have motivated historically powerful groups who perceive a loss of power to reframe these state-led efforts to rectify historical inequities as "unfair." Instead, they suggest that "every man for himself" would be fairer. Despite long-term processes of desegregation and decolonization, neoliberal practices and ideologies have provided an opening for the formation of misogynist, homophobic, and racist political movements of "remasculinization" in each of these regional contexts.

We argue that a new gendered neoliberal cover story, linked to the decreased prominence of the "saving women" script, has emerged: the *manly protector*. Drawing from the rich literature on the "crisis of masculinity," we recenter "manliness." "Masculinity" is a relatively recent term used to separate men from women, whereas manliness is a term bestowed on a subgroup of men.[2] It draws our attention to hierarchies between groups of men and practices categorized as more or less manly. We look at the emergence of authoritarian populism in our regions with a focus on three "strongmen" – Donald Trump in the United States, Vladimir Putin in Russia, and Narendra Modi in India – to garner evidence for the "manly protector" cover story. We show that authoritarian populism results from neoliberalism and the increased anxieties regarding neoliberalism's gender order. Rather than focusing on individual strongmen, we ask what shifts within neoliberalism's gender order make possible the "manly protector" ideal shared by these three men and other modern-day authoritarians. These ideals of manliness find resonance with large segments of the citizenry in all three contexts.

The competitive terrain of manliness has shifted from work and family in the postwar era to the terrain of nationalism and community in the new millennium. Protecting national borders, attending to national and local security, debating about who is included in the nation, and arguing about the nation's values capture the imaginations and aspirations of many men. These masculine projects of anxious nationalisms elevate the international arena as a site of status competition. The construction of borders between home and abroad often paints the foreign as a site of fear and anxiety. However, the international is also a terrain of aspirations. Exercising symbolic power on the international terrain is how politics is done[3] and, we argue, where the competition for manliness and status unfolds. We find, across our three regions, a surprising convergence around competing imperial ambitions, national arguments of exceptionalism, and the enforcement of physical and cultural borders of the nation. These elements provide a moral compass for navigating gendered anxiety that we term the "manly protector" cover story.

The "manly protector" ideal deploys two racialized technologies of Othering – misogyny and homophobia – to effectively articulate the aspirations of many men and some women. These two technologies of Othering facilitate the boundary work performed by manly protectors to construct "the nation," "the people," and "the community." Misogyny technologies punish, through discursive, legal, and physically coercive means, not all women but those who refuse to conform to their caregiving roles by providing social, domestic, reproductive, and emotional labor.[4] Homophobia technologies assert heteronormative manliness as foundational for nationalist modernity, and in so doing punish, exclude, and mock non-normative expressions of gender and sexuality. These state-sponsored technologies assert "traditional values" to counter homonationalism – progressive nationalist projects that appear to protect LGBTQ+ communities while demonizing homophobic, racialized Others as un-modern. As nation-states deploy these technologies, they seek to create an oppositional modernity, one that directly counters the content and claims of western modernity. Such claims lie at the heart of global power politics. Successful modernity claims are powerful political resources that have been used to justify control and perpetuate violence against colonized populations as well as domestic minority groups.[5]

In what follows, we first lay out the economic and geopolitical context that makes the "manly protector" cover story appealing to many men and some women. Men who have experienced a loss of power and women who have been exhausted by empowerment ideologies both experience anxieties around their place in the world. The "manly protector" cover story offers an appealing, comforting, and opposing view of the world that constructs strong boundaries between "us" and "them" as a needed precondition to "freedom." The cover story naturalizes these boundaries through a reassertion of binary biological and social roles for men and women. We then detail the two masculine technologies of Othering – misogyny and homophobia – that allow individual actors and nations to embody the manly protector. Finally, we turn to three examples of authoritarian populists – Putin, Modi, and Trump – to show how these "strongmen" construct and amplify the "manly protector" cover story in their respective contexts. We highlight the inequalities created when competitive manliness is used as the standard for nation-state building projects at home and for constructing the hierarchy of nations internationally.

Anxious men, exhausted women

Even though the heterosexual nuclear family, including the breadwinner/housewife ideal, constitutes the economic and ideological bedrock of neoliberalism, working-class and even middle-class men see the breadwinner ideal as unattainable. Global economic restructuring has shifted the gendered opportunities for work at the bottom of the economic ladder and increased income inequality, a transformation outlined in chapters 4 and 5. Both deindustrialization and the expansion of domestic labor and other "feminine" jobs have created an "hourglass" economy that has made it increasingly difficult for men to secure jobs that provide the middle-class salaries needed to attain the breadwinner ideal. Furthermore, around the world, the globalization of corporations is destabilizing small farm and business ownership. Young men feel entitled to inherit their fathers' businesses in a context where managing and owning property is a powerful symbol of attainment of hegemonic masculine ideals. However, neoliberal policies, which have lifted restrictions on cross-border trade, have increasingly left these young men with nothing to inherit. These downwardly mobile men join a growing "army of angry White men."[6] As men find their pathways to honorable manhood narrowing, they search for other markers of successful masculinity to stabilize their identities and gain a sense of respect and dignity.[7]

Women who have ever-expanding responsibilities under neoliberal capitalism are also beset with anxieties, albeit for different reasons.

Supposedly, women can "have it all" – family and career – if they just "lean in." In practice, this means that women must "do it all" to be considered modern.[8] Undoubtedly, the "empowered women" cover story has made some material changes to our social world. In the United States and Europe, for example, some spaces that used to be reserved for men – sports, workplaces, golf clubs – may now include women. Many milestones that once marked "manhood" today mark "adulthood" for both men and women.[9] The feminist neoliberal cover story has thus been so successful that it has become a truth-making mechanism for individuals on the ground as well as in the arena of geopolitics. In other words, we are not arguing that women have become "empowered" but rather the opposite: this discourse has so successfully obscured the gendered and racial inequalities that exist that the empowered women cover story bolsters neoliberalism. In fact, as we have discussed in earlier chapters, the barriers to advancement in labor markets and the continued expectations to provide free housework and caring labor at home have made some women long for a benevolent protector – a "real" man – who can alleviate their burdens.

Thus the feminist neoliberal cover story also gives rise to its antithesis: the manly protector. Men have felt discursively marginalized by the "empowered women" cover story where "women save themselves."[10] If women can and must "do everything," what tasks are left for men? Where are men needed?

"Irrelevant" men in three regions

In the face of men's decreased economic ability to be the breadwinners in their families, men construct themselves as embodying hegemonic masculinity in alternative ways.[11] In her book *We're Still Here: Pain and Politics in the Heart of America*, Jennifer Silva conducted interviews with over a hundred Black, White, and Puerto Rican working-class people in the United States.[12] She found, like other scholars, that these men expressed gendered pain and anxiety at the gap between their material conditions and the masculine ideal of being the protectors and providers for their families. When White men cannot anchor their identity in the labor market or in authority over their families, her informants reported that "all is left is Whiteness." These men policed the boundaries of masculinity and Whiteness, asserting notions of White supremacy when economic claims to masculine domination seemed untenable.

Although the Soviet Union did not adopt the breadwinner/ housewife ideal, 20 years after the collapse of the Soviet Union, men in Ukraine had assimilated much of the expectations of the neoliberal gender order. This included an understanding that their income and earning potential was linked to their value on the heterosexual marriage market.[13] Since the breadwinner ideal is out of reach for most Ukrainian men, they constructed a "heroic masculinity" that recasts men as the protectors of the ethnonation, rather than protectors of their individual families.[14] This "heroic masculinity" is articulated through the icon of the "Cossack." Cossacks constituted a male-dominated, democratic, military community that formed a Ukrainian–Cossack state in the mid-seventeenth century. In contemporary discourse, Cossacks are credited with founding Ukraine's democratic traditions and are a pre-Soviet symbol of Ukrainian ethnic and national identity. The Cossack movement asserts virile manhood by lower middle- and working-class men whose livelihoods have been undermined by neoliberal economics. This discursive feature of manliness bears some similarities to White nationalism in the United States. The glorification of Cossacks excludes both women and marginalized men (other ethnicities, disabled, and gay men) from nation-state-building processes.[15] In each of these cases, manliness is performed for and judged by other men.

India's anti-colonial nationalist movement, forged in the early twentieth century, contained many strands, one of which was explicitly anti-Muslim Hindu nationalist. This strand was marginalized through much of the twentieth century but rose to prominence during liberalization in the 1990s, having undergone many significant transformations.[16] In the 1980s, the Hindu nationalist party, the Bhartiya Janata Party (BJP), built its ideology upon a sense of masculine discontentment among an amorphous Indian middle class, an anxiety that responded to successful mobilizations of lower-caste groups and protections for religious minorities, and became widely visible through television.[17] Hindutva or radical Hindu nationalist ideology has long been articulated through tropes of virile masculinity aimed at defending Hindu women against especially Muslim men, who are assumed to be predatory.[18] Since liberalization, however, this ideology has become even more explicitly tied to masculine authoritarian power. With the rise of Modi and social media, virulently misogynistic, anti-Muslim media circulates widely to bolster an understanding of gender and nation that is exclusively Hindu and centers manly men.[19]

The existing evidence suggests that in divergent locations, a "manly protector" cover story, the flip side of the "empowered women" cover story, helps solve some of the key gendered contradictions and anxieties tied to neoliberalism. The "manly protector" cover story recenters men as protectors of the nation and their communities, providing a new moral compass that appears more attainable to abide by than breadwinning. This cover story connects everyday men to the emergence of authoritarian populists who have, to varying extents, accepted the neoliberal version of "women's empowerment." Because neoliberal feminism is compatible with the prevailing economic and political system, men can accept the empowered woman cover story while also working to create a space that reclaims men's discursive centrality and amplifies their political dominance. Thus the "manly protector" cover story prompts men to both accept the empowered women ideal and mobilize two technologies of "Othering" – misogyny and homophobia – to create new communities of belonging that center men and hierarchies of manliness. To do this, men and others engage in boundary work along the interconnected areas of policing racial boundaries, securing national borders, and protecting the nation along with a particular iteration of "the people."

Affect and nation: the opening for an oppositional modernity

Understandings of "the nation" are deeply internalized and embodied so that nationalism and its intersections with race, class, gender, and sexuality should be understood as practice.[20] Because nationalism is inherently based on an exclusionary logic of group membership, concerns over moral classification, affective judgment, and emotions should be central to examining nationalist discourses since nationalism is not linked to a specific or coherent ideology.[21] Yet, until recently, nationalism has been viewed as a problem of the past in the established democracies of the United States and Western Europe or, alternatively, as a problem of non-western countries that have experienced an "incomplete" modernization process.[22] Bart Bonikowski identifies a host of triggering events, including what he terms "acute perceptions of collective status threat on the part of national majority-group members (i.e., typically native-born Whites)."[23] These include: economic changes such as unemployment and wage decline, demographic factors such as immigration, cultural changes such as the expansion of LGBTQ+ rights and multiculturalism, the displacement of White working-class culture from the mainstream, and national security threats such as terrorism. These triggering events are not specific to the United States. Perceived status threats, demographic changes, and national security threats have made an embodied conceptualization of nationalism critical to our understanding of global geopolitics, which we continue to neglect at our peril in broader scholarly and public discourse.

The increased salience of authoritarian populism, ethnonationalism, and right-wing populism are linked globally to contentions about the gender order of neoliberalism. Whereas in a previous historical moment, struggles about modernity were linked to discussions about women, today we find that the most significant struggles play out on the terrain of masculinities. Instead of aspiring to breadwinning, the "manly protector" cover story suggests men aspire to be the protectors of the nation and their racial/religious community. They must battle in a competitive field where the characteristics of manliness – dominance, strength, and violence when necessary – are part of the competitive currency in the international arena where nations or organized subgroups within the nation seek to claim superiority or dominance over others. The terrain of competition, therefore, has shifted from economic institutions such as the World Bank and the IMF (see chapter 3), to culture and nationalism, which is elevated as the terrain of competition for political power. In the global arena, the "manly protector" cover story uses nationalism to confirm the superiority of the nation by comparing it to other nations, which are deemed to be masculine yet inferior in their expressions of manliness. For Trump, Putin, and Modi, this is a project of remasculinization that amplifies narratives of national exceptionalism.

When viewed together, these remasculinization projects constitute an oppositional modernity that claims superiority in relation to Euro-American neo-imperialism by asserting a discourse of freedom and modernity that doubles down on biological determinism. Since freedom is a central discourse within neoliberalism, this oppositional modernity, spearheaded by Putin but advanced by Trump, Modi, and other authoritarian dictators around the world, asserts freedom as a central feature of its allure. Oppositional modernity projects assert the freedom of people to be "freely who they are," as determined by biology and the presumption of a binary gender system. In this context, the "traditional family" stands for modernity. Oppositional modernity resists the idea that the meanings of gender are open for negotiation. In the FSU, this discourse is particularly powerful because of the recent experience of the Soviet gender order.

Although western publics view the collapse of the Soviet Union as resulting from the victory of capitalism over communism, within the region the failure is viewed in gendered terms: men were not allowed to "be men" and women were not allowed to "be women" due to Soviet projects of gender egalitarianism. Doubling down on biological determinism and the binary gender system is a break with the Soviet past and thus appears "modern." Oppositional modernity finds resonance in other dominant groups who perceive a loss of power in the United States, India, and elsewhere. US liberalism, the argument goes, has gone "too far," and freedom must be taken back by the groups who naturally deserve power, by force if necessary. Discourses of national exceptionalism bolster these sentiments in culturally and regionally specific ways in these three regions.

A nation is defined by its internal unity and is constructed according to "Others" that are located both inside (i.e., natives vs. immigrants) and outside (i.e., hostile nations that "hate" our way of life).[24] The nation and its "people" are understood as needing protection from enemies both within and without. We identify boundary construction around racial distinctions, sexual politics, and national security as the most salient in defining the community or nation that needs protection in the context of oppositional modernity. Together, misogyny and homophobia produce clear boundaries around race, sexuality, and national security, all of which are needed for contestations of status and hierarchy in domestic and international arenas. These technologies advance projects of remasculinization, while undermining access to meaningful social change that would center human flourishing for marginalized groups. Misogyny and homophobia also create "patterns of useful contradictions"[25] that allow manly protectors to claim to be in favor of women's empowerment while simultaneously undermining women's rights and sustaining the status quo. Similarly, homophobia is deployed in projects of oppositional modernity to promote "freedom" from western hegemony, even while such projects aim to erase minority identities and denigrate "effeminate" men.

Othering through misogyny

The "manly protector" cover story allows authoritarian populists to celebrate, or at least accept, femininity that conforms to a limited understanding of "empowered women" that resonates with narrow notions of freedom and "more choices." But women who resist male dominance or advocate for radical social change are likely to face misogyny from those supportive of authoritarian populism. The "manly protector" cover story allows women to lobby for rights if these are granted on the basis of sexual difference, epitomized in motherhood, without challenging men's collective responsibility for defining, governing, and protecting the nation.[26] It allows for feminist and progressive gains to be used to promote conservative patriarchal ends. Many authoritarian regimes use selective references to gender and "women's rights" as a ruse to entrench themselves.[27] As we have seen, neoliberal capitalism requires women to provide caring labor for free. Special vitriol is unleashed on women who refuse to provide domestic, reproductive, and emotional labor, thus rejecting their caregiving roles.[28] Misogyny is a useful tool for dealing with the fallout of neoliberal policies that reduce or eliminate state-sponsored social services by pressuring women to pick up the slack.

In each of our three regions, misogyny is deployed in a distinct historical context. Nevertheless, in each case it is tied closely to the presence of racialized others against whom "our women" must be protected. As we will show, misogynistic discourses often appear to be pro-women, and in some cases explicitly seek to include women in their movement, though often in carefully demarcated roles. In the postcolonial context, this is particularly apparent because current-day right-wing nationalist ideologies come from a history of anti-colonial nationalism that aimed to construct a culturally distinctive vision of modernity. In India, for example, right-wing Hindutva movements of today have a long historical precedent and centrally rely on conceptions of a virile masculinity that subordinates women to make Hindu culture distinctive from western culture but also from Muslims, a constructed enemy-within that oppresses women. Right-wing Hindutva ideology today involves many prominent women as public figures, but also polices and punishes women who violate patriarchal, ethnocentric norms.[29] Misogyny comprises a key tactic through which politicians and other public figures can effectively draw boundaries between "us" and "them" because its use of naturalized understandings of gender makes affective and embodied "sense."

The "manly protector" cover story that we identify today is a remasculinization project in which the boundaries between men and women, as well as between more or less "manly men," are policed at home, in part, to create a masculine nation capable of dominating the global competition between nations on the terrain of manliness. Women who challenge power are targeted by misogynist projects; but even men who challenge patriarchal norms are delegitimized as being feminine.[30] When we understand gender as a signifier of power, we can see the link between the "individual misogyny of authoritarian leaders" and "the projects of anxious and insecure nationalisms" that are at the heart of right-wing politics.[31]

Othering through homophobia

A new vulnerable subject emerged in the post-1989 context where women no longer need to be saved because they are supposed to save themselves. There was a shift in the field of geopolitics from "saving women" to "saving gays"[32] Although the "saving women" script has not disappeared, a people's fitness for statehood is increasingly measured by the yardstick of their treatment of LGBTQ+ people.[33] In many political discourses, LGBTQ+ inclusion is represented as a marker of European or western advancement and superiority vis-à-vis "intolerant" and "backward" Others, who mistreat or exclude these communities. Jasbir Puar has labeled this tendency "homonationalism."[34] Homonationalism is now a facet of modernity and can be resisted or reframed but not opted out of.[35]

Highlighting this shift in prominence from "saving women" to "saving gays" does not mean that discourses on homosexuality were absent from nineteenth- and twentieth-century European colonial discourse. Homosexuality and gender fluidity were considered evidence of "uncivilized" peoples, whereas a distinct gender binary in which men and women were "opposites" was considered a mark of civilization.[36] Homosexuality has thus switched sides in the familiar dichotomy of modern/backward or civilized/barbaric. Previously a sign of backwardness, under neoliberalism's gender order, acceptance, or at least tolerance, of homosexuality and gender-nonconforming people has become a marker of civilization.[37] This reversal attests to the continued importance of sexual politics as a signifier of political power in global struggles over influence, belonging, and modernity.

Like misogyny, homophobia as a masculine technology of "Othering" creates useful patterns of contradictions.[38] On the one hand, homonationalism marks a homophobic, racialized Other as inherently inferior.[39] In Western European public discourse, for example, LGBTQ+ rights and anti-homophobia serve to denigrate Russia and Eastern Europe.[40] The entire region is framed as permanently "post-communist" and "in transition," as well as "homophobic."[41] This denigration belies the fact that, despite a decline in the use of homophobic language, tolerance of LGBTQ+ people remains superficial in many western contexts, including the

United States and Western Europe.[42] This superficial acceptance comprises an important contradictory pattern of homonationalism around the world since the global neoliberal order offers gay and lesbian citizens the opportunity to form families, so long as those families are configured in ways that are compatible with the prevailing system.[43] In neoliberalism, the inclusion of homosexuals within the imagining of the nation is thus made possible by racialized Othering processes in which non-western cultures are represented as hetero-patriarchal, repressive to both homosexuals and women, and therefore "behind" the West.[44]

The flip side of homonationalism is heteronationalism, which follows the dynamic of a manliness competition and fuels oppositional modernity. Trump, Putin, and Modi all use homophobia as a technology of Othering to help constitute nation-state-building projects. Consider Putin who is operating in a geopolitical field in which sexual rights and the politics of sexual citizenship have emerged as a geopolitical marker between a "liberal" and thus "superior" Western Europe and a "homophobic" and thus "backward" Russia and Eastern Europe. Putin cultivates a geopolitics of "traditional values," in part to address increasing anxiety around masculinity at home where women and men lament what is considered a Soviet legacy of "weak men."[45] At the same time, this articulation seeks to restore Russia's lost status as a superpower abroad.

Putin: fantasies of empire

Russia's president, Vladimir Putin, famously pictured shirtless riding a Siberian horse, is often portrayed as the manly anecdote to the post-Soviet version of the "crisis of masculinity."[46] In post-Soviet discourse, the Soviet modernity project led to the "over-empowerment" of women and produced "masculine" women and "feminine" men.[47] In fact, political elites often blame Soviet collapse on this perceived "distortion" of the "natural" or "traditional" gender order, and the post-Soviet period has been marked by the naturalization of gender essentialism and reification of mothering as women's natural role.[48] Men could not be breadwinners due to unemployment and falling real wages. In Russia, men's life expectancy plummeted during the 1990s, leading to the world's largest gender gap in life expectancy and a crisis of alcoholism among men.[49] Across the region, men's mortality was so concerning that they were considered an "endangered species."[50] A rise in sex trafficking also signaled to Russian men that they were unable to take care of the nation's women. Prostitution became a metaphor for Russia's foreign policy in the 1990s, with many Russians feeling their nation was prostituting itself by kowtowing to western powers.[51]

Most Russians experienced the collapse of the Soviet Union as a profound loss and a blow to Russia's standing in the world that seemed to mirror the humiliation of individual men.[52] To add insult to injury, the coming of capitalist markets did not improve living standards at home as promised. Instead, economic inequality increased dramatically, there was routine nonpayment of wages, institutional collapse, and Russians felt abandoned by the state.[53] In the 1990s, "democracy" became synonymous with social strife, including ethnic and civil wars. Russians experienced the failure of the First Chechen War (1994–1996) and the NATO bombings of Yugoslavia in 1999 as a national humiliation.[54] Thus, when Putin was elected president in March 2000, Russians welcomed him as a force for order in a context of uncertainty and insecurity, and as an example of "real" and sober manhood amidst rampant drunkenness and a pervasive lament that Russia had few "real men."[55] Russians also welcomed Putin's message that he alone, not Russia's weak institutions, was going to "make Russia great again." This was 20 years before Trump adopted MAGA ("Make America Great Again") as his campaign slogan.[56] Putin's narrative of being a working-class, macho kid prone to fighting and playing hockey, not only had populist appeal but signaled "the tough stance of an aggrieved, underdog nation toward outside powers."[57] In 1999, Putin spoke of Russia "rising from its knees," and in 2012, Putin declared that "Russia has once and for all risen from its knees. Now it is taking the next step: putting the rest of the world on its knees."[58]

Putin used both misogyny and homophobia as technologies of Othering to rally, define, and reinvigorate Russian national identity, nationalism, and collective masculine pride. Like other authoritarian populists, Putin did boundary work to define the "real" Russian people and nation and cast out Others at home and abroad. He framed gender conservatism and the "traditional" family in terms of national survival and made hetero- and cis-normativity a condition of national belonging. Putin's popularity is attributed, in part, to this project of remasculinization in which masculine representations of Russia are used to create a positive Russian collective identity. Both misogyny and homophobia as technologies of Othering resonated with Russians in part because of a Soviet past that demonized feminism as a "bourgeois" movement accused of splitting the working class by highlighting the interests of women and similarly associated homosexuality with a "bourgeois" lifestyle.[59] The elevation of traditional values into a key principle for Russia's approach to international politics shows how the defense of the heterosexual family has become not only a matter of global politics and a site for claiming an oppositional modernity against the West, but also is necessarily tied to the feasibility of neoliberal capitalism. Thus "traditional values" enacted through misogyny and homophobia came to signify "Russianness." Not only do images of men and women serve as markers that enable inclusion and exclusion, but they also produce systems of evaluation and hierarchy that assign low and subordinate status to anything typed feminine. Thus the deployment of masculine technologies of Othering can be used to legitimate power, and Putin uses this gendered strategy effectively.[60]

As Russia's relationship with the West soured over the 2000s, the "West" (Europe and the United States) became the most important Other against which Russia defined its collective identity.[61] A quick Google search will turn up images that juxtapose Putin's manliness with US president Barack Obama's supposed femininity, such as Putin shirtless on his Siberian horse placed next to Obama on a bicycle wearing a helmet and "mom jeans," or Putin petting a tiger while Obama holds a white poodle. Whereas American masculinity signaled ideal masculinity in Russia during the 1980s and 1990s, a new image of the Russian *muzhik* (real guy) became the Russian version of the manly protector, beginning in the mid-2000s. According to public opinion polls, Russians have ditched their previous fascination with the "Marlboro man" and now consider their men as more masculine than American men.[62] Interestingly, a *muzhik* values the protection of the nation over breadwinning in determining manliness.[63]

Russia used misogyny and homophobia to substantiate both why western countries should be considered external enemies and justify why political dissidents, enemies within, should be labeled "gay" and thus traitors to the nation.[64] Putin's return to the presidency in 2012 was met with countrywide protests, so the state then fully embraced "traditional values" and remasculinization to reinvigorate Putin's appeal.[65] Pro-LGBTQ+ activism or inclusion was associated with western imperialism and Putin, along with Russian political elites, warned that Gay Europe (shortened to "Gayropa" in Russian) sought to pervert Russian society, undermine its "historic" values, keep ethnic Russians from reproducing, and undercut the state.[66] For example, the Ukrainian 2013–2014 Euromaidan protests that demanded closer ties with Europe and distance from Moscow were labeled "Gayromaidan" in the Russian media, which argued that the protests were organized by LGBTQ+ activist traitors acting as proxies for US or European imperialism.[67] Thus the Russian media linked the supposed "de-masculinization of Ukraine" as a threat to the remasculinization of Russia."[68] Russia argues that the Rose revolution in Georgia, along with the Orange Revolution in Ukraine, were created by LGBTQ+ activists sent by the West to create a "gay revolution" that would throw Russia back into the chaos of the 1990s and perhaps even spark a western-backed revolution in Russia as well.[69] Thus, in Russia, nearly all political dissidents are framed as gay, sexual deviants, and western spies, and thus a threat to the nation.[70] The annexation of Crimea in 2014, Ukraine's southern region, was exalted by Russians as an act of national "restoration." In Putin's February 24, 2022 speech announcing a full-scale invasion of Ukraine (he called it a "special military operation") and in a September 30, 2022 speech announcing the annexation of four Ukrainian regions, Putin railed against the West's supposed undermining of "traditional values" where LGBTQ+ rights, feminism, multiculturalism, and atheism are foreign to Russia's values and both an existential and literal security threat to the nation.[71] One cartoon shows Putin on the phone with a feminized Ukraine who says, "Your tanks are penetrating me deeper and deeper, please don't stop . . ."[72] As part of its messianic mission, Russia argues it is saving Ukraine from western degeneracy.

Deploying homophobia as a masculine technology of Othering within this Gayropa/queer peril framing also allowed for a revival of Russia's messianic idea of "Russian exceptionalism" – Russia is a stronghold of Christianity, a bastion of "traditional values," and Russia will save Europe (and the world) from its own degeneracy characterized by sexual immorality and the dissolution of the "natural gender order.[73] On the one hand, this is an oppositional narrative against western imperialists. On the other hand, Russia has pursued an imperial, "civilizing" mission against Muslims in the Caucasus and Central Asia, who are seen as culturally "backward" and racially inferior. Beginning in 2013, Putin in his speeches sometimes depicts Russia as the "true" Europe which held onto its Christian roots in close alliance with the Russian Orthodox Church.[74] At other times, Putin says Russia does not want to be European at all. Either way, Russia should not imitate the western model of modernity because European modernity has been derailed so that Russia must instead follow a "special path" to an alternate modernity.[75]

Spectacular international events, such as the Olympics and the Eurovision Song Contest, politicize gender nonconformity and LGBTQ+ people, exposing a field of international competition. These mega-events have been used as a "public diplomacy mechanism" for emerging powers and post-socialist cities "keen to prove themselves as sites of global modernity and 'full members' of Europe."[76] Because "neoliberal entrepreneurialism elevates the consumption of images," Putin was able to use the 2014 Sochi Olympic-bidding process as a chance to highlight his own masculine virility, his and Russia's soft power, and show both the world and Russians that Russia has returned to great power status after decades of humiliation.[77] However, western media coverage of Sochi attacked Russia for its 2013 "anti-homosexual propaganda law," its refusal to allow a Pride House at Sochi, and a crackdown on queer activists in Moscow. From Russia's perspective, the western media stoked international calls for boycotting the Sochi Olympics.[78] A few months after the Sochi Olympics, Austria won Eurovision with a song sung and performed by Conchita Wurst, whose drag persona invited audiences to accept gender variance. Fresh off the Sochi Olympics that elevated homo-and heteronationalism as a site of boundary work and collective identity formation, Wurst's win was depicted in the British media as "one in the eye for Putin" and "unwittingly . . . the opening salvo in this culture war," whereas Russian politicians suggested that Wurst's win was a caution at what European integration would bring Russia and demanded Russia stop participating in Eurovision altogether since Wurst's win clearly showed Eastern European supporters of European integration what that future would bring: "a bearded girl" and moral decay.[79] In a caution against Ukraine's bid to join the EU, one of Putin's advisors tweeted: "If Conchita is a woman, then Ukraine is a country."[80] Countless "bearded women jokes" circulated in Russian media, including an image of Wurst in front of an EU flag with the text: "Ukraine – you wanted to go to Europe? Conchita is awaiting Ukraine!"[81] These mega-events solidified Putin's conservative turn and fueled a rejection of Russia as European.[82] This context likely also increased the appeal of the "manly protector" cover story that links misogynist and homophobic technologies of Othering to competition for status on the world stage.

The "manly protector" cover story has shifted the terrain of contestation from global economic institutions to the realm of culture and nationalism. In contrast to homonationalism, which characterizes good statehood and modernity according to how states treat "their gays," heteronationalism, deployed by the "manly protector" cover story, protects "traditional values." The Russian state is thus leading the way in transforming the content of modernity and is staking out a status position that places Russia at the top of the hierarchy of nations. The Russian state is part of a transnational conservative network that allows Russia to create alliances with conservative factions of western powers. The oppositional modernity that Russia spearheads, however, also facilitates alliances with postcolonial global South states, where there is a perception that queer rights have been forced on global South countries by western states and international institutions.[83] In fact, the Russian state supports transnational "profamily" civil society organizations such as the World Congress of Families (WCF), which was cofounded by Russian and US conservatives in 1997, and the US-based ultra-Catholic C-Fam, which had ties to the Trump administration. WCF and C-Fam issued a statement supporting Russia's 2013 law banning "homosexual propaganda."[84] Segments of the White supremacist movement in the United States and Europe, transnational evangelical organizations, and many far-right politicians in the West – Trump in the United States, Le Pen in France, Berlusconi and Salvini in Italy, Abascal in Spain, and Orban in Hungary – see Putin as the international leader in the defense of "traditional values" and the fight against "gender ideology."[85] In December 2022, Russia banned all media portraying or educating the public about LGBTQ+ identities through a 397–0 vote in Russia's parliament. The legislation views any expression of "nontraditional sexual relations" as western propaganda. As Nina Ostanina, chairwoman of Russia's committee on family, women, and children, said during the hearings, "We have our own way of development; we do not need European imposition of nontraditional relations."[86]

Modi: building a "global" Hindu nation from the inside out

Narendra Modi's increasingly radical brand of Hindu nationalism converges with Putin's vision of oppositional modernity, despite some substantive distinctions in presentation. India's history of friendship with the Soviet Union, as well as its status as an "emerging" global South economy and the largest democracy in the world, places India in a somewhat ambiguous geopolitical position. On one hand, India is wedged between the political and economic forces that support US corporate globalization, which has brought tremendous affluence to certain sectors of India's urban population. On the other hand, the increasing influence of Russia and its allies, including China, presents a counter to western global modernity that finds a broad appeal amid the social and political upheavals that neoliberalism has wrought on the country in recent decades.

Neoliberal policies arrived in India in the late 1990s under the leadership of the Congress Party's Rajiv Gandhi, a member of the dynastic Gandhi family that even today represents a secular vision of postcolonial India in which all religious groups are protected under the law. This secular vision of India has been criticized by right-wing Hindu nationalist parties since the inception of the anti-colonial nationalist struggle. Radical Hindu nationalist, or Hindutva, grassroots movements shared key beliefs and attitudes, despite slight variations, that include: hatred of Muslims, and to a lesser extent, Christians, a deep suspicion of western modernity, and a focus on recuperating a manly Hindu masculinity that had been lost first through British colonialism and again through the secular politics that defined the postcolonial period. Extreme right-wing groups such as the Rashtriya Swayasevak Sangh (RSS) and the Shiv Sena gained significant momentum with the rise of neoliberal policies and eventually fused with the ostensibly more moderate Bhartiya Janata Party (BJP) to attain national power first in 1996 and then more significantly in 2004.[87] These groups emphasized the development of a martial masculinity in defense of a Hindu motherland vulnerable to attacks from especially Muslim enemies within the country and outside it (i.e., Pakistan). From the 1990s onward, these conservative, explicitly majoritarian Hindu nationalist ideologies started becoming a dominant force in Indian political life, addressing the anxieties and new political openings offered by economic liberalization, the rise of mass media, and the end of the Cold War.[88] The idea of consolidating a Hindu nation made for Hindus by Hindus has justified the development of the atom bomb in parallel with a steady formalization of anti-Muslim policies, all naturalized through gendered ideologies that assert an aggressive masculinity.[89] Hindu nationalism, thus, has been the crucible in which the "manly protector" discourse has been produced in India.

Like Putin and Trump, Modi has been an authoritarian populist who has melded populist oration, anti-Muslim rhetoric, and a vision of a "new" Hindu masculinity to rise to national-level power. His rise to power in India in the early 2010s represented a consolidation of Hindu nationalist ideology at the highest levels of Indian politics as well as a "masculinization" of Indian politics.[90] Modi's own trajectory as a politician has been deeply embedded in India's political and economic transformations since the 1990s. As a member of a marginalized caste group and the son of a tea seller in a small Gujarat town, he climbed the ranks of the RSS and is represented as the epitome of a self-made man.[91] This myth has been essential to his populist appeal to a younger, ambitious, and underemployed electorate.[92] Modi views urbanization, capitalist development, and economic growth as positive forces. He gained legitimacy with a broad electorate due to his prowess as an administrator and an advocate for national development. This legitimacy allowed him to appropriate and expand understandings of the manly protector that emerged in more radicalized grassroots contexts, especially the RSS, which Modi joined at the age of eight.[93] Modi's increasing control over cultural and social life has effectively transformed India from a secular democracy to what Christophe Jaffrelot has termed an "ethnic democracy."[94] Initially, Modi rose to power on a platform of bureaucratic efficiency and national development in 2014. Upon his re-election in 2019, however, Modi's leadership has become explicitly majoritarian and Hindu nationalist as he has sought to codify cultural ideals in the legal system.[95]

The economic and political conditions of neoliberal capitalism that have marginalized especially lower middle-class men have created an opening for oppositional modernity, which Modi has fully exploited as his power has expanded throughout the country. Whereas the new economy appears to have "emancipated" women of all class backgrounds, a pervasive sense of masculine anxiety has become evident in popular culture as well as in political formations. Liberalization has further differentiated India's middle class by bolstering elite sections that have been able to consolidate historical privileges, especially English fluency, to take advantage of new opportunities in information technology, finance, and consumer-oriented industries. In parallel, due to new forms of affirmative action, lower tiers of India's middle classes have gained greater access to education, a development that has left many communities experiencing a disconnect between aspiration and real material opportunity.[96] The expanded availability of educational opportunities for many lower-tier, middle-class groups, without a corresponding expansion in employment opportunities, has been an engine of masculine suffering and discontent. Craig Jeffrey's landmark study of youth in Meerut found that lower middle-class men with multiple educational qualifications experience what he called "ruptured futures" as they waited endlessly for modernity and development.[97] These young and often not-so-young men were primarily engaged in what they called "timepass," an activity that generated both progressive and regressive masculine cultures that cross caste barriers.[98] These ostensibly class-specific experiences have created a wish for a capable, strong, masculine national culture that can stand up against western culture. But this desire comes along with significant anger about women who defy patriarchal codes of conduct by attempting to assert their own agency. Even Bollywood cinema, in recent years, has started showcasing men protagonists facing a crisis of masculinity because of these anxieties.[99]

Hindutva's "manly protector" cover story addresses these anxieties by allowing men from multiple class and caste backgrounds to reassert virility, masculinity, and patriarchy through multiple strategies that undercut the rights of religious minorities, especially Muslims, and women, all in the name of the upliftment of the Hindu nation. Using universalized language that presumes all inhabitants of India were originally Hindu, Modi's policies and those of the BJP fuse neoliberalism and Hindu nationalism to promote nativist patriarchal values through a marketized empowerment agenda. This empowerment agenda calls upon young, lower-middle class men to be the "strong arm" of the state and act to both protect women's capacity to become virtuous market citizens and punish them when their desires or ambitions expand beyond this narrow role.[100] These empowerment agendas can span the hyper-local, state, or national scales, creating a link between local transgressions around sexuality and foreign policy issues that curtail the autonomy of Kashmir or abrogate the rights of non-Hindus to become citizens of India, both key events that have consolidated and formalized the institutionalization of Hindu nationalism in India since 2020.

In the Indian context, misogyny has been the central technology through which the "manly protector" cover story has been shored up, and this technology is strengthened through Islamophobia, which has become increasingly crystallized and legitimated in legal settings and public discourse. In recent years, right-wing Hindutva media have fabricated a theory that Muslims are plotting to "steal" Hindu girls by romancing them, marrying them, and then forcing them to convert to Islam, which will then produce more Muslim children. Known as Love Jihad, the fabricated plot resonates with racist notions of a demographic threat posed by India's Muslim minority and has fueled widespread harassment against Muslim–Hindu couples in the name of protecting the Hindu nation. Since 2018, these harassing activities have become legitimated through the legal system. The increased formalization of anti-Love Jihad policies is a clear example of this gendered, multi-scalar empowerment agenda and how it targets men and women differently. Anti-Love Jihad campaigns and the laws that have resulted from them in recent years deploy the technology of misogyny to dehumanize and exclude Muslim men while constituting Hindu women as subjects of protection. These processes resonate with the patriarchal common sense prevalent in Indian society that also views Muslims as the enemy within. The campaign against Love Jihad also requires violence and vigilantism to shore up the Hindu nation. Anti-Love Jihad frenzy targeted the celebrity marriage between Kareena Kapoor, a Hindu woman, and Saif Ali Khan, a Muslim man, in 2012. Hindutva media outlets suggested that Kapoor had failed as a role model to young Indian women because of her choice to marry Khan.[101] By 2015, these ideas had gained even more traction and effectively brought together fears of a demographic threat posed by Muslims, the Othering of Muslim men, and the desire to protect Hindu women from what was seen as forced conversion. Never in these conversations has there been a strong voice speaking in favor of a woman's right to marry and change religions if she so desires.

As public sentiment and mobilization against Love Jihad grew, the topic became a central talking point of Hindu nationalists. This produced moves toward legal codification and confidence among Hindu nationalist men activists that vigilante action in such cases would be supported by the state. Indeed, anti-Love Jihad laws in 2020 became formalized in the northern Indian state of Uttar Pradesh, and there were efforts to codify such laws underway in many other states. Chief Minister Adityanath announced at an election rally that his government would act on Love Jihad and warned that "those who hide their name and identity and play with the honour of daughters and sisters . . . if they don't stop, their funeral processions will be carried out."[102] A few days later, an ordinance presented as an outcome of a statewide "Mission Shakti," which translates roughly to "Mission Feminine Power" campaign, ostensibly for women's security was introduced that regulated and partially banned religious conversions in the state. At the launch event, young girls demonstrated self-defense techniques. In a series of tweets about the new program, the chief minister expressed the commitment of his government to ensure that "every woman in the state is respected and can be self-reliant."[103] Women's empowerment programs, thus, became linked to anti-Love Jihad efforts. "Empowered" women could defend themselves against predatory Muslim men, but women who "crossed the line" by engaging in relations with Muslim others would be severely punished. This misogynistic discourse contends that shoring up the rights of Hindu nationalist men to prevent marriages between Muslim men and Hindu women contributes not only to the security of women but to the security of the nation in general.

Without question, the proliferation and expansion of anti-Love Jihad discourses, policies, and vigilante activism infantilizes women and undermines their agency. It empowers extremist men to surveil and police romantic relationships and uses networks of neighborhood informers to punish "mixed" couples. Even a conversation between a Muslim man and a Hindu woman can become a target for a state-sanctioned vigilante group. Anti-Love Jihad discourses, policies, and vigilantism do not target all women, but rather women who dare to challenge the patriarchal Hindu order. Any family member or community member can file a police report on any suspected inappropriate romantic activity. Thus Hindu nationalist activists can openly collaborate with the police to prevent Muslim–Hindu relationships. As a leader from a local right-wing party said to a reporter in 2020, "When a woman puts her foot outside her house without her father's permission, the Bajrang Dal comes into the picture." Thanks to the new law, another leader said, "the work that . . . workers [from my party] used to do on their own . . . now has [the] full support of the police."[104]

Under Modi's leadership, anti-Muslim ideologies have crept to the center of everyday life in many parts of India to replace the secular vision of the nation with a Hindu nationalist one. This has been accomplished through the imposition of a patriarchal Hindu order that works through the technology of misogyny to discipline and infantilize women and to racialize Muslim men. The technology of misogyny, in cooperation with other state-sanctioned anti-Muslim activities, has resulted in "judicial obliteration" for Muslim Indians who have lost their claim to Indianness.[105] Under Modi, Hindu nationalism has become the only framework through which to define national belonging. The strategy of turning latent ideologies and prejudices into official state practice, as has occurred with anti-Love Jihad ordinances, not only has implications for policing sexuality, gender, and the enemy within, but also for regional and international politics. A masculine, capable Hindu state can stand up against the Muslim threat from neighboring countries (Pakistan and Bangladesh) while also saving women in a way that is consistent with maintaining status on a global stage since the language of women's empowerment gets deployed in the context of right-wing nationalist projects.

In the larger international context, India must grapple with representing the conservative "manly protector" identity invested in misogyny while also appearing to aspire to western standards of civilization and modernity. Wedged between the legacies of the Cold War that tie India to the Soviet Union and the present-day friendly trade and policy relationship with the United States, where India's wealthiest and most influential diaspora resides, India's deployment of the second strategy of Othering in the context of the "manly protector" cover story, homophobia, is non-committal. At the level of the UN, India has behaved in an ambivalent manner regarding LGBTQ+ rights. Although India supported gay rights between 2004 and 2010, since then a more homophobic stance that appears to resist the moral legitimacy of the West's support for gay rights has emerged, albeit inconsistently.[106] With the current dominance of Hindu nationalism, India appears poised at times to join a group of reactionary homophobic nations that include Russia and Uganda in pursuit of anti-LGBTQ+ policy goals. At the same time, however, India appears to be receptive to the protests and demands of LGBTQ+ movements within its borders. As a result, there may be a distinction between India's state homophobia at the level of international institutions and within its borders. A recent study suggests that Hindu nationalist groups are in fact wooing LGBTQ+ citizens through a version of Hindu nationalism that appears to accept members of these communities as part of the consumer-oriented, neoliberal Hindu nation, so long as those groups do not push to transform existing patriarchal societal structures.[107]

Modi's politics work in tandem with those of Putin and Trump. Modi's fusion of neoliberalism and right-wing Hindu nationalism appeals to these other two strongmen, and they all view one another favorably. During the 2016 presidential campaign, Hindu supremacist groups supported Trump during political rallies. During the large "Howdy, Modi" rally in Texas, Trump told them that he loves Hindus, he loves India, and he looked forward to working with Modi. After Trump's election, Modi and Trump held spectacular joint rallies packed with multitudes of supporters in India and the United States, including in Gujarat in February 2020 after the onset of the COVID-19 pandemic. Trump also addressed them in Hindi, saying "Ab ki baar, Trump Sarkar" or "this time, a Trump government," referencing a successful slogan for Modi's party campaigning in India in 2014, which had been "Ab ki baar, Modi Sarkar" or "this time, a Modi government."[108]

Trump: uniting the right

In the United States, as in Russia and India, breadwinning has become untenable for working-class and many middle-class men. As men's ability to dominate as breadwinners declines, there is also a perceived sense of status decline among "real" American men that is linked to a decline in US status around the world.[109] In referring to this group of "real" Americans, Donald Trump famously asserted during his presidential campaign, "The only important thing is the unification of the people, because the other people don't mean anything."[110] Misogyny and homophobia are linked in this construction of "the people," which Trump and his supporters believe are under attack by queer and brown "other people."[111] Popular right-wing commentator Rush Limbaugh, upon learning of a "Rural Pride" summit celebrating LGBTQ+ contributions to agriculture in Des Moines, Iowa, warned that the Obama administration had created a sinister plot to "change what it means to be a farmer in America" away from the rugged individual ideal by using government funds to "convince lesbians to become farmers."[112] Limbaugh warned, "No matter where you turn, you can't escape this fact: if you are conservative, Republican, straight and White, you are yesterday. You are so yesterday. You are so irrelevant. You are so unnecessary."[113] This statement encapsulates the concern that men are being left out of modernity discourses altogether and highlights the emotions of pain and fear this worry can illicit.

White, working and middle-class members of the US political right, many of whom were "left behind" in the global economic restructuring of the 1970s (see chapter 4), have created a set of emotion-laden "deep stories," narratives that are felt rather than simply believed, that blame liberal elites, immigrants, queer people, people of color, globalization, and government institutions for a profound sense of loss of both masculine dignity and national belonging.[114] These gendered, racialized, and class anxieties of the majority group view modernity discourses of "women's empowerment," LGBTQ+ rights, and multicultural inclusion as signaling a loss for straight, White men, who argue that men are under attack from leftism, political correctness, and feminism.[115] Evangelical churches aided in developing a victimization narrative for White masculinity and "traditional values" that have been effective mobilizers of both men and women for racist, misogynist, and homophobic projects of remasculinization.[116] Gender, sexuality, and race have historically been interconnected in the exclusionary logic of White men as protectors of the nation.[117] In the contemporary moment, the "manly protector" cover story has helped produce a political polarization where the Democrats are constructed as "un-American," having abandoned "real Americans" in support of immigrants, people of color, and gays as groups considered external to the American nation.[118]

Thus, in the anxious narrative of the majority group, feminism has distorted the natural gender order and de-masculinized men to the detriment of modern society. This "deep narrative" is felt as true, despite our finding that neoliberal feminism has in fact bolstered neoliberalism and provided a cover story for extreme inequality that continues to privilege White, cis, heterosexual men. In a context where many men and working-class folks more generally feel they have been both economically marginalized by neoliberalism and discursively marginalized by a modernity narrative that centers on entrepreneurial, empowered womanhood, the "manly protector" cover story allows for a remasculinization project in the United States as it does in Russia and India. In the United States, a narrative of shared suffering and humiliation of both American men and the nation allows a just deployment of misogyny and homophobia as technologies of Othering against internal and external enemies that simultaneously bolsters a collective identity of "real" men and "real" Americans. The site of competition for manliness, then, has been displaced from breadwinning to protecting the nation. In the United States and across the three regions we examine here, there has been a resurgence of nationalist discourse. Trump has used the "manly protector" ideal to capitalize on this image of a "US under siege" by immigrants, Muslim terrorists, and domestic minority populations in cahoots with US political and cultural elites.[119]

When the "manly protector" cover story is presented as "hard facts" by someone who "tells it like it is," as opposed to "intellectualizing commentators and academics," the cover story is even more convincing.[120] Instead of recognizing the role of neoliberal capitalism in transforming an economy that has disadvantaged some more than others, figures such as Trump claim that abundant state services aid immigrants, women, people of color, or transgender people to unfairly slam shut the door to middle-class lives for "true Americans," understood as heterosexual, native-born, White men with dependents.[121] Trump argued that an "emasculated" United States has made many "bad deals" with other countries so that it is time to put "America First." NAFTA, for example, produced modest positive effects for most US workers, but many middle- and working-class Americans experienced downward economic mobility because of outsourcing and the decline of manufacturing jobs. In his 2019 State of the Union Address, Trump called Americans in states such as Michigan and Ohio the "losers of globalization" who got a raw deal with NAFTA; and, later that year, Trump claimed to have broken "down the doors of Washington backrooms, where deals were cut to close our companies, give away your jobs, shut down our factories, and surrender your sovereignty and your very way of life."[122] Trump's continuous repetition that the United States has been "losing" internationally and his assertion that only he can be the protector of "the people" target a core constituency of White working-class and non-college-educated voters in the American heartland. Trump's rhetoric invites other "real Americans" to join in the task of protecting "America."[123]

Many White, working- and middle-class Americans, especially men, have answered the call. Misogyny and homophobia as technologies of Othering label some men as hypomasculine –at the height of the COVID-19 outbreak Trump's followers suggested Biden carry a purse along with his mask – and other men as hypermasculine so that Muslim, Mexican, and Black men are seen as possessing dangerous masculinities. Various groups of White men have literally embodied the "manly protector" ideal. Its attainability is part of its appeal. Along the Mexican–US border, vigilantes, repeating Trump's "build that wall" rhetoric, have organized to embody the manly protector. Border vigilantes see the "greatness" of America as a gift from God, an extension of the White, heterosexual nuclear family, and something to be protected and defended from those who would diminish it.[124] Trump constructed "illegal immigrants"[125] as possessing a "dangerous masculinity" as "rapists," "criminals," "bad ombres," and "enemies of the American people," and stated that he "traveled all across this country" and "met with many American families whose loved ones were viciously and violently killed by illegal immigrants."[126]

Unsurprisingly, border vigilantes have described Muslims and Mexicans as the biggest threats to the United States and to innocent, hardworking Americans, and they supported Trump's 2017 "Muslim ban" and "building the wall."[127] Border vigilantes saw the government's inability to monitor the southern border as a threefold threat. First, it is a threat to America's economy since vigilantes believe immigrants drive down wages; second, a weak southern border is a threat to national security since it facilitates the entrance of

Muslim terrorists; and, third, it poses a demographic threat of reproduction since vigilantes fear that either through the rape of White American women or the birth of large numbers of brown babies, "real" Americans will become a minority in their own country.[128] Trump suggested that despite winning the presidency in 2016, he lost the popular vote to Hillary Clinton because of 3–5 million illegal immigrants.[129]

Some of these civilian border security groups saw themselves as bolstering the weak US state and helping to restore the government's legitimate capacity to use physical force to capture and deport those who do not belong by making themselves civilian extensions of the Border Patrol.[130] Many of these armed border militias, which gained visibility and legitimacy during the Trump presidency, spread throughout the country and brought with them tactics that had been previously tested at the US–Mexico border, such as harassment of minorities including videotaping day-laborer employment sites, recruitment of military veterans, cultivation of allies in law-enforcement forces and among politicians, and efforts to influence elections.[131] The tactics of armed militias who do not have legal authority but have moral authority as manly protectors of "real" Americans" rallied at Charlottesville, Virginia. White nationalists, neo-Nazis, and other far-right activists gathered for a 2017 Unite the Right march to protest the cultural cleansing of "White history" that would result from local officials' decision to rename two parks named for Confederate generals and remove a park statue of Robert E. Lee.[132] At the height of the Black Lives Matters (BLM) protests in 2020, Trump exclaimed, "Angry mobs are trying to tear down statues of our Founders, deface our most sacred memorials, and unleash a wave of violent crime in our cities."[133] Armed militias have been present at BLM protests, including in Kenosha, Wisconsin, where 17-year-old Kyle Rittenhouse killed two people. Rittenhouse's lawyer said that Rittenhouse was in Kenosha as part of the militia and "as part of his right and duty to protect his community where the state and local government had totally failed in their most basic responsibility to provide law and order."[134] Trump repeatedly called BLM protestors violent "anarchists," "thugs," and "terrorists" who must be put down as a dangerous enemy within because they threatened the traditional American way of life through "socialism" and "cultural Marxism."[135] At the January 6, 2021 "Save America Rally," Trump supporters told the crowd that the election was "stolen" and they had to "show backbone" and "fight for Trump." Trump told the crowd, "And if you don't fight like hell, you're not going to have a country anymore [. . .]. So let's walk down Pennsylvania Avenue . . ." to the Capitol.[136] Ironically, these manly protectors attempted to undermine democracy while believing they were "patriots" protecting "real Americans."

Trump's misogynist rhetoric – "grab 'em by the pussy" – and his project of remasculinization resonated with many segments of the men's rights movement. The Red Pill, an online forum created in 2012 by former Republican lawmaker Robert Fisher, aimed to expose the "true nature of feminism" as "oppressive to men" and help men reclaim their "rightful place" in society.[137] Red Pill adherents state that their goal is to transform men from "betas" to "alphas," and this requires women's sexual subjugation. Trump's portrayal of himself as a ruthless, self-made entrepreneur helped convince Red Pill adherents that Trump was the kind of alpha man who would end the "oppression" of true American men by the "feminist establishment" and "would make America manly again."[138] Whereas this forum had previously advocated for the transformation of individual men, the "manly protector" ideal allowed them to organize around a misogynist and homophobic collective identity. The Red Pill constructed Hillary Clinton as a common enemy, and the group had the collective clout, at least temporarily, to help elect Trump.[139] When Trump demeans women journalists asking difficult questions or lobs misogynist remarks against Hillary Clinton or other women politicians, these acts establish masculine dominance and circumscribe when and where women are to be taken seriously.[140] The 2022 attack on Nancy Pelosi's residence suggests that misogynistic rhetoric continues to motivate right-wing men who identify with White nationalism, even after Trump's departure from the presidential office.[141]

Conclusion

Across these three regions, neoliberal economic transformation has placed breadwinning out of most men's reach and has linked men's perceived humiliation with discourses of national restoration. The competition for manliness has shifted more solidly to the cultural terrain of nationalism and often plays out in cultural sites, whether they are international mega-events such as the Olympics or digital spaces that prioritize images. Putin, Modi, and Trump each make claims to being a "self-made man," and thus embody neoliberalism's entrepreneurial spirit, regardless of whether the "working-class" origin stories are materially accurate. All three "strongmen" embrace the "manly protector" cover story and deploy both misogyny and homophobia and its intersections with race, religion, and citizenship status as technologies of Othering. Many men around the globe feel marginalized economically but also culturally. We can better understand the dire warning that if you are a conservative man "you are so yesterday" if we place it the context of a popular culture of "empowerment" that celebrates "the future is female" slogan on everything from T-shirts to coffee mugs. The "manly protector" cover story allows for a limited acceptance of women's empowerment discourse if those women do not threaten men's political power, renegotiate the gendered arrangement of the heterosexual nuclear family, or challenge norms around who does the unpaid caring labor in both the private and the public spheres. In Russia, the "manly protector" cover story allows for a revival of Russia's messianic and imperial fantasies. In the context of "gay rights as modernity" and the ongoing invasion of Ukraine, Russia has carved out an anti-western stance in alliance with postcolonial African countries and the Christian right across Europe and the United States to position itself as the leader in a transitional conservative network that offers up an oppositional modernity. In India, Hindu nationalism, suspicious of western modernity and eager to remasculinize India and position it for dominance in the international arena after years of colonial subjugation, allows Modi to construct a Hindu nation that needs protection from Muslim enemies both domestic and foreign. In the United States, White nationalism allows men's manliness to be judged by how well they protect "real" Americans from the multiple threats of immigration, Black civil rights activists, queer people, and feminists seeking to destroy an "American way of life" that currently excludes or disadvantages all those marginalized groups.

Conclusion:
A Fairer Multipolar Future

The post-Cold War order, which deemed that "Western liberal democracy and free-market capitalism held all the answers," has been destroyed, wrote Roger Cohen, the *New York Times* Paris bureau chief in the days prior to the World Economic Forum's 2023 meeting in Davos.[1] Cohen identified four prevailing crises that are responsible for this destruction: the COVID-19 pandemic; the Russian war in Ukraine; extreme inequality; and the rise of autocracy, particularly in Russia and China. Cohen argued that the World Economic Forum, built upon the ideals of free trade, globalization, and a convergence in global norms, has faded in its relevance. As a result, countries like Brazil, China, and India would be attending the meeting not to conform but rather to make their distinctive interests known to the rest of the G-20. Russia's war in Ukraine had created food shortages around the world and would be sending Europe into the winter with inadequate energy for heating. This indicates that unfettered trade no longer serves as a reliable safeguard against war and hunger. Brazil is recovering from an insurrection that looked like a copycat of the attack on the US Capitol in 2021. The climate crisis and its effects are apparent, yet there is little political will to build renewable energy at a time when Europe's gas supply is being shut down. Cohen quotes the Indian minister of external affairs, S. Jaishankar, who rejects the post-WWII world order, defined by US dominance, as a geopolitical norm. Jaishankar argues: "Our own complex history underlines that the natural state of the world is multipolarity."[2]

Despite an overwhelming quantity of scholarly analysis on the system of global trade supported by the World Economic Forum, we remain poorly equipped to understand the "natural" multipolarity that is common sense to Jaishankar. This is because our analyses have remained overwhelmingly US-centric. When we do study locales in other parts of the world, we produce illuminating ethnographic studies, but too often the default setting of the nation-state as a unit of analysis has prevented us from seeing the forest for the trees. As we write this concluding chapter at the start of 2023, we are facing the culmination of the historical conditions created by the global neoliberal capitalist order. We have shown, through a multicentric analysis, this order has fostered these four crises and their adverse effects on the most marginalized. Together, these crises are poised to obliterate that existing order, but there are few imaginative possibilities for what might replace it. In the vacuum, authoritarian, misogynistic, and homophobic ideologies are flourishing.

We are in urgent need of a cohesive, critical understanding of this system's past and present, as well as visions for possible futures. In this book, we have attempted to meet the need for an understanding of the past and present of the gender order of neoliberalism. In this conclusion, we broadly outline the key components of a multi-scalar understanding for a fairer multipolar future that links the scale of the personal, the national, and the transnational. We focus particularly on the lessons of the COVID-19 pandemic and Russia's war in Ukraine, while also keeping in mind the other juggernauts of extreme inequality and the rise of autocracy and imperial ambitions. The pandemic has reminded us of the centrality of women's unpaid labor to neoliberalism and how geopolitics continues to organize healthcare, mobility, and life chances. Russia's war in Ukraine has shown us the high price of forgetting the recent pasts of neoliberalism. The oppositional modernity that Putin represents has a history and a global appeal that needs to be understood and historicized. We have shown in this book that when Euro-American academics like us erase key dimensions of our global history, we co-produce outcomes that systematically undermine human thriving, especially for the most marginalized. We suggest that historically grounded, transnational, feminist analysis can pave the way toward a "gender new deal," centering human flourishing, relational and community care, and joy.[3] We call for a new international value system centered on justice, rather than modernity and progress. Recalling anti-imperial, anti-capitalist movements of the past is essential as we do the hard work of imagining the world we would like to see come to fruition.

Gender and national belonging: a view from COVID-19 times

When the COVID-19 crisis shut down the United States in March of 2020, the first distinction made in reorganizing the workforce was between "essential" and "non-essential" workers. "Non-essential" workers were, ironically, the most protected from the spread of the coronavirus, directed to work at home, and, later in the crisis, this group would experience layoffs and furloughs as the scale of the economic disaster grew. In contrast, "essential" workers, including medical personnel, cleaners, and farmworkers, were required to work, risking exposure and death, so that everyone else could continue to eat and, for non-essential workers, work remotely. This essential work, carried out largely by women, especially Black and Latina women, continued to be woefully underpaid. As childcare centers closed, low-wage, essential workers had to make impossible choices, often leaving children unattended to work for poverty wages. In hospitals, nurses cared for those who contracted COVID-19 and experienced severe symptoms. These nurses often also endured the extraordinary emotional burden of being the only ones to say goodbye to COVID-19 patients who died alone because their families could not be with them. While carrying out these burdensome but essential tasks, however, these frontline workers' personal health and safety was put at extreme risk. Despite its status as a global hegemon, the US government and the US hospital system were unable to provide adequate personal protective equipment in the early months of the pandemic. The most essential group of workers thus found themselves unprotected, facing the highest levels of risk.

Countries with less corporate control in their healthcare systems did better with the imperative to provide care for all during the early phase of the pandemic, but the rollout of the vaccine was nonetheless dogged by global inequalities. As vaccine distribution accelerated throughout the United States and Europe in 2021, it stalled in Africa and parts of Asia that lacked a well-developed public health infrastructure. Within the United States and Europe, distribution was uneven, and the uptake was stratified along lines of race, education, age, and political affiliation. These social inequalities, often embedded in geography, were, as ever, a matter of life or death. These varied experiences of the pandemic raised questions about why some nation-states take better care of their citizens than others. Conventional hierarchies between countries were challenged at times, as when, for example, Trump denied COVID-19 existed and later bungled the institutional response, making the United States look "backward." In contrast, Taiwan, South Korea, and New Zealand responded with human-centered policies that were widely praised. Within the United States, anti-Asian racism dogged the everyday experience of the pandemic, as Americans started to associate Asian immigrants and Asian Americans with the virus, which was briefly dubbed "the China virus."[4] The moment of upheaval produced what Arundhati Roy called a "portal" into a new world, a moment of possibility in which the need for collective care, less global hierarchy, and more attention to the marginalized might be put at the forefront of a new system.[5]

But what might that system look like? During the early months of the pandemic, Naomi Klein gave many interviews to media outlets, recalling her earlier research on the imposition of austerity policies across the globe, which occurred across many varied settings during an acute crisis. "Milton Friedman was right," she repeated, "when he said, 'only a crisis – actual or perceived – produces real change. When that crisis occurs, the actions that are taken depend on the ideas that are lying around.'"[6] While we have an abundance of predatory ideas lying around at this moment, we lack the ideas that Klein would call "sensible, fair ones, designed to keep as many people as possible safe, secure, and healthy."[7] But such ideas exist. We have just collectively forgotten them. We have argued in this book that the rich histories of transnational feminist analysis of internationalist gendered struggle are urgent to recall, learn from, and celebrate. In the context of the UN, women from the Soviet bloc in Eastern Europe were active in meeting and sharing ideas with feminists from postcolonial countries in Asia, Africa, and Latin America.[8] These exchanges together formulated a powerful critique of capitalism and a vision for a new world order that did not foreground progress and modernity, but rather foregrounded justice, peace, and reparations. They worked across geographic and ideological lines to forge visions of the future that centered human thriving and amplified the value of egalitarianism across the boundaries of race, class, and gender.[9] These delegates advanced many critical policies and norms supportive of human thriving throughout the four UN conferences on women during 1975–1995, but US delegates constantly countered representatives from Eastern Europe, Asia, and Africa. Activists and human rights advocates around the world accepted the popularity and relevance of socialist feminist projects, even if, as in the case of the US delegates, there were disagreements regarding the organization of work, welfare, and women's rights. In our current moment, however,

Conclusion: A Fairer Multipolar Future

our imaginations have closed in because the predatory reality of neoliberal capitalism appears inevitable and inescapable.

Grassroots movements today also answer the call for a vision of a fairer world, and we as scholars need to amplify their messages to bring their ideas to the forefront of public discourse. For example, movements for racial justice rocked the world in 2020 in response to the brutal police killing of George Floyd and heightened the visibility of abolitionist calls for an anti-racist justice system based on accountability, rather than punishment.[10] In the manifesto *Feminism for the 99%*, the authors elevate militant feminist strikes around the world in which women have withheld paid and unpaid labor and even smiles to make it known how essential the work of all women is to make a country run.[11] They argue that these strikes represent a shift away from the predatory capitalist present to a shared future in which the basic right to flourishing is protected for everyone. What is required, the manifesto authors argue, is the infrastructure and resources for everyday people to realize the rights they have been promised on paper. There are seeds in our current world for an intersectional feminist movement that is radically global and inclusive. The pressing need for gender justice regarding reproduction and labor are central to the crisis faced by neoliberalism as a political movement, and we must recognize it as such.[12]

When we recover feminist histories from internationalist organizing and amplify grassroots struggles around the world, we expand our political and social imaginations to challenge that which appears to be inescapable and inevitable. We can build upon past and current visions of the future to craft a "gender new deal," an agreement that de-genders breadwinning, care work, and domestic labor, and elevates the importance of domestic and care work whether that work is provided publicly or privately. This new deal is not only required to sustain the livelihoods of overburdened working-class women around the world who are shouldering waged work, caring labor, debt, and the unpaid labor of community organizing, but also to curb the expansion of toxic masculine identities that double down on their roles as manly protectors. The expansion of such identities restricts the possibilities for women and gender-nonconforming people to reclaim autonomy over our bodies, communities, economies, and nation-states.

The "portal" that Roy envisioned may be rapidly closing due to the desire for a return to "normal."[13] We have doubled down on our existing predatory patterns. Billionaire profits have ballooned,[14] welfare funds meant for families have been hoarded or embezzled by state governments,[15] and food and housing insecurity has reached unprecedented levels. We are letting the portal pass us by, even at great risk to humanity, because we lack an imagination that excites us to unite for the world we want. As a result, we do not interrupt the endless demand for productivity and outward stability to make the world we want to live in. As sociologists, we are guilty of being part of the problem. As our disciplines and universities have also been absorbed into neoliberal logics and practices, our political will to ally with movements around the world has shrunk along with our imaginations. Going forward, then, we must urgently envision what the template for an anti-capitalist, anti-imperialist, anti-racist vision for feminist political organizing could look like.

The COVID-19 crisis not only made visible the essential character of women's work, but it has also made apparent that geography is a matter of life or death. In our current financialized neoliberal system, the most economically valued activities can undermine human survival and thriving. Thus it is critical to understand why and how inequalities along lines of gender, race, caste, nation, and sexuality are killing us now if we have any hope of generating adequate policy redresses in the future. Social reproduction feminists have been clear about the centrality of women's unpaid work within the family to the functioning of capitalism.[16] As we have shown, this importance is reconfigured and legitimated further in the context of neoliberal capitalism, but we have suggested in this book that the family is not the only critical structure that holds together the global neoliberal system. As feminists, we have paid inadequate attention to the importance of nation as a key site for emotional investment, aspiration, and perception of geopolitical cooperation. The second key crisis of our times further highlights the centrality of geography and nation.

Remembering the historical roots of Russia's war in Ukraine

The Russian invasion of Ukraine in 2022 was anticipated for some time by those familiar with the region, yet many in the US media expressed surprise at what was perceived as Putin's outrageous audacity or arrogance. Russia's invasion of Ukraine has shown us that we ignore the Cold War, its legacies, and its continued presence in our political imaginations at our peril. After the collapse of the Soviet Union in 1991, the US model of capitalism and democracy was hailed the victor. Political forces across the ideological spectrum rushed to erase any memory of

Conclusion: A Fairer Multipolar Future

Cold War geopolitics and of anything about the Soviet Union that worked well.[17] But Russia's new imperial project, now made apparent through Putin's invasion, comes from a Soviet history that is still the object of nostalgia and longing in the region. Putin has a vision of modernity that resonates with millions across many regions, including many political conservatives in the United States and Europe. These aspirations, ostensibly driven by a masculine, authoritarian nationalism, have a history: they aim to restore the imperial power of Russia that grew under Soviet rule not only through territorial expansion but by redefining the international rules by which nation-states are defined as "modern."[18] It is crucial for us to understand that these ambitions are derived from historical experiences that continue to be a vital part of our shared contemporary vision, even if we have stopped naming them as such.

In Putin's vision, Europe is the "backward" one, allied with the American oppressor, whereas Russia is aligned with those parts of the world that have been historically oppressed. This framing comes directly from Cold War politics. In this moment, too, many nations have refused to "take a side" and, in doing so, not only seek to protect their own sovereignty by not antagonizing Russia but recognize the historical ties to the Soviet Union which backed many postcolonial struggles. Putin's invasion of Ukraine was also prefaced by a long period of escalation on the global stage in relation to Donald Trump. Despite the United States and Russia having a tense political relationship, Trump and Putin were strongmen allies. In case we needed another reminder of the centrality of gender and nation to contemporary geopolitics, we need only look at Trump and Putin cultivating popularity as "real men" to promote masculine authority in an uncertain global world.[19] All these conditions created the opening for the Russian invasion and spurred its devastating continuation.

Today, we suffer from a systematic erasure of knowledge about alternatives to unregulated free-market capitalism created within the context of the socialist project and implemented during 75 years of Soviet rule. This erasure also inaccurately separates out the mutual influences of the United States and the Soviet Union. Alongside Soviet repression, there were also some aspects of socialism, such as its commitment to women's emancipation, which significantly improved the everyday lives of Soviet citizens. Indeed, much of what we understand as "modernity" today – gender equality, a stable livelihood, and a government free of corruption that serves all people fairly – was derived from Soviet principles, even if the actual workings of the Soviet state did not deliver on many of those principles. Policies that we today associate with gender equality in the United States – Title IX, paid maternity leave, and workplace legal protections from sexual harassment – came from the Soviet vision of women's emancipation.[20] When the United States implemented some of those principles in the 1960s and 1970s, it was in response to Soviet policy, which at the time appeared to many around the world as a more promising direction for the world than the inegalitarian capitalism of the United States.[21]

Our analysis of the gender order of neoliberalism responds to the pressing reality of how nation, geopolitics, and regional histories get mobilized for political ends, and always leverage gendered language to maximize its affective power. Gender politics can no longer dwell at the edges of our systemic analyses; the "gender lens" becomes the entry point for an intersectional global analysis that can help us build a new moral order centering justice instead of modernity.

Justice not modernity: centering human flourishing and care

As we have uncovered the centrality of gendered nationalism to the maintenance of the neoliberal system, it has become increasingly clear that the narrative of modernity and progress has been antithetical to valuing women's work and to human flourishing in general, even though we often articulate improvements for women in terms of "progress." Initially leveraged by imperial and colonial powers and legitimated by pseudo-science across many disciplines, notions of progress, modernity, and civilization have functioned as a totalizing power and knowledge formation that has justified unconscionable violence and destruction. As one of the key through-lines from colonialism to neoliberalism, our focus on the interconnection between material and symbolic meanings requires us not only to rethink the significance of nations, but how they fit into the cultural story of progress and modernity.

Close at hand is another cultural story that rarely figures in our evaluation of how well a nation is doing relative to others: justice. Used in grassroots movements and constitutions around the world, but seldom in social theory or national political discourse, the framework of justice requires us to rethink everyday forms of violence and replace our prioritization of profit and thirst for power over others with a commitment to fairness. A moral order that centers justice within our politics brings together social movements concerned with labor, the environment, LGBTQ+ rights, and human rights and can be made culturally relevant and salient in many parts of the world. A political orientation toward justice makes space for anti-imperial, anti-racist, and anti-capitalist movements operating at a global scale and involving those international organizations that have the political power to make the world a fairer place for all.

Establishing a new moral order centering justice over modernity or progress requires taking on the status quo at both ends of the political spectrum. In the United States, where we are located, Democrats are even more wedded to the idea of progress than Republicans because of their orientation toward a future temporality when things will be fairer. The recent Supreme Court decision to overturn *Roe v. Wade* was viewed by commentators and everyday people alike as a "step backward." While there is no doubt that this decision, as the first to take away a right previously protected by the judiciary, represents a reversal in the trend of Supreme Court legal decisions, to view it as a "step backward" retains the conviction that the prevailing trajectory of US politics is one of increasing reproductive health access, which represents progress. But the practical truth is that the gap between rights guaranteed on paper and the ability for the majority of the country's residents to access those rights has grown ever larger, as the everyday burdens of livelihoods, debt, and mass incarceration increasingly curb the substantive rights that US residents enjoy. When we center the formal legal system and progress, we shortchange our understanding of what is fair and who actually has access to justice in our country. We nurture the false sense of national exceptionalism that we have found to be detrimental to feminist aims in all the contexts we have examined in this book. The ideology of exceptionalism, inextricably linked to progress, must be explicitly countered and decentered in any global movement for justice that reduces systemic forms of oppression. Our interconnected movements must take this on at multiple scales: the interpersonal, the grassroots, the local, the national, and the international.

Such transformations are possible and being articulated today, in grassroots movements, transnational advocacy movements, and even in the halls of national governments and at the UN. In his July 27, 2021 speech at the G-20 UN meetings in Davos that went viral on social media, economist Jeffrey Sachs called out the interconnections between brutal colonial histories, unfair corporate power in the global food system, and the gross inequalities that determine life or death in rich and poor countries alike. He called for wealthy countries to address the "real financial needs" of poor countries faced with a lack of access to global financial markets and a massive gap between their real needs for food, education, and housing and the existing resources. Sachs shamed the United States and its policies very specifically, as well as the World Bank and the IMF, for failing to provide viable solutions. He argued that they had instead opted to "check a symbolic box" to make it appear that they were doing something. Sachs concluded with a call to greatly strengthen the UN and make it "the core and central institution in our world."[22]

Sachs might appear to be an unlikely advocate for a new world order based on justice, considering his own highly privileged racial, geographic, class, and gender position. Further, in the same speech, he relied on the trope of "civilization" to compel moral action around the issues of food, education, and the environment, a framing that we reject. Yet Sachs's analysis converges with our own in significant ways, reminding us that radical social transformation requires allies from all backgrounds, including the highly privileged speaking out in halls of power.

Indeed, his final call to strengthen the UN reminds us that in the historical moment following WWII, there was a unique historical opening due to the creation of an institution in which all nations had equal representation. The inspiring project of Third World organizing after WWII provides us with a lesson for what transnational, anti-capitalist, and anti-imperial movements can look like. Postcolonial nations organized to push for a new international economic order (NIEO). They challenged western dominance and refused to side with either the Soviets or the United States, seeking instead economic and cultural sovereignty. In our current context, we are unable to even imagine a multipolar world in which nations *can* fairly seek economic sovereignty. We showed in chapter 3 that during the Cold War, the United States hijacked the UN system when it moved the center of power to the World Bank. There, the United States had greater influence and could exercise greater control over the development trajectories of newly independent nations. Nonetheless, the power of the G-77 and the NAM was a significant force in global politics for decades. Strengthening the UN through advocacy and financing can provide an institutional context through which to renegotiate prevailing patterns of financial and human flows such that greater value can be directed toward historically poor countries. In a paradigm that privileges justice, this kind of redirection simply becomes part of the responsibility of all countries, a responsibility that brings us closer to aligning our real actions with our most cherished values and aspirations.

Conclusion: A Fairer Multipolar Future

Even as the nation can be an inspiring basis for critical organizing, national exceptionalism has proven averse to human flourishing and generative of harm for women and marginalized groups. To forge new visions of national belonging that eschew exceptionalism and allow for honest historical reckonings, we must work to redefine national security in a way that centers the labor of social reproduction rather than border control. Security, belonging, health and safety, and social protections must be the values that anchor national imaginings of security. This requires a holistic understanding of environmental threats, rights to land and water, and access to livelihoods that are free from debilitating debt while providing healthcare and childcare as the heart of nations' global and local responsibility to their people and the planet. While notions of progress are compatible with the continued exploitation of the marginalized and natural resources and the perpetuation of geopolitical hierarchies, notions of justice are not.

To undertake this project of expanding our imaginations to reject the harmful narrative of linear progress and embrace justice, there are templates within the history of sociology that we must recuperate. Karl Marx and Émile Durkheim compared societies to one another with linear metrics of relative progress in mind and judged by a European standard. Instead, Harriet Martineau argued that societies should be judged by the standard they set for themselves and thus needed to be evaluated according to the fit between their highest ideals and their lived realities, which she called the gap between "morals" and "manners."[23] Countering racist notions of "civilization" that prevailed during her time, Martineau advocated for the greatest good for the greatest number and for the reduction of domination in society – this resonates with the ideas that Naomi Klein wished we had "lying around" when the pandemic hit. Domination, Martineau believed, prevented everyday people from acting as moral beings.[24] This is because the gap between a society's prevailing ideals and the reality of its practices and lived conditions negatively and disproportionally affected the freedom of marginalized groups and prevented members of the dominant group from acting as moral beings as well. Martineau made significant feminist contributions to social theory but has been marginalized from the sociological canon.[25] When we take her ideas seriously, however, they present an alternative paradigm to those that prevail in the history of the discipline. We must replace positivism and the linear conception of modernity with a more holistic, multipolar, intersectional understanding of truth. Centering justice in the spirit of Martineau, rather than Marx and

Durkheim's linear progress, gets us closer to the values required to address the existential threats of climate change, gendered violence, poverty, and land dispossession.

A final note: the need for joy

As we consider what's needed for broadening our imaginations such that we start to center justice in a new moral order, we need to acknowledge the under-acknowledged necessity of joy. The neoliberal feminist cover story and its flip side, the "manly protector" cover story, are "successful" because those few that do embody those stories can be celebrated. Women who are held up as "success stories" may enjoy the attention, beautiful photos, and the chance to enjoy the limelight, while men who participate in right-wing social movements may experience increased self-regard, a sense of belonging and community, and a sense of empowerment to physically assert themselves against an enemy "Other." All these affective experiences can provide personal motivation to carry on.

Feminist counter-movements for change that center justice must prioritize joy if they are to have any chance of success. Stef Shuster and Laurel Westbrook identify a *joy deficit* in sociology – the unwillingness to ask questions about joy or integrate joy into our discussions of social, economic, and political freedom.[26] But this deficit also has the effect of impoverishing our political imaginations because joy is vital to human sustenance. It makes life worth living. Yet, when we cannot imagine a space outside capitalism, we cannot imagine joy without capitalism, a position that inhibits our thriving and causes "epistemic foreclosures" that reinforce the status quo. The gender order of neoliberalism brings joy to individuals through the consumption of stuff. But the impulse to consume cannot monopolize our imagination of joy and self-care. Joy can also come from self-expression that is received with celebration, radical acceptance of our bodies, rest and renewal, fulfilling relationships of all kinds, artistic endeavors, and learning. We must be joyful in our alliances, loud in our celebrations, and jubilant even in small victories. When we draw from lessons of the past and revitalize our imaginations and social movements to center joy, we advance a path out of neoliberalism and its gender order.

Notes

Chapter 1 Introduction: A Multicentric World Order

1 Solari (2017).
2 Radhakrishnan (2011).
3 For some of the characterizations we found helpful see: Bockman (2013); Brown (2015); Cooper (2017); Harvey (2007); Peck (2010); Prügl (2017); Wacquant (2009).
4 Meghji (2021).
5 See Alden, Morphet, and Vieira (2010).
6 See Ghodsee (2012) and Gradskova (2021).
7 We use the terms "neoliberalism" and "neoliberal capitalism" interchangeably.
8 Hochschild and Machung (1989); Swidler (1986).
9 Lugones (2007).
10 Bockman and Eyal (2002); Grandin (2006); Harvey (2007); Klein (2007); Mirowski and Plehwe (2009); Slobodian (2018).
11 Bockman and Eyal (2002).
12 Slobodian (2018).
13 Rivoli (2014).

Chapter 2 Neoliberalism's Pre-histories

1 This was accomplished by glorifying the figure of the Indian mother, while also creating the possibility of a woman who worked for a wage for the uplift of her family and the nation.
2 Communism was an ideal never achieved in reality. Although many political parties call themselves "communist" and, in the West, communism was the named threat emanating from behind the Iron Curtain, the term "socialism" more accurately describes the economic

organization of the Soviet Union. In this text, we follow this distinction of using "socialist/socialism" to describe an economic system on the ground and "communist/communism" when describing entities that chose this label for themselves or deploy it to describe a threat to capitalism.
3 Weinbaum et al. (2008).
4 Mink (1995); Valocchi (1994).
5 Mink (1995: 156).
6 Mink (1995: 27–9).
7 Odem (1991); Mink (1995: 39–40, 50).
8 Nilsen (2021).
9 Tracy, Sieber, and Moir (2014).
10 Osterman (1999).
11 Smith (2001).
12 Cooper (2017); Milkman (1987).
13 Breines (1992: 2).
14 Milkman (1987).
15 Breines (1992).
16 Kibria, Bowman, and O'Leary (2014).
17 Muschik (2022).
18 To gain a quick and effective overview of this phenomenon, see the statistics and graphic data compiled for this *Washington Post* report during the pandemic: https://www.washingtonpost.com/business/2020/06/04/economic-divide-black-households/
19 Gutterman (2012).
20 Breines (1992: 70).
21 Friedan (1963).
22 Cohen (2013).
23 Harvey (2007).
24 Cooper (2017).
25 The Soviet Union, established in 1922, was a federal union, with Moscow as its capital. It grew to encompass 15 republics and included Eastern European socialist bloc countries in its sphere of influence. The Soviet republics included: Russia, Belarus, Ukraine, and Transcaucasia (Georgia, Azerbaijan, and Armenia), Kazakhstan, Kyrgyzstan, Moldova, Tajikistan, Turkmenistan, Uzbekistan, and the Baltics (Latvia, Lithuania, and Estonia).
26 In 1903, the Russian Socialist Party divided into the Bolsheviks (majority) and Mensheviks (minority). Although both groups sought the overthrow of the Tsarist regime and capitalism, they disagreed on how to attain these goals. The Bolsheviks under Lenin were more willing to use violence to achieve social change, and it was the Bolsheviks that seized power in the Revolution of 1917. The Bolshevik Party then changed its name to the All-Russian Communist Party.
27 Bonnell (1991: 267).
28 Wood (2001: 524).

Notes to pages 30–32

29 Wood (2018).
30 Bonnell (1991); Weitz (2018).
31 Bonnell (1991: 283).
32 Bonnell (1999).
33 Weitz (2018: 329) notes that communist parties "denigrated the household as a backward province of precapitalist social forms and petit-bourgeois values. Individually rather than socially organized, the household was, by definition, a retrograde social organism, hence a site of the most backward political and social ideas." Weitz continues by noting that women and the primary inhabitants of the household were thus seen as threats that could undermine "(male) proletarian resolve forged in the workplace and the streets." This full emancipation for all – not just women – required women's participation in the industrial economy where their political consciousness could be cultivated. The household should simultaneously be transformed from an individualistic to a collective space and reorganized into communal kitchens, nurseries, and laundries.
34 Wood (2001).
35 Ashwin (2000b); Weitz (2018) notes that World War I (1914–1918), the Russian civil war (1917–1922), and World War II (1939–1945) created concerns at different historical moments about bolstering birth rates and created social challenges, due to a gender ratio of significantly more women than men. Still today, the FSU, including Russia and Ukraine, stand out for having far fewer men than women. See: https://www.pewresearch.org/fact-tank/2015/08/14/why-the-former-ussr-has-far-fewer-men-than-women/
36 Ashwin (2000a).
37 Weitz (2018).
38 Ashwin (2000b).
39 Ghodsee (2018).
40 Issoupova (2000).
41 Also of note is that revolutionary laws from the first decrees after October 1917 formally eliminated gender inequalities in marriage, land use, labor policies, and granted women voting rights. In 1919, the Communist Party handed Alexandra Kollantai a mandate to expand her work for Soviet women, and she was able to build a wide network of social services. The state formed the Zhenotdel, the Women's Section, which oversaw the work of implementing a radical program of social reform that would lead to "women's full emancipation" (Ghodsee 2018).
42 An English translation of the Family Code of 1918 can be found here: https://soviethistory.msu.edu/1917-2/the-new-woman/the-new-woman-texts/code-of-laws-concerning-the-civil-registration-of-deaths-births-and-marriages/
43 See Galmarini-Kabala (2018).

44 Keough (2015); Solari (2017); Utrata (2015).
45 Kukhterin (2000).
46 Kiblitskaya (2000); Lissyutkina (1999).
47 Kukhterin (2000).
48 Einhorn (1993); Hankivsky and Salnykova (2012).
49 Ledeneva (1998); Utrata (2019).
50 Afontsev et al. (2008); Rotkirch (2000).
51 Galmarini-Kabala (2018: 8).
52 Galmarini-Kabala (2018).
53 Kuehnast and Nechemias (2004a).
54 Utrata (2015); Solari (2017); Cvajner (2019); Rotkirch and Temkina (1996); Zdravomyslova (2010).
55 Abinales and Amoroso (2017: 167–92); Tharoor (2018).
56 Tadiar (2004).
57 Abinales and Amoroso (2017); Geldart and Lyon (1980); Tadiar (2009).
58 Rotter (1994).
59 Chatterjee (1990); Ray (2000).
60 Ramamurthy (2006).
61 Liddle and Joshi (1989).
62 Chatterjee (1990: 15); Liddle and Joshi (1989); Ray and Katzenstein (2005).
63 Ramaswamy (2010: 2).
64 Ray (2000: 110).
65 Ray and Katzenstein (2005).
66 Schulze (2002).
67 Grewal (2022); Schulze (2002).
68 Rajan (1993: 129–30).
69 Grewal (2022: 17).
70 Fan, Hazell, and Thorat (1999)
71 Roy (2012).
72 Sunil (2013).
73 Chibber (2003).
74 Frankel (2005: 581–91).
75 Roy (2012: 155).
76 Sanyal (2021).
77 Alden, Morphet, and Vieira (2010); Slobodian (2018).

Chapter 3 Investing in "Empowered" Women

1 Tolentino (2016).
2 Dorn and Ghodsee (2012).
3 Ghodsee (2012).
4 Brown (2015)

5 Weber and Berger (2009).
 6 Gandhi (1921).
 7 Marx, Engels, and Tucker (1978: 441).
 8 Andrews and Bawa (2014).
 9 Slobodian (2018).
10 Cornwall and Anyidoho (2010).
11 Batliwala (2007).
12 Sardenberg (2010: 234).
13 Sardenberg (2010: 235).
14 Sardenberg (2008: 25–6).
15 Sen and Grown (1985).
16 Sen and Grown (1985: 85).
17 Gorbachev (1987: 177).
18 Cornwall and Anyidoho (2010: 145).
19 Sardenberg (2008: 19).
20 Cornwall and Anyidoho (2010: 145).
21 Freire (1970); Sen and Grown (1985).
22 Sharma (2008).
23 Simon (1994); Wise (2005).
24 Simon (1994: 2).
25 Abramovitz (2005: 44).
26 Becker (1964); Sweetland (1996).
27 Understanding humans in terms of capital also meant that the varied roles of human beings became distilled into an economistic metaphor, a transformation that Wendy Brown has argued has concretized neoliberal rationality and undermined western democracy. See Brown (2015).
28 Calkin (2018: 46).
29 Kirkendall (2010).
30 Dorn and Ghodsee (2012).
31 Dorn and Ghodsee (2012).
32 Dorn and Ghodsee (2012: 393, 398).
33 Dorn and Ghodsee (2012: 394).
34 McLean (1981).
35 Burnett (1996).
36 Calkin (2018).
37 Calkin (2018: 62).
38 Berkovitch and Bradley (1999).
39 Ghodsee (2012: 59).
40 Ghodsee (2012: 49).
41 Sen and Grown (1985).
42 De Haan (2013); Gradskova (2019).
43 Ghodsee (2012: 66).
44 For example, Kristen Ghodsee documents the significant achievements of the women's movement in Bulgaria, which by 1971 had, through

the Zhivkov Constitution, "elevated maternity leave to a constitutional principle." The constitution guaranteed paid pregnancy leave of 120 days before and after the birth of a child, and an extra six months of leave paid at national minimum wage, in addition to unlimited unpaid leave until the child reached the age of 3 (2012: 57).
45 Boserup (1970).
46 Kabeer (1994: 6).
47 Miller and Razavi (1995: iv).
48 Kabeer (1994: 2).
49 Calkin (2018).
50 Introduced originally during the 1995 Beijing Conference on Women, the measure has been critiqued for certain conceptual shortcomings, but nonetheless adapted to local contexts_(Klasen 2006; Hancock 2005; Mehta 1996).
51 Towns (2009).
52 Kentikelenis and Babb (2019).

Chapter 4 Neoliberalism's Gendered Architecture

1 We follow Foucault who defines discourse as a structured set of statements, rooted in a system of social networks that keep the statements bundled together through repetition so that discourses become truth-making mechanisms. Discourse is power, according to Foucault, because it creates its own actors or subjects.
2 Grandin (2006: 79); Valdés (1995).
3 Bockman (2013); Grandin (2006).
4 Slobodian (2018).
5 Bockman and Eyal (2002)
6 See Bockman and Eyal (2002) for a more nuanced explanation of how the active contributions of Eastern European scholars were erased in the "origin" stories that western scholars most often recount about neoliberalism.
7 Bockman and Eyal (2002); Pula (2018).
8 Marangos (2004).
9 Pula (2018).
10 Dale and Fabry (2018).
11 Slobodian (2018).
12 Bear (2015); Stokke (1995).
13 Bear (2015); Matlon (2016).
14 Cowie (1999); Rivoli (2014).
15 Wright (2006).
16 International Monetary Fund (2022).
17 Della Porta (2015); Walton and Ragin (1990).
18 Slobodian (2018); Yuval-Davis, Wemyss, and Cassidy (2019).

19 Mongia (2018).
20 Mongia (2018).
21 Genschel and Seelkopf (2015: 234).
22 Browning and de Oliveira (2017).
23 Irwin (2020).
24 See, for example, Rivoli (2014).
25 Browning and de Oliveira (2017).
26 Bilgic and Pilcher (2022).
27 Harvey (2007); Standing (2011).
28 Beck, Giddens, and Lash (1994); Rose (1999).
29 Bourdieu (1998).
30 Moore and Anderson (2020).
31 Besley and Peters (2007); Wee and Brooks (2012).
32 Cosic (2017); Pozen (2008).
33 Esnard and Knight (2020).
34 Chant (2016); Rottenberg (2019).
35 Ekinsmyth (2014).
36 Calkin (2018); Roy (2010).
37 Matlon (2016).
38 Kimmel (2013).
39 Syrda (2020) found that men were most comfortable when they were contributing 60% to their wives' 40%. This wage gap allowed men to claim breadwinner status while sharing the emotional and psychological burdens of financially supporting a family in a context of neoliberal job insecurity.
40 Knight (2020).
41 Taylor (2019).
42 Rottenberg (2017).
43 Golash-Boza (2015); Wacquant (2009).
44 Kar (2018).
45 Einhorn (1993: 116).
46 Burawoy, Krotov, and Lytkina (2000).
47 Einhorn (1993); Mink (1995); Zhurzhenko (2001).
48 Mink (1995); Pollitt (2012).
49 Arrighi (2005); Harvey (2007); Krishna (2009).
50 Bilgic and Pilcher (2022).
51 Yuval-Davis (1997).
52 McClintock (1995); Pateman (1988).
53 Bederman (1995).
54 Spivak (1985).
55 Enloe (1990); Scott (1988).
56 Weinbaum et al. (2008: 7).
57 Radhakrishnan and Solari (2015).
58 Keough (2015); Oishi (2005); Rofel (1999).
59 Rottenberg (2014).

60 Solari (2017) found that, for historical reasons, Russia often looks different than other Soviet bloc nations in this regard. Russian women have not experienced the same pressure to be "matriarchs."
61 Radhakrishnan (2011, 2014).
62 Harvey (2007).
63 Enloe (1990); Sassen (1988).
64 Krippner (2005); Osterman (1999).
65 Osterman (1999).
66 Dudley (1997: 74).
67 Dudley (1997).
68 Dudley (1997).
69 Osterman (1999); Wright (2006); Smith (2001).
70 Massey and Denton (1993).
71 Wacquant (2009).
72 Alexander and West (2012); Rios (2011).
73 Ackerman (2013).
74 Roos (2019).
75 Kentikelenis and Babb (2019); Louis and Robinson (1994).
76 Littler (2017).
77 Sandberg (2013).
78 Rosin (2010); Sandberg (2013); Slaughter (2015).
79 Stone (2007); Stone and Lovejoy (2019).
80 Appelbaum et al. (2002).
81 Parreñas (2000).
82 Harvey (2007: 93).
83 Irwin (2020).
84 Zhurzhenko (2001).
85 Kubicek (2008).
86 CIA World Factbook (2011).
87 Shalal (2022).
88 Dale and Fabry (2018).
89 Dale and Fabry (2018); Puglisi (2003).
90 Puglisi (2003: 104).
91 Burawoy (1997); Solari (2017)
92 Reeves (2014).
93 Sakwa (2017); Zinets (2022).
94 Zhurzhenko (2001).
95 Utrata (2015).
96 Zhurzhenko (2001).
97 Alden, Morphet, and Vieira (2010).
98 Heeks (1990); Rajaraman (2015).
99 Veer (2005).
100 Chakravartty (2006); Wise and Martin (2015).
101 Bagchi (2019).
102 Anand (2021); Chancel et al. (2022).

103 Srivastava (2020).
104 Arora and Majumder (2021).
105 Bajpaee (2017); Srikanth (2018).
106 Raju (2020).
107 Chettri (2022); McDuie-Ra (2013).
108 Rai (2022).
109 Chandrachud (2020); Sufian (2022).
110 Raj (2015).
111 Jain and Swamy (2020).
112 Radhakrishnan (2007, 2011).
113 Radhakrishnan (2009)
114 Radhakrishnan (2018)
115 Alden, Morphet, and Vieira (2010: 140–1).
116 Sinha (2016: 30).
117 Alden, Morphet, and Vieira (2010).
118 Alden, Morphet, and Vieira (2010: 105).
119 Alden, Morphet, and Vieira (2010: 101, 105).
120 Dewey (2008); Oza (2006).
121 Radhakrishnan (2011)
122 Patel (2010).
123 Mader (2015).
124 Mankekar (1999); Rajagopal (2001).

Chapter 5 Moving Toward Modernity

1 Gardner and Osella (2003).
2 Sivaramakrishnan and Agrawal (2003).
3 Yuval-Davis (1997).
4 Anthias, Yuval-Davis, and Cain (1992); Radhakrishnan (2011); Solari (2017); Verdery (1994).
5 Oishi (2005).
6 Glenn (1992); Parreñas (2000).
7 Massey, Durand, and Malone (2005).
8 Dudley (1997); Kimmel (2003); Wright and Dwyer (2001).
9 Meerman (2001).
10 Sassen (1988).
11 Sassen (1988).
12 Therefore, the same neoliberal economic processes that have increased migratory streams around the world have also destabilized the class aspirations of previously unionized factory workers, many White native-born men, who now find themselves downwardly mobile and with few options for middle-class salaries (see chapter 6).
13 Lee (1998); Sassen (1998).
14 Enloe (1990); Salzinger (2003).

15 Wright (2006).
16 Sassen (1998, 2003).
17 Oishi (2005); Batalova (2022).
18 Morrison, Schiff, and Sjöblom (2008).
19 Oishi (2005).
20 Chang (2000); Hondagneu-Sotelo (2001); Ramirez (2011); Walter, Bourgois, and Loinaz (2004).
21 Glenn (1992); Parreñas (2000).
22 Hochschild and Machung (1989); Quindlen (2005).
23 Solari (2011)
24 Many post-Soviet countries, such as Ukraine, also think of themselves as postcolonial. See Korek (2007) and Mykola Riabchuk (2012).
25 Solari (2014).
26 Levitt (2001: 24).
27 Fitzgerald (2009); Rodriguez (2002).
28 Rodriguez (2010).
29 Rodriguez (2010); Lindio-McGovern (2003).
30 Rodriguez (2002, 2010).
31 Oishi (2005); Rodriguez (2010).
32 Nyberg-Sørensen, Van Hear, and Engberg-Pedersen (2002); Rodriguez (2002).
33 Rodriguez (2010: ix).
34 See Rodriguez (2002) for a discussion of transnational Filipino organizing that has resisted the state's attempts to shape "docile global Philippine subjects" and refine the term "Filipino" from an ethnic category to a poverty experience manufactured by an exploitative social, economic, and political system imposed on individuals by the Philippine state.
35 Freeman and Ögelman (1998); Levitt and Jaworsky (2007); Oishi (2005).
36 Oishi (2005).
37 Rodriguez (2010: 94).
38 McKay (2007).
39 Nixon (1997); Pateman (1988).
40 Fitzgerald (2009: 16); Gamburd (2000); Sherman (1999).
41 Crewe and Kothari (1998); Gardner and Osella (2003).
42 Gardner and Osella (2003: x).
43 Beck, Giddens, and Lash (1994); Botterill (2014: 235).
44 Meerman (2001). See also Parreñas (2001).
45 Constable (2007: 186).
46 Constable (2007: 187).
47 Gardner and Osella (2003: 16).
48 Gardner and Osella (2003) note that Gujarati migrants were surprised to find both systemic and interpersonal forms of racism they believed would not exist in "modern" countries.

49 Lan (2006: 3).
50 Lan (2006: 128–9). Lan (2006: 128, 5) further notes that this journey of self-transformation, shaped by the "imagining of global modernity among migrant workers," is embedded in "the politics of nationalism and racialization, the restructuring of class relations, and the transformation of family lives."
51 For more on the different moral orders supported by Soviet versus capitalist economic systems, see Mandel and Humphrey (2002); Solari (2019); Wanner (2005); Zavisca (2003).
52 Attwood (1996); Zdravomyslova and Temkina (2013); Zhurzhenko (2001).
53 Janey et al. (2009); Kuehnast and Nechemias (2004b).
54 Gorbachev (1988: 102).
55 Einhorn (1993); Gal and Kligman (2000); Zhurzhenko (2004b). LaFont (2001: 213) notes that the discourse of "return" to a pre-Soviet nuclear family belies the fact that "most of these societies were agricultural, and women worked alongside men in the fields until the communist push for industrialization" and the nuclear family with "man as provider and woman as homemaker was certainly not the norm."
56 Chari and Verdery (2009); Verdery (1996).
57 Gal and Kligman (2000); Kligman (1991); Zhurzhenko (2004a).
58 Palenga-Möllenbeck (2013).
59 Ashwin (2000a); Kuehnast and Nechemias (2004b); Rubchak (2015).
60 Kotusenko (2007); Lutz (2010); Tolstokorova (2010).
61 Keough (2015); Solari (2017).
62 Solari (2017).
63 Solari (2017: 75).
64 Solari (2017: 121).
65 Solari (2017: 99).
66 Botterill (2014).
67 Botterill (2014).
68 Galasińska (2010). Botterill noted that Polish migrants reported feeling guilty if they did not migrate because parents said "you have this passport: use it!" and felt guilty if they did migrate due to the stigmatization by the Polish state:

> choices for mobility are themselves borne out of familial histories and geographies of mobility. These histories and geographies are simultaneously connected to the national habitus, whether related to a heritage of political exile, labour migration or the fate of socialist immobility. Individual experiences of mobility are thus intricately bound to geopolitical structures of post-socialist transformation and relationally constructed around ideologically guided norms, values and experiences. (Botterill 2014: 246)

69 Botterill (2014: 235); Palenga-Möllenbeck (2013).

70 Botterill (2014: 238).
71 Keough (2015).
72 Keough (2015: 19).
73 Keough (2015: 31).
74 Lan (2003); Meszaros (2017).
75 Yeung and Mu (2020).
76 Johnson (2007: 156).
77 Bloch (2010); Constable (2012).
78 Constable (2003); Johnson (2007); Lan (2006: 128).
79 Constable (2003); Kim (2018: 16).
80 Constable (2003).
81 Constable (2003: 66).
82 Bloch (2010); Cvajner (2019).
83 Bloch (2010: 505).
84 Bloch (2010: 507). Soviet projects of gender egalitarianism also resulted in public discussions of eroticism and women's sexual liberation seeking to decenter marriage in understandings of healthy human sexuality. Cvajner (2019: 105) found that middle-aged Ukrainian migrants in Italy continue to draw on Soviet understanding of sexuality and reported that penetrative sex was a requirement for staying healthy, noting that sexual deprivation could cause insomnia, migraines, and wrinkles.
85 Constable (2003).
86 Correll, Benard, and Paik (2007).
87 Constable (2003: 97).
88 Constable (2003); Meszaros (2017); Thai (2002).
89 Constable (2003); Thai (2002).
90 Thai (2002: 250).
91 Thai (2002: 251).
92 Constable (2003: 93); del Rosario (2008); Suzuki (2017).
93 Suzuki (2017: 125).
94 Many Filipina women, through the labor-brokerage process executed by the Philippine state, went to Japan as entertainers and later married Japanese men. On the one hand, in this other version of moving from "maids" to "madams," marriage to Japanese men gave women an opportunity to recreate themselves as respectable and morally worthy wives and mothers. However, it was their labor export as entertainers working in Japanese nightclubs that creating their respectability dilemma in the first place.
95 Kim (2018).
96 Kim (2018: 18).
97 Johnson (2007).
98 For an explanation of Italy's visa regime, see chapter 2 in Solari (2017).
99 Fedyuk (2021).
100 Cvajner (2019: 132).

Notes to pages 116–129

101 Fedyuk (2021).
102 Fedyuk (2021: 40).
103 Bloch (2010).
104 Bloch (2010).
105 Bloch (2010: 509).

Chapter 6 Manly Protectors

1 Hochschild and Machung (1989); Utrata (2015).
2 Bederman (1995).
3 Scott (1988).
4 Kaul (2021).
5 Butler (2008); McClintock (1995).
6 Kimmel (2013).
7 Edin and Nelson (2014); Matlon (2016); Anastasia Riabchuk (2012).
8 Orenstein (2011).
9 Kimmel (2008).
10 Cornwall, Karioris, and Lindisfarne (2016).
11 Ferree (2020); Kimmel (2013); Zdravomyslova and Temkina (2013).
12 Silva (2019).
13 Janey et al. (2009).
14 Bureychak and Petrenko (2015).
15 The Cossack movement is Ukraine's answer to the "crisis of masculinity." It is both a cultural and political project of "remasculinization." This political project includes teaching boys and men combat *hopak* (a mixture of Cossack dance and martial arts), supporting male-dominated contemporary Cossack organizations (a system of NGOs which aim to revive traditional Cossack values as a foundation for the development of contemporary Ukrainian statehood), and the successful campaign to have Ukrainian Cossack Day recognized as a state holiday. Former Ukrainian presidents Viktor Yushchenko and Viktor Yanukovych both had strong ties to Cossack organizations, and Yushchenko claimed to be a direct Cossack descendant.
16 Rajagopal (2001); Upadhyay (2022).
17 Hansen (1999); Rajagopal (2001).
18 Banerjee (2005).
19 Pande (2022).
20 Bonikowski (2016).
21 Bonikowski and DiMaggio (2016); Bonikowski (2016: 443).
22 Bonikowski (2019).
23 Bonikowski (2019).
24 Slootmaeckers (2019).
25 Kaul (2021: 1633).
26 Ferree (2020).

27 Kaul (2021).
28 Kaul (2021).
29 Banerjee (2005).
30 Kaul (2021).
31 Kaul (2021: 1624).
32 Bracke (2012).
33 Schotten (2016).
34 Puar (2007).
35 Puar (2007). See Schotten (2016) for a detailed look at the changing meaning of the term "homonationalism."
36 McClintock (1995); Stryker (2017).
37 Bracke (2012: 248–9); Yuval-Davis (1997).
38 For example, instances where political and religious leaders use anti-western discourses to justify the persecution of LGBTQ+ people are on the rise at the same time as some movements in the West are using pro-LGBTQ+ rhetoric to justify imperial projects to "save gays" that are often anti-Muslim (see Puar 2007).
39 Schotten (2016).
40 Edenborg (2021); Eremin and Petrovich-Belkin (2022).
41 Baker (2017).
42 Orenstein (2011); Slootmaeckers (2019).
43 Schotten (2016).
44 Edenborg (2021); Kaul (2021); Slootmaeckers (2019).
45 Ashwin (2000b); Solari (2017); Utrata (2015).
46 Ashwin and Lytkina (2004); Meshcherkina (2000); Sperling (2015). See here for this image of Putin: https://nypost.com/2014/08/29/putin-its-best-not-to-mess-with-us/
47 To be competitive on the global market, post-Soviet states adopted the neoliberal push to redistribute the reproductive labor the state provided in exchange for the labor force participation of young mothers back onto the shoulders of women, noting that in the West, states call this work "housework," and their women do this labor for free.
48 Solari (2017); Verdery (1994).
49 Gessen (2014); Hinote and Webber (2012); Utrata (2019).
50 Zhurzhenko (2012).
51 Riabov and Riabova (2014a); Zherebkin (2006).
52 Kiblitskaya (2000).
53 Burawoy, Krotov, and Lytkina (2000).
54 Ekşi and Wood (2019).
55 Utrata (2015). See the pop song "A Man Like Putin" (*Takogo kak Putin*) released in 2002, written by Alexander Elin and performed by the all-girl band, Singing Together, that rose to the top of Russia's pop charts and was appropriated by that state as a "propaganda song" at pro-Putin rallies: https://www.youtube.com/watch?v=qtZUeHmpV6A, accessed August 17, 2022. Sperling (2015) notes that the song

constructs Putin as an ideal man: athletic, strong, sober, and responsible, unlikely to up and leave, despite Russia's soaring divorce rates.
56 Ashwin and Utrata (2020); Ekşi and Wood (2019).
57 Ekşi and Wood (2019: 738).
58 Riabov and Riabova (2014a: 28).
59 Wood (2018); Sperling (2015); Eremin and Petrovich-Belkin (2022). Also see Eremin and Petrovich-Belkin (2022) for a historical look at how Russian laws around homosexuality went from being more progressive than Europe to less progressive.
60 Sperling (2015); Riabov and Riabova (2014a); Wood (2016).
61 Edenborg (2018); Eremin and Petrovich-Belkin (2022).
62 Riabov and Riabova (2014a: 29).
63 For more the origins of the term *muzhik*, see Sperling (2015) and Riabov and Riabova (2014a). For a more popular explanation of why it is cool to be a *muzhik* in Russia, see Manaev (2022).
64 Eremin and Petrovich-Belkin (2022).
65 Ashwin and Utrata (2020); Edenborg (2021).
66 Eremin and Petrovich-Belkin (2022); Ekşi and Wood (2019).
67 Shevtsova (2020).
68 Riabov and Riabova (2014b).
69 Riabov and Riabova (2014a); Edenborg (2022).
70 Riabov and Riabova (2014b).
71 See here for the translations of these two speeches: https://www.bloomberg.com/news/articles/2022-02-24/full-transcript-vladimir-putin-s-televised-address-to-russia-on-ukraine-feb-24 and https://www.miragenews.com/full-text-of-putins-speech-at-annexation-866383/
72 Edenborg (2017: 159).
73 Riabov and Riabova (2014b) find the idea of Russia as an international beacon of "traditional values" echoes older missionary narratives of Russia's role in the world, such as the pre-revolutionary idea of Moscow as a "Third Rome" embodying true Christianity after the fall of the Roman and Byzantine Empires, as well as the Soviet rhetoric of liberating workers across the world.
74 Edenborg (2021).
75 Edenborg (2018).
76 Baker (2017: 104).
77 Alekseyeva (2014).
78 Edenborg (2017).
79 Baker (2017).
80 Baker (2017).
81 Edenborg (2017).
82 Torbakov (2014).
83 Edenborg (2021); Feder (2014).
84 Edenborg (2021).

85 Moreton (2022).
86 Bubola (2022).
87 Hansen (1996); Corbridge and Hariss (2000).
88 Corbridge and Hariss (2000); Rajagopal (2001, 2019).
89 Corbridge (2002); Hansen (1999).
90 Kinnvall (2019).
91 Jaffrelot (2021); Saxena (2016).
92 Malik (2015).
93 Jaffrelot (2021).
94 Jaffrelot (2021).
95 Nielsen and Nilsen (2021).
96 Fernandes and Heller (2006).
97 Jeffrey (2010).
98 Jeffrey (2010).
99 Jha (2022); Paunksnis and Paunksnis (2020).
100 Chacko (2020).
101 Strohl (2019).
102 Nielsen and Nilsen (2021: 1–2).
103 Financial Express Online (2020).
104 Nielsen and Nilsen (2021).
105 Jaffrelot (2021: 406).
106 Yadav and Kirk (2018).
107 Banerjea (2022).
108 Kaul (2021: 1630).
109 Silva (2019); Fuist and Williams (2019).
110 Muller (2016).
111 Gökarıksel, Neubert, and Smith (2019).
112 Gökarıksel, Neubert, and Smith (2019: 575).
113 Limbaugh (2016).
114 Carlson (2015); Hochschild (2016).
115 Dignam and Rohlinger (2019).
116 Ferree (2020).
117 Bederman (1995).
118 Bonikowski (2019); Fabregat (2021). Bonikowski (2019: 126) writes, "Whether calling Mexicans rapists, smearing National Football League players protesting police brutality, vilifying Muslims after terrorist attacks, or embracing neo-Nazis after the Charlottesville attack, President Trump, with the passive approval of the Republican Party, has portrayed minority groups as fundamentally un-American."
119 Bonikowski (2016: 428).
120 Gökarıksel, Neubert, and Smith (2019: 566).
121 Bjork-James (2020).
122 Löfflmann (2022: 551).
123 Fuist and Williams (2019).
124 Crockford (2018: 225).

125 See De Genova (2004) and Ackerman (2014) for a historical account of how the category "illegal immigrant" was produced by US immigration policy and came to be racialized.
126 Löfflmann further writes:

> Trump thereby frequently resorted to emotion-filled representations of victimhood, referring to "countless innocent Americans", 'grieving mothers and fathers", and American families whose "loved ones" had been killed by "illegal immigrants" in a vicious and violent fashion. This imaginary of shared victimization and injustice invoked the locale of an innocent heartland and its people as a mythologized space that had fallen victim to foreign aggression, alien invasion, and complicitous elites at home. (Löfflmann 2022: 552)

127 Crockford (2018).
128 Crockford (2018); Gleeson and Sampat (2018).
129 Antonio (2022: 942). Bonikowski writes:

> It is no surprise, then, that in its first year the Trump administration has sought to build a border wall with Mexico, impose a travel ban on people from Muslim-majority countries, investigate affirmative-action admission practices at elite universities, defund the Civil Rights Division and curtail oversight of discriminatory police departments at the Department of Justice, repeal the Deferred Action for Childhood Arrivals (DACA) program for undocumented migrants brought to the US as children, and pursue draconian law enforcement measures against undocumented migrants. All these initiatives have signaled to Trump's ethnonationalist supporters that the administration is delivering on its promises to champion the interests of white Americans, which have been portrayed as mutually exclusive with the interests of non-whites. (Bonikowski 2019: 125)

130 Elcioglu (2015).
131 Felbab-Brown and Norio (2021).
132 Phillips and Yi (2018).
133 Löfflmann (2022: 549).
134 Ali (2020).
135 Antonio (2022); Löfflmann (2022).
136 Antonio (2022: 946).
137 Dignam and Rohlinger (2019).
138 Dignam and Rohlinger (2019: 605).
139 Dignam and Rohlinger (2019).
140 Kaul (2021: 1632).
141 Klar and Kagubare (2022).

Chapter 7 Conclusion: A Fairer Multipolar Future

1 Cohen (2023).
2 Cohen (2023).

3 Ashwin and Utrata (2020).
4 Kania (2022); Zhang (2022).
5 Roy (2020).
6 Americanswhotellthetruth.org (2020).
7 Americanswhotellthetruth.org (2020).
8 Adami and Plesch (2021).
9 Gradskova (2021).
10 Arruzza, Bhattacharya, and Fraser (2019); Kaba, Murakawa, and Nopper (2021).
11 Arruzza, Bhattacharya, and Fraser (2019).
12 Ferree (2020).
13 Roy (2020).
14 Myriad reports about billionaire profits abounded during the pandemic. See Oxfam International (2022).
15 In a particularly egregious case in Mississippi, the state has sued 38 defendants for embezzling funds meant for the poorest for fraudulent purposes unrelated to poverty reduction. See Wolfe (2022).
16 Ferguson (2020).
17 Ghodsee (2018).
18 Woolley (2022).
19 Sperling (2015); Ferree (2020).
20 Ghodsee (2018).
21 Ghodsee (2018: 12–13).
22 For the full video of Sachs's July 27, 2021 speech, see https://www.youtube.com/watch?v=WZ1xc491mnU&t=282s. For the transcript, see https://www.jeffsachs.org/recorded-lectures/5jf86pp5lxch35e6z3nct6xnmb8zy5.
23 Martineau (1838).
24 For Martineau, the supreme right of all individuals, the key to each person's pursuit of happiness within the general good, is the right to act as a moral being.
25 See Lengermann and Niebrugge-Brantley (1998).
26 Shuster and Westbrook (2022).

References

Abinales, Patricio N. and Amoroso, Donna J. 2017. *State and Society in the Philippines*. Rowman & Littlefield.
Abramovitz, Mimi. 2005. "The Largely Untold Story of Welfare Reform and the Human Services." *Social Work* 50(2): 175–86.
Ackerman, Edwin F. 2013. "The Rise of the 'Illegal Alien.'" *Contexts* 12(3): 72–4.
Ackerman, Edwin. 2014. "'What Part of Illegal Don't You Understand?': Bureaucracy and Civil Society in the Shaping of Illegality." *Ethnic & Racial Studies* 37(2): 181–203.
Adami, Rebecca and Plesch, Daniel. 2021. "Women and the UN: A New History of Women's International Human Rights," Routledge Explorations in Development Studies series. Routledge.
Afontsev, Sergey, Kessler, Gijs, Markevich, Andrei, Tyazhelnikova, Victoria, and Valetov, Timur. 2008. "The Urban Household in Russia and the Soviet Union, 1900–2000: Patterns of Family Formation in a Turbulent Century." *The History of the Family* 13(2): 178–94.
Alden, Chris, Morphet, Sally, and Vieira, Marco. 2010. *The South in World Politics*. Palgrave Macmillan.
Alekseyeva, Anna. 2014. "Sochi 2014 and the Rhetoric of a New Russia: Image Construction through Mega-Events." *East European Politics* 30(2): 158–74.
Alexander, Michelle and West, Cornel. 2012. *The New Jim Crow: Mass Incarceration in the Age of Colorblindness*. New Press.
Ali, Safia Samee. 2020. "Where Protesters Go, Armed Militias, Vigilantes Likely to Follow with Little to Stop Them." NBC News, September 1.
Americanswhotellthetruth.org. 2020. "Only a Crisis Produces a Real Change." https://truthout.org/video/naomi-klein-makes-the-case-for-transformative-change-amid-coronavirus-pandemic/
Anand, J. C. 2021. "India Amongst the Most Unequal Countries in the World, says Report." *Economic Times Online*.

References

Andrews, Nathan and Bawa, Sylvia. 2014. "A Post-development Hoax? (Re)-examining the Past, Present and Future of Development Studies." *Third World Quarterly* 35(6): 922–38.

Anthias, Floya, Yuval-Davis, Nira, and Cain, Harriet. 1992. *Racialized Boundaries: Race, Nation, Gender, Colour, and Class and the Anti-racist Struggle*. Routledge.

Antonio, Robert J. 2022. "Democracy and Capitalism in the Interregnum: Trump's Failed Self-Coup and After." *Critical Sociology* 48(6): 937–65.

Appelbaum, Eileen, Bailey, Thomas, Berg, Peter, and Kalleberg, Arne L. 2002. "Shared Work-valued Care: New Norms for Organizing Market Work and Unpaid Care Work." *Economic and Industrial Democracy* 23(1): 125–31.

Arora, Shubhda and Majumder, Mrinmoy. 2021. "Where is My Home? Gendered Precarity and the Experience of COVID-19 among Women Migrant Workers from Delhi and National Capital Region, India." *Gender, Work & Organization* 28(S2): 307–20.

Arrighi, Giovanni. 2005. "Hegemony Unravelling (I and II)." *New Left Review* 32(33): 23–80.

Arruzza, Cinzia, Bhattacharya, Titho, and Fraser, Nancy. 2019. *Feminism for the 99%: A Manifesto*. Verso.

Ashwin, Sarah (ed.). 2000a. *Gender, State, and Society in Soviet and Post-Soviet Russia*. Routledge.

Ashwin, Sarah. 2000b. "Introduction: Gender, State and Society in Soviet and Post-Soviet Russia," in Sarah Ashwin (ed.), *Gender, State and Society in Soviet and Post-Soviet Russia*. Routledge, 1–29.

Ashwin, Sarah and Lytkina, Tatyana. 2004. "Men in Crisis in Russia: The Role of Domestic Marginalization." *Gender & Society* 18(2): 189–206.

Ashwin, Sarah and Utrata, Jennifer. 2020. "Masculinity Restored? Putin's Russia and Trump's America." *Contexts* 19(2): 16–21.

Attwood, Lynne. 1996. "The Post-Soviet Woman in the Move to the Market: A Return to Domesticity and Dependence?" in Rosalind Marsh (ed.), *Women in Russia and Ukraine*. Cambridge University Press, 255–66.

Bagchi, Amiya Kumar. 2019. "Neoliberalism and Globalisation in India," in Pradip Kumar Biswas and Panchanan Das (eds), *Indian Economy: Reforms and Development: Essays in Honour of Manoj Kumar Sanyal*. Springer Singapore, 11–24.

Bajpaee, Chietigj. 2017. "Dephasing India's Look East/Act East Policy." *Contemporary Southeast Asia* 39(2): 348–72.

Baker, Catherine. 2017. "The 'Gay Olympics'? The Eurovision Song Contest and the Politics of LGBT/European Belonging." *European Journal of International Relations* 23(1): 97–121.

Banerjea, Niharika. 2022. "Homopopulism: A New Layer of LGBTQ Politics in India." *Sexualities*: OnlineFirst.

Banerjee, Sikata. 2005. *Make Me a Man! Masculinity, Hinduism, and Nationalism in India*. State University of New York Press.

References

Batalova, Jeanne. 2022. "Top Statistics on Global Migration and Migrants." Migration Policy Institute.
Batliwala, Srilatha. 2007. "Taking the Power Out of Empowerment – An Experiential Account." *Development in Practice* 17(4/5): 557–65.
Bear, Laura. 2015. *Navigating Austerity: Currents of Debt along a South Asian River*. Anthropology of Policy series. Stanford University Press.
Beck, Ulrich, Giddens, Anthony, and Lash, Scott. 1994. *Reflexive Modernization: Politics, Tradition and Aesthetics in the Modern Social Order*. Polity Press.
Becker, Gary S. 1964. *Human Capital: A Theoretical and Empirical Analysis, with Special Reference to Education*. National Bureau of Economic Research General series. National Bureau of Economic Research; distributed by Columbia University Press.
Bederman, Gail. 1995. *Manliness and Civilization: A Cultural History of Gender and Race in the United States, 1880–1917*. University of Chicago Press.
Berkovitch, Nitza and Bradley, Karen. 1999. "The Globalization of Women's Status: Consensus/Dissensus in the World Polity." *Sociological Perspectives* 42(3): 481–98.
Besley, Tina and Peters, Michael A. 2007. "Enterprise Culture and the Rise of the Entrepreneurial Self." *Counterpoints* 303: 155–74.
Bilgic, Ali and Pilcher, Jordan. 2022. "Desires, Fantasies and Hierarchies: Postcolonial Status Anxiety through Ontological Security." *Alternatives: Global, Local, Political* 48(1): 1–17.
Bjork-James, Sophie. 2020. "White Sexual Politics: The Patriarchal Family in White Nationalism and the Religious Right." *Transforming Anthropology* 28(1): 58–73.
Bloch, Alexia. 2010. "Intimate Circuits: Modernity, Migration and Marriage Among Post-Soviet Women in Turkey." *Global Networks* 11(4): 502–21.
Bockman, Johanna. 2013. "Neoliberalism." *Contexts* 12(3): 14–15.
Bockman, Johanna and Eyal, Gil. 2002. "Eastern Europe as a Laboratory for Economic Knowledge: The Transnational Roots of Neoliberalism." *American Journal of Sociology* 108(2): 310–52.
Bonikowski, Bart. 2016. "Nationalism in Settled Times." *Annual Review of Sociology* 42(1): 427–49.
Bonikowski, Bart. 2019. "Trump's Populism: The Mobilization of Nationalist Cleavages and the Future of US Democracy," in Kurt Weyland and Raúl L. Madrid (eds), *When Democracy Trumps Populism: European and Latin American Lessons for the United States*. Cambridge University Press, 110–31.
Bonikowski, Bart and DiMaggio, Paul. 2016. "Varieties of American Popular Nationalism." *American Sociological Review* 81(5): 949–80.
Bonnell, Victoria E. 1991. "The Representation of Women in Early Soviet Political Art." *The Russian Review* 50(3): 267–88.
Bonnell, Victoria E. 1999. *Iconography of Power: Soviet Political Posters under Lenin and Stalin*. University of California Press.

Boserup, Esther. 1970. *The Role of Women in Economic Development*. New York: St. Martin's Press.

Botterill, Katherine. 2014. "Family and Mobility in Second Modernity: Polish Migrant Narratives of Individualization and Family Life." *Sociology* 48(2): 233–50.

Bourdieu, Pierre. 1998. *Acts of Resistance: Against the Tyranny of the Market*. New Press.

Bracke, Sarah. 2012. "From 'Saving Women' to 'Saving Gays': Rescue Narratives and Their Dis/continuities." *European Journal of Women's Studies* 19(2): 237–52.

Breines, Wini. 1992. *Young, White, and Miserable: Growing up Female in the Fifties*. Beacon Press.

Brown, Wendy. 2015. *Undoing the Demos: Neoliberalism's Stealth Revolution*. Zone Books.

Browning, Christopher S. and de Oliveira, Antonio Ferraz. 2017. "Introduction: Nation Branding and Competitive Identity in World Politics." *Geopolitics* 22(3): 481–501.

Bubola, Emma. 2022. "Putin Signs Law Banning Expressions of LGBTQ Identity in Russia." *New York Times*, December 5.

Buck, Pearl S. 1931. *The Good Earth*. John Day Co.

Burawoy, Michael. 1997. "The Soviet Descent into Capitalism: Review Essay." *American Journal of Sociology* 102(5): 1430–44.

Burawoy, Michael, Krotov, Pavel, and Lytkina, Tatyana. 2000. "Involution and Destitution in Capitalist Russia." *Ethnography* 1(1): 43–65.

Bureychak, Tetyana and Petrenko, Olena. 2015. "Heroic Masculinity in Post-Soviet Ukraine: Cossacks, UPA and 'Svoboda.'" *East/West: Journal of Ukrainian Studies* 2(2): 3–27.

Burnett, Nicholas. 1996. "Priorities and Strategies for Education – A World Bank Review: The Process and the Key Messages." *International Journal of Educational Development* 16(3): 215–20.

Butler, Judith. 2008. "Sexual Politics, Torture, and Secular Time." *British Journal of Sociology* 59(1): 1–23.

Calkin, Sydney. 2018. *Human Capital in Gender and Development*. Routledge Studies in Gender and Global Politics. Routledge, Taylor & Francis Group.

Carlson, Jennifer. 2015. *Citizen-Protectors: The Everyday Politics of Guns in an Age of Decline*. Oxford University Press.

Chacko, Priya. 2020. "Gender and Authoritarian Populism: Empowerment, Protection, and the Politics of Resentful Aspiration in India." *Critical Asian Studies* 52(2): 204–25.

Chakravartty, Paula. 2006. "Symbolic Analysts or Indentured Servants? Indian High-Tech Migrants in America's Information Economy." *Knowledge, Technology, and Policy* 19(3): 27–43.

Chancel, Lucas, Piketty, Thomas, Saez, Emmanuel, and Zucman, Gabriel. 2022. *World Inequality Report 2022*. https://wir2022.wid.world/: World Inequality Lab.

References

Chandrachud, Abhinav. 2020. "Secularism and the Citizenship Amendment Act." *Indian Law Review* 4(2): 138–62.
Chang, Grace. 2000. *Disposable Domestics: Immigrant Women Workers in the Global Economy*. South End Press.
Chant, Sylvia. 2016. "Women, Girls and World Poverty: Empowerment, Equality or Essentialism?" *International Development Planning Review* 38(1): 1–24.
Chari, Sharad and Verdery, Katherine. 2009. "Thinking between the Posts: Postcolonialism, Postsocialism, and Ethnography after the Cold War." *Comparative Studies in Society and History* 51(1): 6–34.
Chatterjee, Partha. 1990. "The Nationalist Resolution of the Women's Question," in Kumkum Sangari and Sudesh Vaid (eds), *Recasting Women: Essays in Indian Colonial History*. Rutgers University Press, 233–53.
Chettri, Mona. 2022. "Next-gen Precarity: Gender and Informal Labor in the Eastern Himalaya." *Gender, Technology and Development* 26(1): 96–115.
Chibber, Vivek. 2003. *Locked in Place: State-building and Late Industrialization in India*. Princeton University Press.
CIA World Factbook. 2011. "Population Below Poverty Line (2003) by Country." http://www.NationMaster.com/graph/eco_pop_bel_pov_lin-economy-population-below-poverty-line&date=2003.
Cohen, Nancy L. 2013. "Why America Never Had Universal Child Care." *New Republic*, April 24.
Cohen, Roger. 2023. "Davos Confronts a New World Order." *New York Times*, January 14.
Constable, Nicole. 2003. *Romance on a Global Stage: Pen Pals, Virtual Ethnography, and "Mail Order" Marriages*. University of California Press.
Constable, Nicole. 2007. *Maid to Order in Hong Kong: Stories of Filipina Workers*. Cornell University Press.
Constable, Nicole. 2012. "International Marriage Brokers, Cross-Border Marriages and the US Anti-Trafficking Campaign." *Journal of Ethnic and Migration Studies* 38(7): 1137–54.
Cooper, Melinda. 2017. *Family Values: Between Neoliberalism and the New Social Conservatism*. MIT Press.
Corbridge, Stuart. 2002. "Cartographies of Loathing and Desire: The Bhartiya Janata Party, the Bomb, and the Political Spaces of Hindu Nationalism," in Yale H. Ferguson and R. J. Barry Jones (eds), *Political Space: Frontiers of Change and Governance in a Globalizing World*. State University of New York Press, 151–72.
Corbridge, Stuart and Hariss, John. 2000. *Reinventing India: Liberalization, Hindu Nationalism, and Popular Democracy*. Polity Press.
Cornwall, Andrea and Anyidoho, Nana Akua. 2010. "Introduction: Women's Empowerment: Contentions and Contestations." *Development* 53(2): 144–9.
Cornwall, Andrea, Karioris, Frank G., and Lindisfarne, Nancy (eds). 2016. *Masculinities under Neoliberalism*. Zed Books.

Correll, Shelley J., Benard, Stephen, and Paik, In. 2007. "Getting a Job: Is There a Motherhood Penalty?" *American Journal of Sociology* 112(5): 1297–338.

Cosic, Miriam. 2017. "'We Are All Entrepreneurs': Muhammad Yunus on Changing the World, One Microloan at a Time." *Guardian*, March 28.

Cowie, Jefferson. 1999. *Capital Moves: RCA's 70-year Quest for Cheap Labor.* Cornell University Press.

Crewe, Emma and Kothari, Uma. 1998. "Gujurati Migrants' Search for Modernity in Britain." *Gender & Development* 6(1): 13–20.

Crockford, Susannah. 2018. "Thank God for the Greatest Country on Earth: White Supremacy, Vigilantes, and Survivalists in the Struggle to Define the American Nation." *Religion, State and Society* 46(3): 224–42.

Cvajner, Martina. 2019. *Soviet Signoras: Personal and Collective Transformations in Eastern European Migration.* University of Chicago Press.

Dale, Gareth and Fabry, Adam. 2018. "Neoliberalism in Eastern Europe and the Former Soviet Union," in Gareth Dale and Adam Fabry (eds), *The SAGE Handbook of Neoliberalism*, SAGE Publications, 234–47.

De Genova, Nicholas. 2004. "The Legal Production of Mexican/Migrant 'Illegality.'" *Latino Studies* 2(2): 160–85.

De Haan, Francisca. 2013. "Eugénie Cotton, Pak Chong-ae, and Claudia Jones: Rethinking Transnational Feminism and International Politics." *Journal of Women's History* 25(4): 174–89.

del Rosario, Teresita C. 2008. "Bridal Diaspora: Migration and Marriage among Filipino Women," in Rajni Palriwala and Patricia Uberoi (eds), *Marriage, Migration and Gender*. SAGE Publications India, 78–97.

Della Porta, Donatella. 2015. *Social Movements in Times of Austerity: Bringing Capitalism Back into Protest Analysis.* John Wiley & Sons.

Dewey, Susan. 2008. *Making Miss India Miss World: Constructing Gender, Power, and the Nation in Postliberalization India.* Syracuse University Press.

Dignam, Pierce Alexander and Rohlinger, Deana A. 2019. "Misogynistic Men Online: How the Red Pill Helped Elect Trump." *Signs: Journal of Women in Culture and Society* 44(3): 589–612.

Dorn, Charles and Ghodsee, Kristen. 2012. "The Cold War Politicization of Literacy: Communism, UNESCO, and the World Bank." *Diplomatic History* 36(2): 373–98.

Dudley, Kathryn Marie. 1997. *The End of the Line: Lost Jobs, New Lives in Postindustrial America.* University of Chicago Press.

Edenborg, Emil. 2017. *Politics of Visibility and Belonging: From Russia's "Homosexual Propaganda" Laws to the Ukraine War.* Routledge.

Edenborg, Emil. 2018. "Homophobia as Geopolitics: 'Traditional Values' and the Negotiation of Russia's Place in the World," in Jon Mulholland, Nicola Montagna, and Erin Sanders-McDonagh (eds), *Gendering Nationalism: Intersections of Nation, Gender and Sexuality*. Palgrave Macmillan.

Edenborg, Emil. 2021. "'Traditional Values' and the Narrative of Gay Rights

as Modernity: Sexual Politics beyond Polarization." *Sexualities*: 1–17. https://doi.org/10.1177/13634607211008067.
Edenborg, Emil. 2022. "Putin's Anti-Gay War on Ukraine." *Boston Review*, March 14.
Edin, Kathryn and Nelson, Timothy J. 2014. *Doing the Best I Can: Fatherhood in the Inner City*. University of California Press.
Einhorn, Barbara. 1993. *Cinderella Goes to Market: Citizenship, Gender, and Women's Movements in East Central Europe*. Verso.
Ekinsmyth, Carol. 2014. "Mothers' Business, Work/Life and the Politics of 'Mumpreneurship.'" *Gender, Place & Culture: A Journal of Feminist Geography* 21(10): 1230–48.
Ekşi, Betül and Wood, Elizabeth A. 2019. "Right-wing Populism as Gendered Performance: Janus-faced Masculinity in the Leadership of Vladimir Putin and Recep T. Erdogan." *Theory and Society* 48: 733–51.
Elcioglu, Emine F. 2015. "Popular Sovereignty on the Border: Nativist Activism among Two Border Watch Groups in Southern Arizona." *Ethnography* 16(4): 438–62.
Enloe, Cynthia H. 1990. *Bananas, Beaches, & Bases: Making Feminist Sense of International Politics*. University of California Press.
Eremin, Arkadiy and Petrovich-Belkin, Oleg Konstantinovich. 2022. "State Policies Regarding Sexual Minorities in Russia: From Russian Empire to Modern-Day Russian Federation." *Sexuality & Culture* 26: 289–311.
Esnard, Talia and Knight, Melanie. 2020. "Shifting the Lens: The Complexity of Space and Practice for Entrepreneurial Mothers," in Talia Esnard and Melanie Knight (eds), *Mothering and Entrepreneurship: Global Perspectives, Identities, and Complexities*. Demeter Press, 293–307.
Fabregat, Eduard. 2021. "The Role of Boundary Objects in Trump's Speech: The Results of Coloniality and the Processes of Othering Towards Latin American People in US Politics." *Social Identities* 27(1): 3–19.
Fan, Shenggen, Hazell, Peter, B. R., and Thorat, Sukhadeo. 1999. *Linkages between Government Spending, Growth, and Poverty in Rural India*, Vol. 110. International Food Policy Research Institute.
Feder, J. Lester. 2014. "The New Cold War over Human Rights." https://www.buzzfeednews.com/article/lesterfeder/the-new-cold-war-over-human-rights.
Fedyuk, Olena. 2021. "Moral Economies of Intimacy: Narratives of Ukrainian Solo Female Migrants in Italy," in Haldis Haukanes and Frances Pine (eds), *Intimacy and Mobility in an Era of Hardening Borders: Gender, Reproduction, Regulation*. Manchester University Press, 33–50.
Felbab-Brown, Vanda and Norio, Elisa. 2021. "What Border Vigilantes Taught US Right-Wing Armed Groups." *Mexico Today*, https://www.brookings.edu/articles/what-border-vigilantes-taught-us-right-wing-armed-groups/.
Ferguson, Susan. 2020. *Women and Work: Feminism, Labour, and Social Reproduction*. Pluto Press.

Fernandes, Leela and Heller, Patrick. 2006. "Hegemonic Aspirations: New Middle-Class Politics and India's Democracy in Comparative Perspective." *Critical Asian Studies* 38(4): 495–522.

Ferree, Myra Marx. 2020. "The Crisis of Masculinity for Gendered Democracies: Before, During, and After Trump." *Sociological Forum* 35(S1): 898–917.

Financial Express Online. 2020. "Uttar Pradesh: Yogi Adityanath Launches Mission Shakti for Security of Women in the State." *Financial Express*, October 17.

Fitzgerald, David. 2009. *A Nation of Emigrants: How Mexico Manages its Migration*. University of California Press.

Frankel, Francine R. 2005. *India's Political Economy 1947–2004: The Gradual Revolution*. Oxford University Press.

Freeman, Gary and Ögelman, Nedim. 1998. "Homeland Citizenship Policies and the Status of Third Country Nationals in the European Union." *Journal of Ethnic and Migration Studies* 24(4): 769–88.

Freire, Paulo. 1970. *Pedagogy of the Oppressed*. Continuum.

Friedan, Betty. 1963. *The Feminine Mystique*. W. W. Norton.

Friedman, Thomas L. 2000. *The Lexus and the Olive Tree: Understanding Globalization*: Farrar, Straus and Giroux.

Friedman, Thomas L. 2006. *The World is Flat: A Brief History of the Twenty-first Century*, updated and expanded edn. Macmillan.

Fuist, Todd and Williams, Rhys. 2019. "'Let's Call Ourselves the Super Elite': Using the Collective Behavior Tradition to Analyze Trump's America." *Sociological Forum* 34(S1): 1132–52.

Gal, Susan and Kligman, Gail (eds). 2000. *Reproducing Gender: Politics, Publics and Everyday Life after Socialism*. Princeton University Press.

Galasińska, Aleksandra. 2010. "Leavers and Stayers Discuss Returning Home: Internet Discourses on Migration in the Context of the Post-communist Transformation." *Social Identities* 16(3): 309–24.

Galmarini-Kabala, Maria Cristina. 2018. *The Right to be Helped: Deviance, Entitlement, and the Soviet Moral Order*. Cambridge University Press.

Gamburd, Michele Ruth. 2000. *The Kitchen Spoon's Handle: Transnationalism and Sri Lanka's Migrant Housemaids*. Cornell University Press.

Gandhi, Mohandas Karamchand. 1921. *Hind Swaraj or Indian Home Rule*: GA Natesan.

Gardner, Katy and Osella, Filippo. 2003. "Migration, Modernity and Social Transformation in South Asia: An Overview." *Contributions to Indian Sociology* 37(1–2): v–xxviii.

Geldart, Carol and Lyon, Peter. 1980. "The Group of 77: A Perspective View." *International Affairs* 57(1): 79–101.

Genschel, Philipp and Seelkopf, Laura. 2015. "The Competition State," in Stephan Leibfried, Evelyne Huber, Matthew Lange, Jonah D. Levy, and John D. Stephens (eds), *The Oxford Handbook of Transformations of the State*, 1–23.

Gessen, Masha. 2014. "The Dying Russians." *New York Times*, September 2.
Ghodsee, Kristen. 2012. "Rethinking State Socialist Mass Women's Organizations: The Committee of the Bulgarian Women's Movement and the United Nations Decade for Women, 1975–1985." *Journal of Women's History* 24(4): 49–73.
Ghodsee, Kristen. 2018. *Why Women Have Better Sex Under Socialism: And Other Arguments for Economic Independence*. Random House.
Gleeson, Shannon and Sampat, Prerna. 2018. "Immigrant Resistance in the Age of Trump." *New Labor Forum* 27(1): 86–95.
Glenn, Evelyn Nakano. 1992. "From Servitude to Service Work – Historical Continuities in the Racial Division of Paid Reproductive Labor." *Signs* 18(1): 1–43.
Gökarıksel, Banu, Neubert, Christopher, and Smith, Sara. 2019. "Demographic Fever Dreams: Fragile Masculinity and Population Politics in the Rise of the Global Right." *Signs: Journal of Women in Culture and Society* 44(3): 561–87.
Golash-Boza, Tanya Maria. 2015. *Deported: Immigrant Policing, Disposable Labor, and Global Capitalism*. Latina/o Sociology series. New York University Press.
Gorbachev, Mikhail. 1987. "Mikhail Gorbachev on Women and the Family." *Population and Development Review* 13(4): 757–9.
Gorbachev, Mikhail. 1988. *Perestroika: New Thinking for our Country and the World*. Harper & Row.
Gradskova, Yulia. 2019. "Women's International Democratic Federation, the 'Third World' and the Global Cold War from the late 1950s to the mid-1960s." *Women's History Review* 29(2): 270–88.
Gradskova, Yulia. 2021. *The Women's International Democratic Federation, the Global South, and the Cold War: Defending the Rights of Women of the "Whole World"?* Routledge.
Grandin, Greg. 2006. *Empire's Workshop: Latin America, the United States, and the Rise of the New Imperialism*. Metropolitan Books.
Grewal, Anup. 2022. "From *The Good Earth* to *Mother India*: Esthetic Circulations of Peasant Womanhood between India and China." *International Journal of Asian Studies* 19(2): 283–302.
Gutterman, Lauren Jae. 2012. "Another Enemy Within: Lesbian Wives, or the Hidden Threat to the Nuclear Family in Post-war America." *Gender & History* 24(2): 475–501.
Hancock, Peter. 2005. "Power, Women's Empowerment and the Gender Empowerment Measure: Voices from Sri Lankan Factory Women who Work in Export Processing Zones." *Labour Management in Development* 6(1): 3–23.
Hankivsky, Olena and Salnykova, Anastasiya. 2012. *Gender, Politics and Society in Ukraine*. University of Toronto Press.
Hansen, Thomas Blom. 1996. "Recuperating Masculinity: Hindu Nationalism, Violence and the Exorcism of the Muslim 'Other.'" *Critique of Anthropology* 16(2): 137–72.

Hansen, Thomas Blom. 1999. *The Saffron Wave: Democracy and Hindu Nationalism in Modern India*. Princeton University Press.
Harvey, David. 2007. *A Brief History of Neoliberalism*: Oxford University Press.
Heeks, Richard. 1990. "Technology Policy Making as a Social and Political Process: Liberalizing India's Software Policy." *Technology Analysis & Strategic Management* 2(3): 275–92.
Hinote, Brian P. and Webber, Gretchen R. 2012. "Drinking Toward Manhood: Masculinity and Alcohol in the Former USSR." *Men and Masculinities* 15(3): 292–310.
Hochschild, Arlie Russell. 2016. *Strangers in Their Own Land: Anger and Mourning on the American Right*. New Press.
Hochschild, Arlie Russell and Machung, Anne. 1989. *The Second Shift: Working Families and the Revolution at Home*. Avon Books.
Hondagneu-Sotelo, Pierrette. 2001. *Domestica: Immigrant Workers Cleaning and Caring in the Shadows of Affluence*. University of California Press.
International Monetary Fund. 2022. "Subsidies, Trade, and International Cooperation." Washington, DC: International Monetary Fund.
Irwin, Douglas A. 2020. *Free Trade Under Fire*, 5th edn. Princeton University Press.
Issoupova, Olga. 2000. "From Duty to Pleasure? Motherhood in Soviet and Post-Soviet Russia," in Sarah Ashwin (ed.), *Gender, State and Society in Soviet and Post-Soviet Russia*. Routledge, 30–54.
Jaffrelot, Christophe. 2021. *Modi's India: Hindu Nationalism and the Rise of Ethnic Democracy*. Princeton University Press.
Jain, Sonali and Swamy, Arun. 2020. "Hindu Nationalism, Identity Politics, and the Indian Diaspora in the United States," in John Stone, Rutledge M. Dennis, Polly Rizova, and Xiaoshuo Hou (eds), *The Wiley Blackwell Companion to Race, Ethnicity, and Nationalism*. Wiley-Blackwell, 165–81.
Janey, Bradley A., Plitin, Sergei, Muse-Burke, Janet L., and Vovk, Valintine M. 2009. "Masculinity in Post-Soviet Ukraine: An Exploratory Factor Analysis." *Culture, Society and Masculinities* 1(2): 137–54.
Jeffrey, Craig. 2010. "Timepass: Youth, Class, and Time among Unemployed Young Men in India." *American Ethnologist* 37(3): 465–81.
Jha, Sonal. 2022. "Unbecoming Men." *Third Text* 36(3): 278–92.
Johnson, Ericka. 2007. *Dreaming of a Mail-Order Husband: Russian–American Internet Romance*. Duke University Press.
Kaba, Mariame, Murakawa, Naomi, and Nopper, Tamara K. 2021. *We Do This 'til We Free Us : Abolitionist Organizing and Transforming Justice*. Haymarket Books.
Kabeer, Naila. 1994. *Reversed Realities: Gender Hierarchies in Development Thought*: Verso.
Kania, Ursula. 2022. "'Snake Flu,' 'Killer Bug,' and 'Chinese Virus': A Corpus-assisted Critical Discourse Analysis of Lexical Choices in Early UK Press Coverage of the COVID-19 Pandemic." *Frontiers in Artificial Intelligence* 5.

Kar, Sohini. 2018. *Financializing Poverty: Labor and Risk in Indian Microfinance*. Stanford University Press.

Kaul, Nitasha. 2021. "The Misogyny of Authoritarians in Contemporary Democracies." *International Studies Review* 23: 1619–45.

Kentikelenis, Alexander E. and Babb, Sarah. 2019. "The Making of Neoliberal Globalization: Norm Substitution and the Politics of Clandestine Institutional Change." *American Journal of Sociology* 124(6): 1720–62.

Keough, Leyla J. 2015. *Worker-Mothers on the Margins of Europe: Gender and Migration Between Moldova and Istanbul*. Indiana University Press.

Khan, Mehboob (dir.). 1957. *Mother India*. Mehboob Productions Private Ltd.

Kiblitskaya, Marina. 2000. "Russia's Female Breadwinners: The Changing Subjective Experience," in Sarah Ashwin (ed.), *Gender, State and Society in Soviet and Post-Soviet Russia*, Routledge, 55–70.

Kibria, Nazli, Bowman, Cara, and O'Leary, Megan. 2014. *Race and Immigration*. Polity Press.

Kim, Minjeong. 2018. *Elusive Belonging: Marriage Immigrants and "Multiculturalism" in Rural South Korea*. University of Hawai'i Press.

Kimmel, Michael S. 2003. "Globalization and its Mal(e)contents: The Gendered Moral and Political Economy of Terrorism." *International Sociology* 18(3): 603–20.

Kimmel, Michael S. 2008. *Guyland: The Perilous World Where Boys Become Men*. New York: HarperCollins.

Kimmel, Michael. 2013. *Angry White Men: American Masculinity at the End of an Era*. Nation Books.

Kinnvall, Catarina. 2019. "Populism, Ontological Insecurity and Hindutva: Modi and the Masculinization of Indian Politics." *Cambridge Review of International Affairs* 32(3): 283–302.

Kirkendall, Andrew J. 2010. *Paulo Freire and the Cold War Politics of Literacy*. University of North Carolina Press.

Klar, Rebecca and Kagubare, Ines. 2022. "Hillicon Valley – Pelosi Attack Raises Risks of Online Misogyny." *The Hill*, November 2.

Klasen, Stephan. 2006. "UNDP's Gender-related Measures: Some Conceptual Problems and Possible Solutions." *Journal of Human Development* 7(2): 243–74.

Klein, Naomi. 2007. *The Shock Doctrine: The Rise of Disaster Capitalism*. Picador.

Kligman, Gail. 1991. "Women and Reproductive Legislation in Romania: Implications for the Transition," in George W. Breslauer (ed.), *Dilemmas of Transition in the Soviet Union and Eastern Europe*. Center for Slavic and East European Studies and the Berkeley-Stanford Program in Soviet Studies, 141–66.

Knight, Melanie. 2020. "Reclaiming Motherhood and Family: How Black Mothers Use Entrepreneurship to Nurture Family and

Community," in Talia Esnard and Melanie Knight (eds), *Mothering and Entrepreneurship: Global Perspectives, Identities, and Complexities*. Demeter Press, 143–70.

Korek, Janusz (ed.). 2007. *From Sovietology to Postcoloniality: Poland and Ukraine from a Postcolonial Perspective*. Södertörns Högskola.

Kotusenko, Victor. 2007. "Labour Migration from Ukraine and its Ethical Implications." *Oikonomia* 3: 9–13.

Krippner, Greta R. 2005. "The Financialization of the American Economy." *Socio-economic Review* 3(2): 173–208.

Krishna, Sankaran. 2009. *Globalization and Postcolonialism: Hegemony and Resistance in the Twenty-first Century*. Rowman & Littlefield.

Kubicek, Paul. 2008. *The History of Ukraine*. The Greenwood Histories of the Modern Nations. Greenwood Press.

Kuehnast, Kathleen and Nechemias, Carol. 2004a. "Introduction: Women Navigating Change in Post-Soviet Currents," in Kathleen Kuehnast and Carol Nechemias (eds), *Post-Soviet Women Encountering Transition: Nation Building, Economic Survival, and Civic Activism*. Johns Hopkins University Press, 1–20.

Kuehnast, Kathleen and Nechemias, Carol (eds). 2004b. *Post-Soviet Women Encountering Transition: Nation Building, Economic Eurvival, and Civic Activism*. Johns Hopkins University Press.

Kukhterin, Sergei. 2000. "Fathers and Patriarchs in Communist and Post-Communist Russia," in Sarah Ashwin (ed.), *Gender, State and Society in Soviet and Post-Soviet Russia*. Routledge, 71–89.

LaFont, Suzanne. 2001. "One Step Forward, Two Steps Back: Women in Post-Communist Societies." *Communist and Post-Communist Studies* 34: 203–20.

Lan, Pei-Chia. 2003. "Maid or Madam? Filipina Migrant Workers and the Continuity of Domestic Labor." *Gender & Society* 17(2): 187–207.

Lan, Pei-Chia. 2006. *Global Cinderellas: Migrant Domestics and Newly Rich Employers in Taiwan*. Duke University Press.

Ledeneva, Alena V. 1998. *Russia's Economy of Favours: Blat, Networking, and Informal Exchange*. Cambridge University Press.

Lee, Ching Kwan. 1998. *Gender and the South China Miracle*. University of California Press.

Lengermann, Patricia M. and Niebrugge-Brantley, Jill. 1998. *The Women Founders: Sociology and Social Theory, 1830–1930: A Text/Reader*. McGraw-Hill.

Levitt, Peggy. 2001. *The Transnational Villagers*. University of California Press.

Levitt, Peggy, and Jaworsky, B. Nadya. 2007. "Transnational Migration Studies: Past Developments and Future Trends." *Annual Review of Sociology* 33(1): 129–56.

Liddle, Joanna and Joshi, Rama. 1989. *Daughters of Independence: Gender, Caste, and Class in India*. Rutgers University Press.

Limbaugh, Rush. 2016. "Latest Lib Assaults: Lesbian Farmers, Transgender Homeless Shelters, American Flag Ripped from Trucks, aired August 17, 2016." https://www.rushlimbaugh.com/daily/2016/08/17/.

Lindio-McGovern, L. 2003. "Labor Export in the Context of Globalization – The Experience of Filipino Domestic Workers in Rome." *International Sociology* 18(3): 513–34.

Lissyutkina, Larissa. 1999. "Empancipation without Feminism: The Historical and Socio-cultural Context of the Women's Movement in Russia," in Sue Bridger (ed.), *Women and Political Change: Persepctives from East-Central Europe*. St. Martin's Press, 168–87.

Littler, Jo. 2017. *Against Meritocracy*. Routledge.

Löfflmann, Georg. 2022. "'Enemies of the People': Donald Trump and the Security Imaginary of America First." *British Journal of Politics and International Relations* 24(3): 543–60.

Louis, W. M. Roger and Robinson, Ronald. 1994. "The Imperialism of Decolonization." *Journal of Imperial and Commonwealth History* 22(3): 462–511.

Lugones, María. 2007. "Heterosexualism and the Colonial/Modern Gender System." *Hypatia* 22(1): 186–219.

Lutz, Helma. 2010. "Gender in the Migratory Process." *Journal of Ethnic and Migration Studies* 36(10): 1647–63.

McClintock, Anne. 1995. *Imperial Leather: Race, Gender, and Sexuality in the Colonial Contest*. Routledge.

McDuie-Ra, Duncan. 2013. "Beyond the 'Exclusionary City': North-east Migrants in Neo-liberal Delhi." *Urban Studies* 50(8): 1625–40.

McKay, Steven C. 2007. "Filipino Sea Men: Constructing Masculinities in an Ethnic Labour Niche." *Journal of Ethnic and Migration Studies* 33(2): 617–33.

McLean, Martin. 1981. "The Political Context of Educational Development: A Commentary on the Theories of Development Underlying the World Bank Education Sector Policy Paper." *Comparative Education* 17(2): 157–62.

McClintock, Ann. 1995. *Imperial Leather: Race, Gender and Sexuality in the Colonial Contest*. Routledge.

Mader, Philip. 2015. *The Political Economy of Microfinance: Financializing Poverty*, in Toby Carroll, M. Ramesh, Darryl S. L. Jarvis, and Paul Cammack (eds), *Studies in the Political Economy of Public Policy*. Palgrave Macmillan.

Malik, Ashok. 2015. "The India that Made Modi," in François Godement (ed.), *What Does India Think?* European Council on Foreign Relations.

Manaev, Georgy. 2022. "What is 'Muzhik' in Russian, and Why is it Cool to Be One?" Russia Beyond. https://www.rbth.com/lifestyle/334708-what-is-muzhik-in-russian.

Mandel, Ruth and Humphrey, Caroline. 2002. *Markets and Moralities: Ethnographies of Postsocialism*. Berg.

Mankekar, Purnima. 1999. *Screening Culture, Viewing Politics: An Ethnography of Television, Womanhood, and the Nation in Postcolonial India.* Duke University Press.

Marangos, John. 2004. "Was Shock Therapy Consistent with Democracy?" *Review of Social Economy* 62(2): 221–43.

Martineau, Harriet. 1838. *How to Observe: Morals and Manners.* Anthon's Series of Classical Works for Schools and Colleges. Harper & Bros.

Marx, Karl, Engels, Friedrich, and Tucker, Robert C. 1978. *The Marx–Engels Reader*, 2nd edn. Norton.

Massey, Douglas S. and Denton, Nancy A. 1993. *American Apartheid: Segregation and the Making of the Underclass.* Harvard University Press.

Massey, Douglas S., Durand, Jorge, and Malone, Nolan J. 2005. "Principles of Operation: Theories of International Migration," in Marcelo M. Suárez-Orozco, Carola Suárez-Orozco, and Desirée Baolian Qin (eds), *The New Immigration: An Interdisciplinary Reader.* Routledge, 21–33.

Matlon, Jordanna. 2016. "Racial Capitalism and the Crisis of Black Masculinity." *American Sociological Review* 81(5): 1014–38.

Mayo, Katherine. 1927. *Mother India.* Harcourt, Brace & Co.

Meerman, Marije (dir.). 2001. *Chain of Love/Kenten van Liefde. A Film by Mariki Meerman.* Brooklyn, NY: First Run/Icarus Films.

Meghji, Ali. 2021. *Decolonizing Sociology : An Introduction, Decolonizing the Curriculum.* Polity Press.

Mehta, Aasha Kapur. 1996. "Recasting Indices for Developing Countries: A Gender Empowerment Measure." *Economic and Political Weekly*: WS80–WS86.

Meshcherkina, Elena. 2000. "New Russian Men: Masculinity Regained?" in Sarah Ashwin (ed.), *Gender, State and Society in Soviet and Post-Soviet Russia.* Routledge.

Meszaros, Julia. 2017. "Marriage Migration as a Pathway to Citizenship: Filipina Brides, Economic Security, and Ideas of Global Hypergamy," in Anne J. Kershen, Asuncion Fresnoza-Flot, and Gwénola Ricordeau (eds), *International Marriages and Marital Citizenship: Southeast Asian Women on the Move.* Routledge.

Miller, Carol and Razavi, Shahra. 1995. "Gender Mainstreaming: A Study of Efforts by the UNDP, the World Bank and the ILO to Institutionalize Gender Issues." UNRISD Occasional Paper.

Milkman, Ruth. 1987. *Gender at Work.* Urbana: University of Illinois Press.

Mink, Gwendolyn. 1995. *The Wages of Motherhood: Inequality in the Welfare State, 1917–1942.* Cornell University Press.

Mirowski, Philip and Plehwe, Dieter. 2009. *The Road from Mont Pèlerin: The Making of the Neoliberal Thought Collective.* Harvard University Press.

Mongia, Radhika. 2018. *Indian Migration and Empire: A Colonial Genealogy of the Modern State.* Duke University Press.

Moore, Joseph and Anderson, Gillian. 2020. "Reproducing Precarity: Representations of Mompreneurship, Family, and Work in a British Columbian Parenting Magazine," in Talia Esnard and Melanie Knight (eds), *Mothering and Entrepreneurship: Global Perspectives, Identities and Complexities*. Demeter Press, 42–71.

Moreton, Bethany. 2022. "The US Christians Who Pray for Putin: The Mystical Connection between White Southern Nostalgia, the Global Family Values, and Russia." *Boston Review.*

Morrison, Andrew R., Schiff, Maurice, and Sjöblom, Mirja (eds). 2008. *The International Migration of Women*. World Bank and Palgrave Macmillan.

Muschik, Eva-Maria. 2022. "Towards a Global History of International Organizations and Decolonization." Special issue introduction, *Journal of Global History* 17(2): 173–90.

Muller, Jan-Werner. 2016. "Real Citizens: Democracy, Elections, Politics, Populism." *Boston Review*, October 26.

Nielsen, Kenneth Bo and Nilsen, Alf Gunvald. 2021. "Love Jihad and the Governance of Gender and Intimacy in Hindu Nationalist Statecraft." *Religions* 12(12): 1068.

Nilsen, Ella. 2021. "These Workers Were Left Out of the New Deal. They've Been Fighting for Better Pay Ever Since." *vox.com*, May 18.

Nixon, Rob. 1997. "Of Balkan and Bantustans: Ethnic Cleansing and the Crisis in National Legitimation," in Anne McClintock, Aamir Mufti and Ella Shoh (eds), *Dangerous Liaisons: Gender, Nation, and Postcolonial Perspectives*. University of Minnesota Press, 69–88.

Nyberg-Sørensen, Ninna, Van Hear, Nicholas, and Engberg-Pedersen, Poul. 2002. "The Migration–Development Nexus Evidence and Policy Options State-of-the-Art Overview." *International Migration* 40(5): 3–47.

Odem, Mary. 1991. "Single Mothers, Delinquent Daughters, and the Juvenile Court in Early 20th Century Los Angeles." *Journal of Social History* 25(1): 27–43.

Oishi, Nana. 2005. *Women in Motion: Globalization, State Policies, and Labor Migration in Asia*. Stanford University Press.

Orenstein, Peggy. 2011. *Cinderella Ate My Daughter: Dispatches from the Front Lines of the New Girlie-Girl Culture*. Harper Paperbacks.

Osterman, Paul. 1999. *Securing Prosperity: The American Labor Market, How It Has Changed and What We Can Do about It*. Princeton University Press.

Oxfam International. 2022. "Ten Richest Men Double their Fortunes in Pandemic while Incomes of 99 percent of Humanity Fall." Oxfam International. https://www.oxfam.org/en/press-releases/ten-richest-men-double-their-fortunes-pandemic-while-incomes-99-percent-humanity

Oza, Rupal. 2006. *The Making of Neoliberal India: Nationalism, Gender, and the Paradoxes of Globalization*. Routledge.

Palenga-Möllenbeck, Ewa. 2013. "Care Chains in Eastern and Central Europe: Male and Female Domestic Work at the Intersections of Gender, Class, and Ethnicity." *Journal of Immigrant & Refugee Studies* 11(4): 364–83.

Pande, Mrinal. 2022. "Gendered Analysis of Hindutva Imaginaries:

Manipulation of Symbols for Ethnonationalist Projects." *Journal of Modern European History* 20(3): 407–22.

Parreñas, Rhacel Salazar. 2000. "Migrant Filipina Domestic Workers and the International Division of Reproductive Labor." *Gender & Society* 14(4): 560–80.

Parreñas, Rhacel. 2001. *Servants of Globalization: Women, Migration and Domestic Work*. Stanford University Press.

Patel, Reena. 2010. *Working the Night Shift: Women in India's Call Center Industry*. Stanford University Press.

Pateman, Carole. 1988. *The Sexual Contract*. Stanford University Press.

Paunksnis, Runa Chakraborty and Paunksnis, Šarūnas. 2020. "Masculine Anxiety and 'New Indian Woman' in the Films of Anurag Kashyap." *South Asian Popular Culture* 18(2): 149–62.

Peck, Jamie. 2010. *Constructions of Neoliberal Reason*. Oxford University Press.

Phillips, Joe and Yi, Joseph 2018. "Charlottesville Paradox: The 'Liberalizing' Alt-Right, 'Authoritarian' Left, and Politics of Dialogue." *Society* 55(3): 221–8.

Pollitt, Katha. 2012. "Ann Romney, Working Woman?" *The Nation*, April 18.

Pozen, David E. 2008. "We Are All Entrepreneurs Now." *Wake Forest Law Review* 43: 283–40.

Prügl, Elisabeth. 2017. "Neoliberalism with a Feminist Face: Crafting a New Hegemony at the World Bank." *Feminist Economics* 23(1): 30–53.

Puglisi, Rosaria. 2003. "The Rise of the Ukrainian Oligarchs." *Democratization* 10(3): 99–123.

Puar, Jasbir K. 2007. *Terrorist Assemblages: Homonationalism in Queer Times*. Duke University Press.

Pula, Besnik. 2018. *Globalization Under and After Socialism: The Evolution of Transnational Capital in Central and Eastern Europe*. Stanford University Press.

Quindlen, Anna. 2005. "The Good Enough Mother." *Newsweek*, February 20.

Radhakrishnan, Smitha. 2007. "Rethinking Knowledge for Development: Transnational Knowledge Professionals and the New India." *Theory and Society* 36(2): 141–59.

Radhakrishnan, Smitha. 2009. "Professional Women, Good Families: Respectable Femininity and the Cultural Politics of a 'New' India." *Qualitative Sociology* 32(2): 195–212.

Radhakrishnan, Smitha. 2011. *Appropriately Indian: Gender and Culture in a New Transnational Class*. Duke University Press.

Radhakrishnan, Smitha. 2014. "Subverting the Microfinance Myth: Gendered Livelihoods in Urban India's Slums." *Oppositional Conversations* 1(3).

Radhakrishnan, Smitha. 2018. "Empowerment, Declined: Paradoxes of

Microfinance and Gendered Subectivity in Urban India." *Signs: Journal of Women, Culture, and Society* 44(1): 83–105.

Radhakrishnan, Smitha and Solari, Cinzia. 2015. "Empowered Women, Failed Patriarchs: Neoliberalism and Global Gender Anxieties." *Sociology Compass* 9(9): 784–802.

Rai, Rohini. 2022. "From Colonial 'Mongoloid' to Neoliberal 'Northeastern': Theorising 'Race', Racialization and Racism in Contemporary India." *Asian Ethnicity* 23(3): 442–62.

Raj, Dhooleka Sarhadi. 2015. "The Overseas Citizen of India and Emigrant Infrastructure: Tracing the Deterritorializations of Diaspora Strategies." *Geoforum* 59: 159–68.

Rajagopal, Arvind. 2001. *Politics after Television: Religious Nationalism and the Reshaping of the Indian Public*. Cambridge University Press.

Rajagopal, Arvind. 2019. "The Cold War as Nightmare Envy: A View from India." India Seminar, https://www.india-seminar.com/2019/719/719_arvind_rajagopal.htm.

Rajan, Rajeshwari Sunder. 1993. *Real and Imagined Women: Gender, Culture, and Postcolonialism*. Routledge.

Rajaraman, V. 2015. "History of Computing in India: 1955–2010." *IEEE Annals of the History of Computing* 37(1): 24–35.

Raju, K. D. 2020. "Doklam and Beyond: Revisiting the India–China Territorial Disputes: An International Law Perspective." *India Review* 19(1): 85–105.

Ramamurthy, Priti. 2006. "The Modern Girl in India in the Interwar Years: Interracial Intimacies, International Competition, and Historical Eclipsing." *Women's Studies Quarterly* 34(1/2): 197–226.

Ramaswamy, Sumathi. 2010. *The Goddess and the Nation: Mapping Mother India*. Duke University Press.

Ramirez, Hernan. 2011. "Masculinity in the Workplace: The Case of Mexican Immigrant Gardeners." *Men and Masculinities* 14(1): 97–116.

Ray, Raka and Katzenstein, Mary. 2005. "In the Beginning, There Was the Nehruvian State," in Raka Ray and Mary Fainsod Katzenstein (eds), *Social Movements in India: Poverty, Power, and Politics*. Oxford University Press, 1–31.

Ray, Sangeeta. 2000. *En-gendering India: Woman and Nation in Colonial and Postcolonial Narratives*. Duke University Press.

Reeves, Madeleine. 2014. *Border Work: Spatial Lives of the State in Rural Central Asia*. Culture and Society after Socialism series. Cornell University Press.

Riabchuk, Anastasia. 2012. "Homeless Men and the Crisis of Masculinity in Contemporary Ukraine," in Olena Hankivsky and Anastasia Salnykova (eds), *Gender, Politics and Society in Ukraine*. Toronto Press, 204–21.

Riabchuk, Mykola. 2012. "Ukraine's 'Muddling Through': National Identity and Postcommunist Transition." *Communist and Post-Communist Studies* 45(3–4): 439–46.

Riabov, Oleg and Riabova, Tatiana. 2014a. "The Remasculinization of Russia? Gender, Nationalism, and the Legitimation of Power Under Vladimir Putin." *Problems of Post-Communism* 61(2): 23–35.
Riabov, Oleg and Riabova, Tatiana. 2014b. "The Decline of Gayropa? How Russia Intends to Save the World." *Eurozine*, February 5.
Rios, Victor M. 2011. *Punished: Policing the Lives of Black and Latino Boys*. New York University Press.
Rivoli, Pietra. 2014. *The Travels of a T-Shirt in the Global Economy: An Economist Examines the Markets, Power, and Politics of World Trade. New Preface and Epilogue with Updates on Economic Issues and Main Characters*: John Wiley & Sons.
Rodriguez, Robyn M. 2002. "Migrant Heroes: Nationalism, Citizenship and the Politics of Filipino Migrant Labor." *Citizenship Studies* 6(3): 341–56.
Rodriguez, Robyn M. 2010. *Migrants for Export: How the Philippine State Brokers Labor to the World*. University of Minnesota Press.
Rofel, Lisa. 1999. *Other Modernities: Gendered Yearnings in China after Socialism*. University of California Press.
Roos, Jerome E. 2019. *Why Not Default? The Political Economy of Sovereign Debt*. Princeton University Press.
Rose, Nikolas. 1999. *Powers of Freedom: Reframing Political Thought*. Cambridge University Press.
Rosin, Hanna. 2010. "The End of Men." *The Atlantic*, July/August.
Rotkirch, Anna. 2000. *The Man Question: Loves and Lives in Late 20th Century Russia*. University of Helsinki.
Rotkirch, Anna and Temkina, Anna. 1996. "What Does the (Russian) Woman Want? – Women Psychoanalysts Talk," in Anna Rotkirch and Elina Haavio-Mannila (eds), *Women's Voices in Russia Today*. Darmouth, 49–68.
Rottenberg, Catherine. 2014. "The Rise of Neoliberal Feminism." *Cultural Studies* 28(3): 418–37.
Rottenberg, Catherine. 2017. "Neoliberal Feminism and the Future of Human Capital." *Signs: Journal of Women in Culture and Society* 42(2): 329-48.
Rottenberg, Catherine. 2019. "Women Who Work: The Limits of the Neoliberal Feminist Paradigm." *Gender, Work & Organization* 26(8): 1073–82.
Rotter, Andrew J. 1994. "Gender Relations, Foreign Relations: The United States and South Asia, 1947–1964." *Journal of American History* 81(2): 518–42.
Roy, Ananya. 2010. *Poverty Capital: Microfinance and the Making of Development*. Routledge.
Roy, Ananya. 2012. "Subjects of Risk: Technologies of Gender in the Making of Millennial Modernity." *Public Culture* 24(1/66): 131–55.
Roy, Arundhati. 2020. "The Pandemic is a Portal." *Financial Times Online*, April 3.

Roy, Srila. 2012. *Remembering Revolution: Gender, Violence, and Subjectivity in India's Naxalbari Movement*. Oxford University Press.
Rubchak, Marian (ed.). 2015. *New Imaginaries: Youthful Reconstruction of Ukraine's Cultural Paradigm*. Berghahn Press.
Sakwa, Richard. 2017. "The Ukraine Syndrome and Europe: Between Norms and Space." *Soviet & Post-Soviet Review* 44(1): 9–31.
Salzinger, Leslie. 2003. *Genders in Production: Making Workers in Mexico's Global Factories*. University of California Press.
Sandberg, Sheryl. 2013. *Lean In: Women, Work, and the Will to Lead*. Alfred A. Knopf.
Sanyal, Devapriya. 2021. *Gendered Modernity and Indian Cinema: The Women in Satyajit Ray's Films*: Routledge.
Sardenberg, Cecília. 2008. "Liberal vs. Liberating Empowerment: A Latin American Feminist Perspective on Conceptualising Women's Empowerment 1." *IDS Bulletin* 39(6): 18–27.
Sardenberg, Cecília. 2010. "Women's Empowerment in Brazil: Tensions in Discourse and Practice." *Development* 53(2): 232–38.
Sassen, Saskia. 1988. *The Mobility of Labor and Capital: A Study in International Investment and Labor Flow*. Cambridge University Press.
Sassen, Saskia. 1998. *Globalization and its Discontents*. New Press.
Sassen, Saskia. 2003. "Strategic Instantiations of Gendering in the Global Economy," in Pierrette Hondagneu-Sotelo (ed.), *Gender and US Immigration: Contemporary Trends*. University of California Press, 43–60.
Saxena, Swati. 2016. "Revisiting Charles Dickens' *Hard Times*: Narendra Modi and the Myth of a Self-made Man." *Indian Express*, May 2.
Schotten, C. Heike. 2016. "Homonationalism: From Critique to Diagnosis, or, We are All Homonational Now." *International Feminist Journal of Politics* 18: 351–70.
Schulze, Brigitte. 2002. "'The Cinematic 'Discovery of India': Mehboob's Re-Invention of the Nation in Mother India." *Social Scientist* 30 (9/10): 72–87.
Scott, Joan. 1988. *Gender and the Politics of History*. Columbia University Press.
Sen, Gita and Grown, Caren. 1985. "Development Alternatives, Crises and Alternative Visions." *New Delhi: DAWN Secretariat*.
Shalal, Andrea. 2022. "World Bank Says Ukraine Has Tenfold Increase in Poverty Due to War." *Reuters*, October 15.
Sharma, Aradhana. 2008. *Logics of Empowerment: Development, Gender, and Governance in Neoliberal India*. University of Minnesota Press.
Sherman, Rachel. 1999. "From State Introversion to State Extension in Mexico: Modes of Emigrant Incorporation, 1900–1997." *Theory and Society* 28(6): 835–78.
Shevtsova, Maryna. 2020. "Fighting 'Gayropa': Europeanization and Instrumentalization of LGBTI Rights in Ukrainian Public Debate." *Problems of Post-Communism* 67(6): 500–10.
Shuster, Stef M. and Westbrook, Laurel. 2022. "Reducing the Joy Deficit in

Sociology: A Study of Transgender Joy." *Social Problems.* https://doi.org/10.1093/socpro/spac034.
Silva, Jennifer M. 2019. *We're Still Here: Pain and Politics in the Heart of America.* Oxford University Press.
Simon, Barbara Levy. 1994. *The Empowerment Tradition in American Social Work: A History.* Columbia University Press.
Sinha, Aseema. 2016. *Globalizing India: How Global Rules and Markets are Shaping India's Rise to Power.* Cambridge University Press.
Sivaramakrishnan, K. and Agrawal, Arun. 2003. *Regional Modernities: The Cultural Politics of Development in India.* Oxford University Press.
Slaughter, Anne-Marie. 2015. *Unfinished Business: Women, Men, Work, Family.* Random House.
Slobodian, Quinn. 2018. *Globalists: The End of Empire and the Birth of Neoliberalism.* Harvard University Press.
Slootmaeckers, Koen. 2019. "Nationalism as Competing Masculinities: Homophobia as a Technology of Othering for Hetero- and Homonationalism." *Theory and Society* 48: 239–65.
Smith, Vicki. 2001. *Crossing the Great Divide: Worker Risk and Opportunity in the New Economy.* ILR Press.
Solari, Cinzia. 2011. "Between 'Europe' and 'Africa': Building the New Ukraine on the Shoulders of Migrant Women," in Marian J. Rubchak (ed.), *Mapping Difference: The Many Faces of Women in Ukraine.* Berghahn Books, 23–46.
Solari, Cinzia. 2014. "'Prostitutes' and 'Defectors': How the Ukrainian State Constructs Women Emigrants to Italy and the USA." *Journal of Ethnic and Migration Studies* 40(11): 1817–35.
Solari, Cinzia D. 2017. *On the Shoulders of Grandmothers: Gender, Migration, and Post-Soviet Nation-state Building.* Routledge.
Solari, Cinzia D. 2019. "Transnational Moral Economies: The Value of Monetary and Social Remittances in Transnational Families." *Current Sociology* 67(5): 760–77.
Sperling, Valerie. 2015. *Sex, Politics, and Putin: Political Legitimacy in Russia.* Oxford University Press.
Spivak, G. C. 1981. "'Draupadi' by Mahasveta Devi," trans. with a foreword by Gayatri Chakravorty Spivak. *Critical Inquiry.* University of Chicago Press. https://www.journals.uchicago.edu/doi/10.1086/448160.
Spivak, G. C. 1985. "Can the Subaltern Speak?" in Patrick Williams and Laura Chrisman (eds), *Colonial Discourse and Postcolonial Theory.* Columbia University Press, 66–111.
Srikanth, H. 2018. "Look East Policy, Sub-regional Connectivity Projects and Northeast India," in Atul Sarma and Saswati Choudhury (eds), *Mainstreaming the Northeast in India's Look and Act East Policy.* Springer Singapore, 213–31.
Srivastava, Ravi. 2020. "Growing Precarity, Circular Migration, and the Lockdown in India." *Indian Journal of Labour Economics* 63(1): 79–86.

References

Standing, Guy. 2011. *The Precariat: The New Dangerous Class*. Bloombury.
Stokke, Olav. 1995. *Aid and Political Conditionality*. Routledge.
Stone, Pamela. 2007. *Opting Out? Why Women Really Quit Careers and Head Home*. University of California Press.
Stone, Pamela and Lovejoy, Meg. 2019. *Opting Back In: What Really Happens When Mothers Go Back to Work*. University of California Press.
Strohl, David James. 2019. "Love Jihad in India's Moral Imaginaries: Religion, Kinship, and Citizenship in Late Liberalism." *Contemporary South Asia* 27(1): 27–39.
Stryker, Susan. 2017. *Transgender History*. Seal Press.
Sufian, Abu. 2022. "Geopolitics of the NRC-CAA in Assam: Impact on Bangladesh–India Relations." *Asian Ethnicity* 23(3): 556–86.
Sunil, Babu C.T. 2013. "Sociology, Village Studies and the Ford Foundation." *Economic and Political Weekly* 48(52): 113–18.
Suzuki, Nobue. 2017. "Postcolonial Desires, Partial Citizenship, and Transnational 'Un-mothers': Contexts and Lives of Filipina Marriage Migrants in Japan," in Anne J. Kershen, Asuncion Fresnoza-Flot, and Gwénola Ricordeau (eds), *International Marriages and Marital Citizenship: Southeast Asian Women on the Move*. Routledge.
Sweetland, Scott R. 1996. "Human Capital Theory: Foundations of a Field of Inquiry." *Review of Educational Research* 66(3): 341–59.
Swidler, Ann. 1986. "Culture in Action: Symbols and Strategies." *American Sociological Review* 51: 273–6.
Syrda, Joanna. 2020. "Spousal Relative Income and Male Psychological Distress." *Personality and Social Psychology Bulletin* 46: 976–92.
Tadiar, Neferti Xina M. 2004. *Fantasy Production: Sexual Economies and Other Philippine Consequences for the New World Order*. Hong Kong University Press.
Tadiar, Neferti Xina M. 2009. *Things Fall Away: Philippine Historical Experience and the Makings of Globalization*. Post-contemporary Interventions series. Duke University Press.
Taylor, Keeanga-Yamahtta. 2019. *Race for Profit: How Banks and the Real Estate Industry Undermined Black Homeownership*. University of North Carolina Press.
Thai, Hung Cam. 2002. "Clashing Dreams: Highly Educated Overseas Brides and Low-Wage US Husbands," in Barbara Ehrenreich and Arlie Hochschild (eds), *Global Woman: Nannies, Maids, and Sex Workers in the New Economy*. Metropolitan Books, 230–53.
Tharoor, Shashi. 2018. *Inglorious Empire: What the British Did to India*. Penguin.
Tolentino, Jia. 2016. "How 'Empowerment' Became Something for Women to Buy." *New York Times Magazine*, April 12.
Tolstokorova, Alissa. 2010. "Where Have all the Mothers Gone? The Gendered Effect of Labour Migration and Transnationalism on the Institution of Parenthood in Ukraine." *Anthropology of East Europe Review* 28(1): 184–214.

Torbakov, Igor. 2014. "This is a Strife of Slavs among Themselves": Understanding Russian–Ukrainian Relations as the Conflict of Contested Identities," in Klaus Bachmann and Igor Lyubashenko (eds), *Maidan Uprising, Separatism and Foreign Intervention: Ukraine's Complex Transition*. Peter Lang, 183–205.

Towns, Ann. 2009. "The Status of Women as a Standard of 'Civilization.'" *European Journal of International Relations* 15(4): 681–706.

Tracy, Natalicia, Sieber, Tim, and Moir, Susan. 2014. "Invisible No More: Domestic Workers Organizing in Massachusetts and Beyond." *ScholarWorks: University of Massachusetts Boston*.

Upadhyay, Smriti. 2022. "'(Hindu) Workers of India, Unite!': How Class Politics Shape the Consolidation of Right-Wing Hegemony in India," in Smitha Radhakrishnan and Gowri Vijayakumar (eds), *Sociology of South Asia: Postcolonial Legacies, Global Imaginaries*. Palgrave Macmillan, 93–119.

Utrata, Jennifer. 2015. *Women Without Men: Single Mothers and Family Change in the New Russia*. Cornell University Press.

Utrata, Jennifer. 2019. "Invisible Labor and Women's Double Binds: Collusive Femininity and Masculine Drinking in Russia." *Gender & Society* 33: 911–34.

Valdés, Juan Gabriel. 1995. *Pinochet's Economists: The Chicago School of Economics in Chile*. Cambridge University Press.

Valocchi, Steve. 1994. "The Racial Basis of Capitalism and the State, and the Impact of the New Deal on African Americans." *Social Problems* 41(3): 347–62.

Veer, Peter van der. 2005. "Virtual India: Indian IT Labor and the Nation-State," in Thomas Blom Hansen and Finn Stepputat (eds), *Sovereign Bodies: Citizens, Migrants, and States in a Postcolonial World*. Princeton University Press, 276–90.

Verdery, Katherine. 1994. "From Parent-State to Family Patriarchs: Gender and Nation in Contemporary Eastern Europe." *East European Politics and Societies* 8(2): 225–55.

Verdery, Katherine. 1996. "Nationalism, Postsocialism, and Space in Eastern Europe." *Social Research* 63(1): 77–95.

Wacquant, Loïc J. D. 2009. *Punishing the Poor: The Neoliberal Government of Social Insecurity*. Politics, History, and Culture series. Duke University Press.

Walter, Nicholas, Bourgois, Philippe, and Loinaz, H. Margarita. 2004. "Masculinity and Undocumented Labor Migration: Injured Latino Day Laborers in San Francisco." *Social Science & Medicine* 59: 1159–68.

Walton, John and Ragin, Charles. 1990. "Global and National Sources of Political Protest: Third World Responses to the Debt Crisis." *American Sociological Review* 55(6): 876–90.

Wanner, Catherine. 2005. "Money, Morality and New Forms of Exchange in Postsocialist Ukraine." *Ethnos* 70(4): 515–37.

References

Weber, Heloise and Berger, Mark T. 2009. "Human (In)Security and Development in the 21st Century." *Third World Quarterly* 30(1): 263–70.
Wee, Lionel and Brooks, Ann. 2012. "Negotiating Gendered Subjectivity in the Enterprise Culture: Metaphor and Entrepreneurial Discourses." *Gender, Work & Organization* 19(6): 573–91.
Weinbaum, Alys Eve, Thomas, Lynn M., Ramamurthy, Priti, Poiger, Uta G., Dong, Madeleine Yue, and Barlow, Tani. 2008. *The Modern Girl Around the World: Consumption, Modernity, and Globalization*. Duke University Press.
Weitz, Eric D. 2018. "The Heroic Man and the Ever-Changing Woman: Gender and Politics in European Communism, 1917–1950," in Laura L. Frader and Sonya O. Rose (eds), *Gender and Class in Modern Europe*. Cornell University Press, pp. 311–52.
Wise, Judith Bula. 2005. *Empowerment Practice with Families in Distress*. Columbia University Press.
Wise, Raúl Delgado and Martin, David T. 2015. "The Political Economy of Global Labour Arbitrage," in Kees van der Pijl (ed.), *Handbook of the International Political Economy of Production*. Edward Elgar Publishing, pp. 59–75.
Wolfe, Anna. 2022. "State Files Lawsuit to Recoup $24 Million in Welfare Funds from Brett Favre, WWE Wrestlers and 34 Other People or Companies." *Mississippi Today*, May 9.
Wood, Elizabeth A. 2001. "The Trial of the New Woman: Citizens-in-Training in the New Soviet Republic." *Gender & History* 13(3): 524–45.
Wood, Elizabeth A. 2016. "Hypermasculinity as a Scenario of Power: Vladimir Putin's Iconic Rule, 1999–2008." *International Feminist Journal of Politics* 18(3): 329–50.
Wood, Elizabeth A. 2018. "Class and Gender at Loggerheads in the Early Soviet State: Who Should Organize the Female Proletariat and How?" in Laura L. Frader and Sonya O. Rose (eds), *Gender and Class in Modern Europe*. Cornell University Press, pp. 294–310.
Woolley, Ursula. 2022. "Ukraine and Putin's Post-Soviet Imperialism." *Political Insight* 13(1): 15–17.
Wright, Erik Olin and Dwyer, Rachel. 2001. "The American Jobs Machine: Is the New Economy Creating Good Jobs?" *Boston Review* 25, December 1.
Wright, Melissa. 2006. *Disposable Women and Other Myths of Global Capitalism*. Routledge.
Yadav, Vikash and Kirk, Jason A. 2018. "State Homophobia? India's Shifting UN Positions on LGBTQ Issues." *Globalizations* 15(5): 670–84.
Yeung, Wei-Jun Jean and Mu, Zheng. 2020. "Migration and Marriage in Asian Contexts." *Journal of Ethnic and Migration Studies* 46(14): 2863–79.
Yuval-Davis, Nira. 1997. *Gender and Nation*. Sage Publications.
Yuval-Davis, Nira, Wemyss, Georgie, and Cassidy, Kathryn. 2019. *Bordering*. Polity Press.
Zavisca, Jane. 2003. "Contesting Capitalism at the Post-Soviet Dacha: The

Meaning of Food Cultivation for Urban Russians." *Slavic Review* 62(4): 786–810.
Zdravomyslova, Elena. 2010. "Working Mothers and Nannies: Commercialization of Childcare and Modifications in the Gender Contract (A Sociological Essay)." *Anthropology of East Europe Review* 28(2): 200–25.
Zdravomyslova, Elena and Temkina, Anna. 2013. "The Crisis of Masculinity in Late Soviet Discourse." *Russian Social Science Review* 54(1): 40–61.
Zhang, D. 2022. "The Construction of National Image of China by English World Media in Public Health Emergencies." *Journal of Environmental and Public Health* 2022: 9669941.
Zherebkin, Sergei. 2006. "'Male Fantasies' in Ukraine: 'Fucking Women and Building Nation,'" in Edith Saurer, Margareth Lanzinger, and Elisabeth Frysak (eds), *Women's Movements: Networks and Debates in Post-Communist Countries in the 19th and 20th Centuries*. Böhlau Verlag, 268–79.
Zhurzhenko, Tatiana. 2001. "Free Market Ideology and New Women's Identities in Post-socialist Ukraine." *European Journal of Women's Studies* 8(1): 29–49.
Zhurzhenko, Tatiana. 2004a. "Families in the Ukraine: Between Postponed Modernization, Neo-Familialism and Economic Survival." *Contemporary Perspectives in Family Research* 5: 187–209.
Zhurzhenko, Tatiana. 2004b. "Strong Women, Weak State: Family Politics and Nation Building in Post-Soviet Ukraine," in Kathleen Kuehnast and Carol Nechemias (eds), *Post-Soviet Women Encountering Transition: Nation Building, Economic Survival, and Civic Activism*. Johns Hopkins University Press, 23–43.
Zhurzhenko, Tatiana. 2012. "Gender, Nation, and Reproduction: Demographic Discourses and Politics in Ukraine after the Orange Revolution," in Olena Hankivsky and Anastasiya Salnykova (eds), *Gender, Politics, and Society in Ukraine*. University of Toronto Press. 131–52.
Zinets, Natalia. 2022. "Ukraine Appoints Anti-corruption Prosecutor, Vows to Meet EU Entry Demands." *Reuters*, July 28.

Index

Asian immigrants, US
   Asian Americans and COVID-19 pandemic 152
   Hart–Celler Act (1965) 27
austerity policies 70, 71, 152
authoritarian populism *see* Modi, N.; Putin, V.; Trump, D.

Becker, G. 54, 63
Black Americans and people of color
   Civil Rights Movement 26–7
   men 76, 80–1, 124, 145–7
   women 23, 24–5, 26, 28–9, 76
   Black Lives Matter (BLM) protests 146
Bloch, A. 117
Bockman, J. and Eyal, G. 67
Bonikowski, B. 126
Brazil 50, 91, 149
breadwinner status 75, 123, 125, 127
Breines, W. 26

Calkin, S. 62
capitalism 5
   consumer-oriented nuclear family 27–8
   India: forging nationalism between socialism and 34–9
   socialism and postcoloniality 20–2
   see also modernity/modernization
childcare *see* hetero-patriarchal/nuclear family; motherhood
Chile 67

China 84, 89, 91, 149
"choices"
   full-time motherhood 76–7, 79
   marriage migrants 112–13
   post-Soviet and postcolonial countries 33–4, 76, 86–7, 96–8
Christianity
   Eastern Europe 110
   Russia 134
   United States 136, 143
Civil Rights Movement, US 26–7
Clinton, B. 82
Clinton, H. 146, 147
Cohen, R. 149
Cold War 4–5, 42
   competing visions/ideologies 20–2, 44–8
   end of 58, 66
   see also Soviet Union, collapse of
   human capital theory 55
   Latin America 67
   South and Southeast Asian countries 34–5
   US policies 27, 28, 29, 158
colonialism 3–4
   anti-colonial movements 35–6, 45, 125
   binary gender identities 8
   decolonization 27
   status of women 77–8
   see also imperialism and hegemony, US; postcolonial countries; *specific countries*

"competition state" 72
Constable, N. 105
Contemplacion, F. 104
Cornwall, A. and Anyidoho, N.A. 49, 51
Cossack movement, Ukraine 125
COVID-19 pandemic era 151–4
and contemporary crises 149

Davos: World Economic Forum 149–50, 157–8
decolonization (1960s) 27
deindustrialization, US 80–1
Development Alternatives with Women for a New Era (DAWN) 50, 51, 59
Devi, M. 38–9
domestic workers, migration of 102–11
Dudley, K. 80

East–West circuits of expertise and power 67–9
economic growth
  and gender equality 58–62
  India 90–1
  postwar US 25
education
  for all 51–3, 55–8
  Soviet women 50–1
elites *see* states protect elites and global capital
"emerging economies" 91
  see also specific countries
empowerment 78–9
  India 91–2
  mompreneurs 74–5
  US model 83–4
empowerment, investing in 41–4, 62–4
  competing ideologies 44–8
  genealogy of discourse 49–54
  and human capital 54–62
entrepreneurs 8, 74–7, 87, 92, 104, 107
Eurasian Economic Union (EAEU) 86
European Union (EU) 86, 106–7, 111, 135
Eurovision Song Contest and Russia 135

exhausted women and anxious men 123–4
Export Processing Zones (EPZs) 79, 88, 99

family forms 7–8
  see also hetero-patriarchal/nuclear family
feminist perspectives
  1970s 23, 26, 28–9
  empowerment and global development discourse 51
  "new feminism" 74–5
  transnational 59–60, 152–3
  see also neoliberal feminist "cover story"
Fisher, R. 147
Freire, P. 51–3, 55–6
Friedan, B. 28
Friedman, T. 48

G-77 countries 34–5, 40, 91, 158
  see also empowerment, investing in
Gandhi, I. 38
Gandhi, M. K. 45
Gandhi, R. 39, 88, 137
Gender Empowerment Measure (GEM) 78
  and related indices 62
gender equality and economic growth 58–62
gender and national belonging 151–4
gendered architecture 65–7, 92–4
  East–West circuits of power and expertise 67–9
  India 87–92
  key actors 73–9
  post-Soviet countries 84–7
  structuring conditions 69–73
  US 79–84
global economic restructuring and limits of human capital theory 98–102
global South, women's empowerment in 49–50
Gorbachev, M. 50, 108, 109
Grandin, G. and Valdéz, J.G. 67
Great Depression and New Deal, US 23–4
Great Society, US 26–7

Hart–Celler Act (1965), US 27
hetero-patriarchal/nuclear family
  breadwinner status 75, 123, 125, 127
  and individual achievement 73–7
  and non-heteronormative 7–8
  Soviet model 30–4, 107–8
  US "liberal" ideal 23–30
heteronationalism 131, 135–6
Hindu nationalism, India 89–90, 92, 125, 129, 136–42
Hochschild, A. 6
homonationalism 130–1
homophobia 122, 128, 130–1
  India 142
  US 28, 143–5
Hong Kong: Filipina domestic workers 105
"hourglass" economy 80, 83, 98, 99, 101, 123
human capital theory 43
  and empowerment 54–62
  global economic restructuring and limits of 98–102
human flourishing and care 156–60

immigrants *see* migration/immigrants
imperialism and hegemony, US 79–84
India 149
  entrepreneurs 76, 92
  forging nationalism between capitalism and socialism 34–9
  Hindu nationalism/Modi leadership 89–90, 92, 125, 129, 136–42
  Mahila Samiti (MS) movement 52
  meritocracy, free markets and emerging economy 87–92
  and Ukraine 1–2, 9
  individual and collective understandings of empowerment 49–50, 51, 52, 53
individuals as key actors 73–7, 86–7
industrialization
  and deindustrialization, US 80–1
  India 38
  science and technology 47
International Labor Organization (ILO) 51

International Monetary Fund (IMF) 70, 71, 81, 82, 90–1, 103, 158
"irrelevant" men in three regions 124–6
Italy, Ukrainian migrants in 109–10, 116–17

Jaishankar, S. 149–50
Japan, marriage migrants in 115
Johnson, L.B. 26–7, 45–7
joy, need for 160
justice vs modernity 156–60

Kabeer, N. 61
Keough, L. 111
Kim, M. 115–16
Klein, N. 152

labor
  deindustrialization, US 80–1
  India 88, 90
  postwar US 25–6, 79–80
  women
    post-Soviet and postcolonial countries 76, 79
    Soviet "mother-worker" 31–3, 107, 110
    US 25–6, 29, 83–4
  see also entrepreneurs; migration/immigrants
Lan, P. 106
Lavender Scare, US 28
Lenin, V. 30, 31
LGBTQ+ individuals *see* homophobia
Limbaugh, R. 143
Love Jihad, India 139–41

Macapagal-Arroyo, G. 104
McCarthy, J. 28
McNamara, R. 57
Mahila Samiti (MS) movement, India 52
manly protectors 120–3, 147–8
  affect and nation 126–8
  anxious men, exhausted women 123–4
  "irrelevant" men in three regions 124–6
  see also homophobia; misogyny; Modi, N.; Putin, V.; Trump, D.

marriage migrants 111–17
Martineau, H. 159–60
Marx 47
Marxist–Leninism 30, 31
masculine anxiety
  and exhausted women 123–4
  India 138–9
  US 75, 124, 143–4
men
  breadwinner status 75, 123, 125, 127
  and marriage migrants 113, 114–15
  Soviet 30–1
meritocracy 80, 82–3, 84
  free markets and emerging economy, India 87–92
  see also entrepreneurs
Mexican–US border 145, 146
microfinance programs, India 92
migration/immigrants 95–8, 117–19
  COVID-19 pandemic 152
  domestic workers 102–11
  early twentieth century 24, 25, 26, 27
  global economic restructuring and limits of human capital theory 98–102
  and manly protectors 145–7
  marriage 111–17
  restricting 71–3, 81
misogyny 122, 128–30
  India 139–42
  US 143–5, 147
modernity/modernization
  and competing ideologies 44–8
  rethinking theories 52–3
  status of countries and women 73, 77–8
  through economic opportunity for White families 23–30, 39–40
  vs justice 156–60
  see also oppositional modernity
Modi, N. 92, 125, 127, 131, 136–42
Moldova: migration 108, 111, 113
Mother India (film) 37–8
motherhood
  "choice" 76–7, 79
  mompreneurs 74–5
  post-Soviet 79, 86–7

Soviet "mother-worker" 31–3, 107, 110
  state welfare 29, 32, 33
  see also hetero-patriarchal/nuclear family
multicentric world order 1–6
  and fairer future 149–60
  theorizing gendered and 9–12
  see also neoliberal feminist "cover story"
Muslims
  –Hindus relations, India 125, 137, 139–41
  US 145–6

NAFTA 81, 144–5
nation and affect 126–8
nation and gender, horizontal and vertical analysis of 9–12
nation-states 72–3, 84
  as key actors 77–9
national belonging and gender: COVID-19 pandemic era 151–4
national borders, strengthened 71–3
  India 89–90
  post-Soviet countries 86
  US 81, 145–6
nationalism
  forged between capitalism and socialism 34–9
  Hindu 89–90, 92, 125, 129, 136–42
  homonationalism and heteronationalism 130–1, 131, 135–6
Nehru, J. 36–7
neoliberal feminist "cover story" 6–9, 12
  and manly protectors 124, 126, 144–5, 160
  postcolonial and post-Soviet countries 95–6
  see also "choices"; empowerment
New Deal, US 23–5
new international economic order (NIEO) 48, 158
Nixon, R.M. 27, 29, 45–7
non-aligned movement (NAM) 35, 90, 158

non-heteronormal relationships 7–8
nuclear family *see* hetero-patriarchal/
nuclear family

Obama, B. 133, 143
Olympic Games, Sochi, Russia 135
oppositional modernity 126–8
   India 138
   Russia 131, 133, 136
ordoliberals 48
Ostanina, N. 136
Othering *see* homophobia; misogyny

Parreñas, R. 105
people of color *see* Black Americans
and people of color
Philippines
   Cold War relations 34–5
   marriage migrants 112–13,
115–16
   migrant domestic workers 103–7
Pinochet, A. 67
Poland: migration 110–11
post-Soviet countries
   "choices" 33–4, 76, 86–7, 96
   gendered architecture 84–7
   marriage migrants 113, 116–17
   migrant domestic workers 107–11
   see also Ukraine
postcolonial countries
   United States and Soviet Union
6–7, 10–11, 34–5, 37–8, 42–4,
49
   see also empowerment, investing in;
G-77 countries; India
postcoloniality and competing visions/
ideologies 20–2, 44–8
poverty alleviation
   India 36–8, 92
   "Women in Development" (WID)
perspective 60–2
power
   East–West circuits of expertise and
67–9
   gender as signifier of 78
   imperialism and hegemony, US
79–84
   see also colonialism
pre-histories 20–2, 39–40
   India 34–9
   Soviet Union 30–4
   United States 23–30
Putin, V. 127, 131–6, 154, 155

Ray, S. 39
Reagan, R. 29, 60, 79
Red Pill (online forum) 147
religion *see* Christianity; Hindu
nationalism; Muslims
Rodriguez, R. 103
Roe v. Wade 157
Roosevelt, F.D. 23–4, 27
Roy, A. 152, 153
Russia
   Putin leadership 127, 131–6, 154,
155
   war in Ukraine 133–4, 149, 154–6

Sachs, J. 157–8
Sandberg, C. 83
Sardenberg, C. 51
Sen, G. and Grown, C. 50
Sharma, A. 52
shock therapy 68–9, 84–5
Shuster, S. and Westbrook, L. 160
Silva, J. 124
Singapore: Filipina domestic workers
104
"smart economics" 55, 58–9
social work theories, US 53–4
socialism
   break with 84–7
   and competing visions/ideologies
20–2, 44–8
   India: forging nationalism between
capitalism and 34–9
   as "laboratory of economic
knowledge" 67–8
   see also Soviet Union
Solari, C. 109
South Korea
   COVID-19 response 152
   marriage migrants 115–16
South and Southeast Asia (SSEA)
20–2, 34–5
   see also India; Philippines;
Singapore; Vietnam
Soviet Union
   collapse of 5, 69, 73, 86, 128, 132,
154–5

Soviet Union (*cont.*)
  deal with women: "build socialism alongside men" 30–4
  empowerment discourse 50–1
  funding education programs 56, 58
  "mother-worker" 31–3, 107, 110
  and US consumerism 28
  United States and postcolonial countries 6–7, 10–11, 34–5, 37–8, 42–4, 49
  see also Cold War; socialism
Spivak, G. 77
state welfare
  Soviet Union 32, 33
  United States 23–5, 29
states protect elites and global capital 69–71, 79–81, 85
  India 88–9
Suzuki, N. 115
Sydra, J. 75

Taiwan
  COVID-19 response 152
  Filipina domestic workers 106
technology sector, India 88, 90
Thai, H. 114
transnational networks
  East–West circuits of power and expertise 67–9
  feminist 59–60, 152–4
Trump, D. 127, 131, 136, 142, 143–7, 151–2
  "America First" agenda 84, 144–5
  individualism and meritocracy 82
Turkey: migration 111, 113, 117

Ukraine 85–6, 87
  and India 1–2, 9
  manly protectors 125
  migration 108, 109–10, 116–17
  Russia's war in 133–4, 149, 154–6
United Nations (UN) 27, 41–3, 44–5
  conferences on women's rights and equality 59–60, 152–3
  Development Project (UNDP) 62
  Research Institute for Social Development (UNRISD) 51
  UNESCO 56, 57
  World Economic Forum, Davos 149–50, 157–8

United States
  COVID-19 pandemic 151–2
  East–West circuits of expertise and power 67–9
  and education for all policy 55–8
  imperialism, hegemony, and aspiration 79–84
  and India 142
  labor market and labor migration 98, 99–100, 101–2
  "liberal" ideal: modernity through economic opportunity for White families 23–30
  "liberated" women 78–9
  masculine anxiety 75, 124
  masculinity 133
  migrant marriage 114–15
  reproductive health access 157
  and Russia 133, 155–6
  social work theories 53–4
  Soviet Union and postcolonial countries 6–7, 10–11, 34–5, 37–8, 42–4, 49
  "Women in Development" (WID) perspective 60–1
  see also Cold War; empowerment, investing in; *specific presidents*
Utrata, J. 86

Vietnam: marriage migrants 114–15

White families: US "liberal" ideal 23–30
White Supremacy 124, 136
"Women in Development" (WID) perspective 60–2
Women's International Democratic Forum (WIDF) 59
World Bank 48, 71, 81, 82, 100, 158
  empowerment discourse 51, 52, 53
  gender equality and economic growth 58–9, 61–2
  investments in education 56–8
World Congress of Families (WCF) 136
World Economic Forum, Davos 149–50, 157–8
World Trade Agreements (1995) 81–2
World Trade Organization (WTO) 71, 81, 84
Wurst, C. 135